JOURNAL FOR THE STUDY OF THE OLD TESTAMENT SUPPLEMENT SERIES

77

Editors
David J A Clines
Philip R Davies

JSOT Press
Sheffield

Edom
and the
Edomites

John R. Bartlett

Journal for the Study of the Old Testament
Supplement Series 77

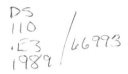

Published by JSOT Press
in association with
the Palestine Exploration Fund
JSOT Press is an imprint of
Sheffield Academic Press Ltd
The University of Sheffield
343 Fulwood Road
Sheffield S10 3BP
England

Typeset by Sheffield Academic Press
and
printed in Great Britain
by Billing & Sons Ltd
Worcester

British Library Cataloguing in Publication Data

Bartlett, John R. (John Raymond)
    Edom and the Edomites.—(Journal for the study of the
    Old Testament)
    1. Jordan. East Jordan. Edom. Antiquities.
    Archaeological investigation
    I. Title   II. Series
    933

    ISSN 0309-0787
    ISBN 1-85075-205-2

CONTENTS

PREFACE

It is nearly a hundred years since Frants Buhl published his *Geschichte der Edomiter* in Leipzig in 1893. The monograph is a minor classic of its kind and it remains valuable to the scholar. Since 1893, the archaeological exploration of Jordan has made available to the historian a vast amount of material evidence, adding an extra dimension to the task of reconstructing Edom's history. The archaeological evidence shows every sign of annual increase; in 1986 an archaeologist working in Edom commented to me that it would not be possible to write a history of Edom for at least another six years. Perhaps he had in mind what his own excavations might reveal, but he might as well have said for at least another sixty years, for the archaeological exploration of Edom is even now still in its infancy.

The present study, then, can hardly be definitive, and I am already aware of some of its limitations. We still know little for certain of the origins of the Edomites or of their early history. It is not always easy to define the boundaries of our study. Geographically, Edom shades into Arabia on one side and into the Negev on the other; historically, it emerges from the obscurity of the Late Bronze Age and the Early Iron Age in southern Jordan and disappears half a millennium later into the equal obscurity of southern Jordan and north-west Arabia under the Persian empire. How the early Edomites were related (if at all) to the Israelites, and how the later Edomites were related (if at all) to the Nabataeans are still matters of debate to which it is possible to give simple but very unsatisfactory answers: for example, that Edom was 'brother' to Israel, and that the Edomites were driven from their territory by incoming Nabataean Arabs. Such answers beg too many questions, and the historian's answers take more complex form; ancient folk-lore and modern text-books alike, for reasons of clarity and brevity, have tended to simplify international relationships and political events.

I have tried in this work to reconstruct the history of the place called Edom in the ancient texts by careful use of both the archaeological evidence so far known and the literary and documentary evidence. Archaeologists who draw on biblical evidence, and biblical scholars who draw on archaeological evidence, are often criticised for their handling of materials outside their own expertise, and any attempt at synthesis, even by one who can claim at least some experience on each side of the fence, is fraught with risk. But when the evidence comes, as it does, from two different sources, the attempt at synthesis must be made, and the historian must be fully aware of the limitations of each type of evidence. This is easier said than done; but in the case of the biblical material, for example, it is clearly important to be aware that the references to Edom's history have been shaped by centuries of hostility between Judah and Edom, and that Edom is generally portrayed as seen through Judaean eyes. We have always to ask of our biblical sources 'Who wrote this? When? And why?' Failure to ask these questions—for example of references to Edom in the Pentateuch—has led to some highly improbable reconstructions of Edomite history.

It is impossible to thank all who have at various time and in various ways helped me in the preparation of this book. I have always been particularly grateful to the late E.G. Collieu, Senior Tutor and Fellow of Brasenose College, Oxford, who originally encouraged me to undertake research, and the Revd J.R. Porter, subsequently Professor of Theology at Exeter, who supervised it. The late Crystal-M. Bennett, Litt.D., F.S.A., O.B.E., with whom I first discussed Edom in 1962, gave constant encouragement; her excavations in Jordan and her part in the establishment of the British Institute at Amman for Archaeology and History have made a major contribution to our understanding of ancient Edom. The focus of all archaeological work in Jordan is the Department of Antiquities of Jordan in Amman, and I am grateful to several of its members for their welcome hospitality, and in particular to its Director, Dr Adnan Hadidi, for the generosity of his assistance with archaeological maps and other publications of the Department. It is a pleasure to thank Professor P.R. Ackroyd for interest and encouragement over many years. I am grateful to Margaret Spencer for the final typescript, and to Helen Oxley for much valuable help with the bibliography. I am grateful also to Alison Maybury for the index of biblical references. It remains for me to thank my colleagues in the Department of Hebrew, Biblical and Theological Studies, and my family at home, for their long-suffering support.

Trinity College Dublin
September 1987

ABBREVIATIONS

AASOR	*Annual of the American Schools of Oriental Research*
ABSA	*Annual of the British School at Athens*
ADAJ	*Annual of the Department of Antiquities of Jordan*
AJA	*American Journal of Archaeology*
AJSL	*American Journal of Semitic Languages and Literature*
*ANET*³	*Ancient Near Eastern Texts relating to the Old Testament*, ed. J.B. Pritchard. 3rd ed. with Supplement. Princeton, N.J.: Princeton University Press. 1969.
AOAT	Alter Orient und Altes Testament
AUSS	*Andrews University Seminary Studies*
BA	*Biblical Archaeologist*
BASOR	*Bulletin of the American Schools of Oriental Research*
BE	*Babylonian Expedition of the University of Pennsylvania. Series A: Cuneiform Texts*, ed. H.V. Hilprecht. Philadelphia: Department of Archaeology, University of Pennsylvania. 1893-1911.
BIAUL	*Bulletin of the Institute of Archaeology*, University of London.
BIES	*Bulletin of the Israel Exploration Society*
Bib	*Biblica*
BiOr	Bibliotheca Orientalis, Leiden
BN	*Biblische Notizen*
BRCI	*Bulletin of the Research Council of Israel*
BZAW	Beihefte zur Zeitschrift für die alttestamentliche Wissenschaft
CAH	*The Cambridge Ancient History*. 3rd ed. Cambridge: Cambridge University Press. 1973-1975.
CB	Coniectanea Biblica
CBQ	*Catholic Biblical Quarterly*
CPJ	*Corpus Papyrorum Judaicarum*
CQR	*Church Quarterly Review*

CTR	*Calvin Theological Journal*
DBS	*Dictionnaire de la Bible, Supplément*
DOTT	*Documents from Old Testament Times.* Ed. D.W. Thomas. London: T. Nelson. 1958.
EAEHL	*Encyclopedia of Archaeological Excavations in the Holy Land*, I-IV. Eds. M. Avi-Yonah and E. Stern. London: Oxford University Press. 1975-1978.
EEP	*Explorations in Eastern Palestine*, I, II, III (= AASOR 14, 15, 18-19)
EI	*Eretz Israel*
ERE	*Encyclopaedia of Religion and Ethics.* Ed. J. Hastings. Edinburgh: T. & T. Clark, 1908-1926.
ESI	*Explorations and Surveys in Israel*
GJ	*Geographical Journal*
GM	Göttinger Miscellen
HUCA	*Hebrew Union College Annual*
ICC	International Critical Commentary
IDB	*Interpreter's Dictionary of the Bible.* Nashville, N.Y.: Abingdon, 1962
IEJ	*Israel Exploration Journal*
ILN	*Illustrated London News*
JAOS	*Journal of the American Oriental Society*
JBL	*Journal of Biblical Literature*
JEA	*Journal of Egyptian Archaeology*
JEOL	*Jaarbericht van het vooraziatisch-egyptisch genootschap 'Ex Oriente Lux'*
JESHO	*Journal of the Economic and Social History of the Orient*
JFA	*Journal of Field Archaeology*
JNES	*Journal of Near Eastern Studies*
JPOS	*Journal of the Palestine Oriental Society*
JRAS	*Journal of the Royal Asiatic Society of Great Britain and Ireland*
JRGS	*Journal of the Royal Geographical Society*
JSOT	*Journal for the Study of the Old Testament*
JSS	*Journal of Semitic Studies*
JTS	*Journal of Theological Studies*
MIOF	*Mitteilungen des Institutes für Orientforschung*
MNDPV	*Mitteilungen und Nachrichten des deutschen Palästina-Vereins*

NEB	New English Bible
OrAnt	*Oriens Antiquus*
OTL	Old Testament Library
OTS	*Oudtestamentische Studiën*
PEFQS	*Palestine Exploration Fund Quarterly Statement*
PEQ	*Palestine Exploration Quarterly*
PJB	*Palästinajahrbuch*
PSAS	*Proceedings of the Seminar for Arabian Studies*
PSBA	*Proceedings of the Society of Biblical Archaeology*
QDAP	*Quarterly of the Department of Antiquities in Palestine*
RAr	*Revue archéologique*
RB	*Revue biblique*
REJ	*Revue des études juives*
RivBib	*Rivista Biblica*
RPh	*Revue de philologie, de littérature et d'histoire anciennes*
RSV	Revised Standard Version of the Bible
SBFLA	*Studii Biblici Franciscani Liber Annuus*
SHAJ	*Studies in the History and Archaeology of Jordan*, I, II. Ed. A. Hadidi. Amman: Department of Antiquities of Jordan. 1982, 1985.
StOr	Studia Orientalia (Helsingfors)
TA	*Tel Aviv*
ThLZ	*Theologische Literaturzeitung*
ThStKr	*Theologische Studien und Kritiken*
ThZ	*Theologische Zeitschrift*
TRE	*Theologische Realenzyklopädie*
UF	*Ugarit-Forschungen*
VT(S)	*Vetus Testamentum* (Supplement)
ZAW	*Zeitschrift für die alttestamentliche Wissenschaft*
ZDMG	*Zeitschrift der deutschen Morgenländischen Gesellschaft*
ZDPV	*Zeitschrift des deutschen Palästina-Vereins*
ZKKB	*Zeitschrift für Kunst und Kultur im Bergbau*

Chapter 1

THE EXPLORATION OF EDOM

The Early Nineteenth Century

Between the Crusades and the beginning of the nineteenth century, Edom lay beyond the reach of European travellers. Reland, in his *Palaestina ex monumentis veteribus illustrata* (1714: 66-73), relied entirely on the ancient sources for his chapter on Edom. Men like Henry Maundrell, 'late Fellow of Exeter Coll, and Chaplain to the Factory at Aleppo', who travelled from Aleppo to Jerusalem in 1697, could reach Jericho, the Jordan and the Dead Sea with reasonable ease (Maundrell, 1703: 78-86), but travel beyond the Jordan was a different matter. Transjordan was a wild region, of little interest either to pilgrims or businessmen from Europe; the former focused on Jerusalem and the latter on the routes to India. Transjordan was no place for the European Christian; along its desert edge ran the Muslim pilgrim's route from Damascus to Mecca, a route on which Christians were not welcome. C.-F. Volney, travelling in Egypt and Syria in 1783-85, relied on reports of Arabs from Bakir and Gaza for his information that there were 'to the south-west of Lake Asphaltites, within three days' journey, upwards of thirty ruined towns, absolutely deserted' (Volney, 1793: II.464).

The first modern European traveller in this region to leave a record of his journey was Ulrich Jasper Seetzen, '*Conceiller d'Embassade de S.M. l'Empereur de Russie*'. On 19 January 1806 he left Damascus, travelled south via Paneion, the upper Jordan, the west coast of the Sea of Galilee to Tiberias, and then via Edrei, Jerash, Salt (with an excursion to Amman), Elealeh, Madaba, Dhiban, Karak, the southern end of the Dead Sea, and on to Jerusalem, which he reached on 6 April 1806. He did not enter Edom, reaching only its north-western borders in the Ghor, but in the brief account of his journey published in English in 1810 (his

journal was published, with a commentary, in German in 1854-59),
he notes as follows:

> The southern limit of the country of Karrak is marked by the Wady
> el-Hessa, which divides it from the district of Jebbal, and which
> under the name of el-Karahhy empties itself into the southern
> extremity of the Dead Sea. Three more villages in Karrak are
> occupied by Mussulmen. The extent of the country of Jebbal is
> about two or three days journey, but it contains only seven
> inhabited villages.
>
> I enquired for Petra ... and I was assured that it was at the
> distance of one day's journey; but I afterward learned from the
> Bishop of Karrak at Jerusalem, that Petra is two leagues distant
> from the Dead Sea. Further on, south of Jebbal, is the mountain of
> Sharah, which is likewise two days' journey in extent, and with
> only one inhabited village, known by the same name (Seetzen,
> 1810: 39-40).

Although Seetzen did not travel in Edom, by careful enquiry he was
able to compile lists of inhabited and uninhabited or ruined villages.
While at Karak, he listed in his journal (28 March, 1806; Seetzen,
1854-59: I. 418) the following inhabited villages in northern Edom:
Eïme, Taphíle, Scháubak, es Szúunne, es Szille, es Szúnnefhá, el
Bzéra. A year later, on his journey from Hebron to Sinai, he noted
from his informant (17 March 1807) a longer list of ten inhabited
towns and some seventy-four unoccupied or ruined sites. Seetzen
suggested that Taphile was perhaps the Tophel of Deut. 1.1 and Szille
the Sela of 2 Kings 14.7 (this identification is thus not as recent as
has often been suggested), and that Bzéra was the Old Testament
Bozrah (Jer. 14.13). He identified Jebbal with the Gebalene of
Eusebius and Jerome, and in this he was followed by Burckhardt,
Robinson, and others (Seetzen, 1854-59: III.17).

J.L. Burckhardt's journey through this region in 1812 is famous for
his visit to Petra, but useful above all for the detailed description of
the land of Edom and its villages. Burckhardt noted that the waters
of the wadi el Ahsa (el-Ḥasā), which divided Karak from Djebal,
were tepid from the presence of a hot spring. He apparently climbed
out of the valley into Edom by way of the Wadi 'Afra, for he mentions
passing the spring El Kaszrein ('Ain el Qasrein). He next mentions
'the ruins of an ancient city of considerable extent called El Karr,
ancient Kara', and then Ayme (Seetzen's Eime, now 'Eimah). On the

next day, 8 August, he reached Tafyle (Tafila) and noted its fruit plantations, the export of its figs to Gaza, and the presence in this region of traders from Hebron. South of Tafila, he mentions the valley and village of Szolfehe. On 11 August he reached Beszeyra (Seetzen's Bzéra, now Buseira), and on 13 August Ain Djedolat (probably 'Ain Jaladāt, south of Rashadiya) and Wadi Dhana, with its gardens and tobacco plantations, and El Dhahel. On 14 August he skirted the eastern edge of the Wady Ghoeyr (Wady Ghuweir), which he crossed, noting that it divided the district of Djebal from that of Djebel Shera (which he identified with the Old Testament Mount Seir). On 16 August he 'passed the ruined place called Szyhhan' (Sihan), reaching Shaubak castle on 19 August and Wady Nedjed (Wady Nijil?) on 21 August. The next day he reached 'Ain Musa (above which he noted the abandoned village of Badabda (Badibda), Eldjy (Elji), and Petra; he spent the night on the plain at the foot of Jebel Harun, leaving Petra the next morning. On 23 August he reached Betahy (Bitahi), and on the 24th 'Ain Mafrak (Mabrak?) and el-Szadeke (Sadaqa). Here he turned west off the road that ran south to Naqb esh-Shtar, and on 26 August passed the spring at Ibn Reszeysz (er-Rasis) to reach Ain Delegha (Dilagha). He passed Djebel Koula, 'which appears to be the highest summit of Djebel Shera' (presumably Jebel el-Khalal) to reach Gharendel (ancient Arindela, now Gharandal) on 27 August. The accuracy of Burckhardt's pioneering observation and notes can be readily seen by comparing his account with a modern map. (For this account, see Burckhardt, 1822: 401-04). Between Tafila and Sadaqa his route lay along the line of the modern road popularly called 'The King's Highway'; whether or not this route is to be identified with that mentioned in Num. 20.17, it must certainly be ancient.

Burckhardt was soon followed along this route by two English naval officers, the Hon. Captain C.L. Irby and Captain J. Mangles, accompanied by a Mr Legh and Mr W.J. Banks, with several attendants and two guides (Irby and Mangles, 1844: 102). They left Jerusalem on 6 May 1818 and travelled via Solomon's Pools, Tekoa, Hebron, the southern end of the Dead Sea and the Wadi Karak to Karak. Here 'Four hundred piastres were paid down as the price of a safe conduct through several places, specified in a list, as far as Wady Mousa, to the south, and Szalt, to the north; but the old man [Sheik Yousouf] could not undertake to free us from some incidental tribute on the road' (*ibid.*, 112). The party left Karak on 14 May, and travelled past Mote (Mauta) to Dettrass (Dhat Ras). From here, on 16 May, they descended to the Wady-el-Ahsa (el-Ḥasā), passing an ancient fortress, Acoujah (Khirbet el 'Akkuza) on their left, and a volcanic outrop on their right (probably the basalt outcrop opposite Kh. eṭ-Ṭannur on the northern slope of the Wadi e-Ḥasā). On the way up the southern slope of the wadi, they noted the ruins of a small but richly decorated temple. The description of 'rich arabesque borders of vines and foliage, much in the taste of Diocletian's buildings at Palmyra' (*ibid.*, 114) suggests that Irby and Mangles had found the temple at Jebel eṭ-Ṭannur, later to be excavated by Nelson Glueck (Glueck, 1966; 1937a, 1937b, 1938a). They shortly turned south off the road in order to avoid visiting 'the town of Djebel', by which is probably meant Tafila. Nearby they passed some 'uninteresting ruins' called El-Hagre. On the following day, 17 May, they passed Bseida village (probably Buseira is meant) about a mile to the west and came to Gharundel (Gharandal), where parallel rows of columns were to be seen among its ruins. They met 'an ancient Roman highway paved with black stone', passed the ruins of El Gaig (Khirbet Abū 'Ajāj?) to the south-west, and came to Shaubak.

Leaving Shaubak on 18 May, they stayed overnight at an Arab camp on high ground to the west-southwest where they met Abou Raschid, who accompanied them south against the opposition of Abou Zatoun, the sheik of Wadi Mousa, and his people. On 19 May they reached the spring of Sammack (Shammakh), south of Shaubak. They found traces of a paved way like that met before Shaubak, and they camped that night above Dibdeba (Badibda), and on 20 May above Wadi Musa. After much negotiation, they explored Petra on 24-25 May, departing again for Shaubak on 26 May. The next day they left Shaubak and reached Ipseyra/Bseida, 'a miserable village, and the people a fanatical and surly sect'; here they were told that 'Burckhardt had made a very hasty survey of the ruins'. On 28 May they reached Tafyle (Tafila), and the next day crossed the Wadi el-Ahsa, 'probably the Zared of Scripture, the boundary of the Edomites and Moabites'; they bathed 'in the hot spring which the Arabs call the bath of Solomon', and so returned to Karak (Irby and Mangles, 1844: 102-37). Irby and Mangles had taken a slightly different route from that of Burckhardt, entering Edom by the Wadi La'ban rather than by Wadi 'Afra, and by-passing Tafila. Burckhardt had gone further, travelling on from Petra, but Irby and Mangles had greater success in Petra itself; as Robinson noted, they were 'the first Frank travellers to ascend Mount Hor and visit the Wely Nebi Harun' (Robinson and Smith, 1841: II. 548, n. 2).

From now on the chief attraction of the region to the European traveller was Petra, and the next important visitor was M. Léon de Laborde. (He mentions as his predecessors Burckhardt, 'Mr Banks and his companions', and 'Messrs Strangways and Anson', who 'reached Wady Mousa under the guidance of a single Arab from Gaza' (de Laborde, 1830: 52; 1836: 132). M. de Laborde, unlike Burckhardt, travelled in style, with 'a caravan of sixteen dromedaries; a number sufficient, indeed, to tempt the avarice of the Arabs, but at the same time to compel them to treat me with respect' (de Laborde, 1836: 44). He left Cairo on 25 February 1828, and after crossing Sinai set out from 'Aqaba for Petra in late March or early April 1828. He travelled north through the Wadi 'Araba, past Gharandal, and then eastward through the Wadi Pabouchebe (Wadi Abū Khusheiba) towards Jebel Harun and Petra. This was to become a regular route to Petra. After exploring Petra and making a number of sketches and plans, de Laborde and his party left by the Wadi Sabra, ascended a mountain called El Naqb (probably Ras en-Naqb, immediately south of Jebel Harun), and travelled across high country to the well of Dalege (Dilagha). Here de Laborde's path crossed Burckhardt's route from Sadaqa to Gharandal. From Dilagha they travelled roughly southeast to the wells of Gana (perhaps Bir el-Hiyad, Bir el Mārī, Bir el Fuweilī and Bir Abū el Lusan near Ras el Qana), and then down the mountain to Ameime (Humeima), then Wadi Jetoum (Wadi el Yutm), and 'Aqaba. De Laborde's journey thus broke new ground, and his map opened the Wadi 'Araba and the Ḥismā region to subsequent travellers, while his sketches of Petra illustrated the reports of Burckhardt and Irby and Mangles for thousands of biblical scholars and armchair travellers. Of particular interest and importance is de Laborde's visit to the Isle of Graia, now Jezirat Fara'un, which he planned and measured as accurately as he could before planting a standard on the highest rock and taking possession of the island in the name of France (de Laborde, 1836: 114). De Laborde anticipated recent suggestions by noting that the Edomite capital, Petra, 'had for auxiliaries two maritime cities situated at the northern point of the Gulf of Akaba, one on the coast, which was Ela, and the other on a neighbouring island, called Ezion-Gaber' (de Laborde, 1836: 290).

The Gulf of 'Aqaba had already been visited by Eduard Rüppell, who arrived there from Suez on 4 May 1822 (Rüppell, 1829: 248-52). He noted a ruined settlement, perhaps ancient Ailat, west of the modern settlement of 'Akaba and its castle, and connects the name Ailat or Eilat with the reported name of the district, Gelana (*ibid.*, 250). He further noted the island Gelat Emrag at the entry to a small bay offering good shelter a few miles down the west coast of the Gulf of 'Aqaba (*ibid.*, 252). Rüppell pictures the island and its ruins on plate 7 of his work; his 'Karte des Petraischen Arabien' (Taf.11, dated 1826) shows the Gulf of 'Akaba with the island of Emrag, 'Akaba, and the Wadi 'Araba, but shows nothing of the hinterland to the north. In January 1833 Lt. J.R. Wellsted also visited 'Aqaba and described the ruins of Jezirat Pharoun (Wellsted, 1838: II.142-46). Wellsted notes that D'Anville and other geographers had located Elath and Ezion-geber near 'Aqaba, and that the area had been minutely investigated by de Laborde and Rüppell; and also that Pietro della Valle had visited the Gulf in 1615.

The next visits to Petra were also made via the Wadi 'Araba. In 1836 John Lloyd Stephens travelled from Sinai to 'Aqaba, and then up the Wadi 'Araba, from which he turned east past Mount Hor (Jebel Harun) into Petra. He took little note of the route or its details, but does comment that 'Three different parties, at different times, and under different circumstances, after an interval of twenty years from its discovery by Burckhardt, had entered the city of Petra, but not one of them had passed through the land of Idumaea. The route of the two Englishmen and Italian before referred to was not precisely known; and with the exception of these three, I was the first traveller who had ever attempted to pass through the doomed and blighted Edom' (Stephens, 1838: II. 102). Stephens here probably shows his awareness of Alexander Keith's studies of biblical prophecies, particularly those against Edom; their influence is also clear in the translator's preface to the English edition of de Laborde (pp. x-xvi) and in S. Olin's account of his travels (Olin, 1843). Stephens seems to have allowed the prophetic view of Edom to colour his own, for he notes that 'On the very borders of Edom I noticed a change for the worse in the appearance of the Bedouins' (Stephens, 1838: II.33). The identity of the two Englishmen and the Italian remains uncertain; later, Stephens notes that they had started from Cairo about a year before, 'and as they had been heard of afterwards in Europe, it was known that they had succeeded, but no account of their journey had been published' (*ibid.*, I. 214). A graffito found in Petra by Lord Melchett's party in 1930 appears to evidence the presence in Petra in 1836 of an English group which included one Charlotte Rowley, perhaps the first European woman to visit Petra (the next was probably Harriet Martineau in 1847) (Wellesley, 1938: 63). In April 1837 Lord Lindsay set out from 'Aqaba northwards up the Wadi 'Araba, turning east to Petra through the Wadi Aboughsheibi (Abū Khusheiba), as de Laborde had done, and then returning through a district called Brayitha, the Wadi Seeg, the Wadi Nummula (Namala), and then across the Wadi 'Araba to El Uebe (el-Weibeh) (Lindsay, 1847: 215-32). The previous month Petra had been visited by a German man of letters, G.H. von Schubert, accompanied by the artist J.M. Bernatz, whose *Bilder aus dem heiligen Land* (Stuttgart, 1839) provided an important pictorial introduction to Petra for German readers. The sub-title described these pictures as 'Vierzig ausgewählte Original-Ansichten biblisch-wichtiger Orte, treu nach der Natur aufgenommen'.

The Wadi 'Araba itself attracted scholarly interest. In April 1838 the Comte de Bertou travelled from Jerusalem via Hebron, the Ghor and the Wadi 'Araba to 'Aqaba; then via 'Ain Ghadyan and Wadi Dilagha to Petra, returning to the 'Araba by Wadi er-Rubā'i (de Bertou, 1839: 277-86). His journey gave him

the gratification of knowing that we were the first Europeans who in modern times had traversed the whole extent of the Wadi, from the Dead Sea to Akabah, and have proved that, in the present state of things, the river Jordan could never have flowed into the Aelanitic Gulf (*ibid.*, 286).

De Bertou attempted in particular to pinpoint the watershed of the Wadi 'Araba, but his findings met with some criticism, especially from E. Robinson, who followed de Bertou along the Wadi 'Araba a month later, and challenged the accuracy of many of de Bertou's observations (Robinson and Smith, 1841: II. 659-69). Robinson and his party left Jerusalem on Friday 26 May 1838, passing the southwest corner of the Dead Sea at 8.30 a.m. the following Tuesday. They noted the line of cliffs marking the end of the Lisan marl deposit and dividing the Ghor valley at the southern end of the sea from the Wadi 'Araba. Robinson comments that

Thus far we had followed the route of the few former travellers
who had passed between Hebron and Kerak around the south end
of the Dead Sea. But from this point we were about to enter a new
region, and to follow along a portion of the great valley (no very
extensive one, indeed), into which until a few weeks before, the foot
of no Frank traveller had ever penetrated (*ibid.*, II. 490-91).

They passed 'Ain 'Arus and the opening of the Wadi el-Jeib ('the vast
drain of all the 'Arabah'), along which they travelled south, passing
the wadi that enters the el-Jeib from 'Ain Hasb, until they halted for
the evening. They set out again just after midnight on the Wednesday
morning; with the range of Hamra el-Fidān on their left, they passed
'Ain el-Hufeira, travelling south up the Wadi el-Buweirida and then
up 'the long, wild, romantic Wadi Namala' (II. 506), at the top of
which they camped for the night. From here, on Thursday 21 May,
they travelled past Beida with the village of Dibdiba (Badibda) above
them to their left, turned southeast across the hills to Elji and then
west to the Sik of Wadi Musa and so into Petra. They departed on
Friday 1 June at 11.00 a.m., reaching the 'Araba by Wadi Namala
and Wadi Abū Sakākin; on the Saturday they arrived at 'Ain el-
Weibeh. Their return from Petra thus followed much the same route
as Lord Lindsay had taken in April 1837.

From now on it became easier, though not always easy, to visit
Petra, and an increasing number of travellers did so. One of the first
was the artist David Roberts (1839) (see Bannister, 1866: 116-26).
(For a short study of Roberts and other artists of the nineteenth
century who illustrated this region, see Llewellyn, 1980: 123-28.)
Roberts' name was later found inscribed in the Deir by H. Formby,
travelling with S. Olin (Formby, 1843: 287). Roberts was soon
followed by another artist, W.H. Bartlett (October, 1845). Bartlett
took the now standard route from the south; he came from Sinai,
past the head of the Gulf of 'Aqaba and 'the mounds of Aila, or Elath'
(Bartlett, 1867: 106), up the Wadi 'Araba, and then up the ravine of
the Wadi Abū Khusheiba, as had de Laborde and Lindsay, and past
Mount Hor, where he visited Aaron's tomb, into Petra itself, where
he dined off Irish stew in the Corinthian Tomb. After two days and
nights in Petra, he returned by the same route to the Gulf of 'Aqaba.
Roberts and Bartlett are important because their illustrations and
travel accounts reached a wider public than the more scholarly works
of Burckhardt and Robinson. Another artist who later reached Petra

was Edward Lear, travelling in the east between 1848 and 1858 (Lear, 1897: 410-30).

It is impossible to detail all who travelled to Petra in the mid-nineteenth century; not all travellers left records, and of those who did, not all had scholarly interests or sufficient knowledge of Arabic to record accurately what they were told. Not all scholarly travellers had biblical or archaeological interests. One who had was Arthur Penrhyn Stanley, the Dean of Canterbury, who reached Petra in 1852 and commented disparagingly of the Khazneh that 'There is nothing of peculiar grace or grandeur in the temple itself—it is of the most debased style of Roman architecture'. His book, *Sinai and Palestine*, from which that quotation comes (1856: 90), was to become the Victorian churchman's main guide to the Holy Land (the British Library Catalogue notes three editions in 1856, the fourth in 1857, another in 1862, a 'new' edition in 1866, another 'new' edition in 1881, a further edition in 1910, while extracts were published under the title *The Bible in the Holy Land* in 1862 and 1863 for the use of schools). Stanley's comment, however, did nothing to reduce public interest in Petra, which had been stimulated earlier by Dean Burgon's famous line, 'A rose-red city, half as old as time' (from his prize poem 'Petra', published in 1845).

The Late Nineteenth Century

The second half of the nineteenth century saw the arrival in the land of Edom of a number of individual travellers and expeditions with serious scientific objectives. One of the first was G.A. Wallin, who published his 'Narrative of a journey from Cairo to Medina and Mecca by Suez, Araba, Tawila, al-Jauf, Jubba, Hail and Nejd in 1845' in 1854. Wallin was less concerned with biblical history than with the tribal relationships among the Arabs of his own day. He crossed the Wadi 'Araba and climbed into the mountains of Edom by Wadi Gharandal, and travelled eastwards into the Wadi Dilagha, northeast to Wadi Mabrak, Basta, and Ma'an. From Ma'an he turned northwest to Udhruh, Shaubak and Wadi Nijil, and then north past Shajarāt al-Taiyar to Tafila before turning eastwards into the Syrian desert. Wallin was thus the first after Burckhardt to explore the eastern slopes of the Edomite highlands.

In 1864-66 a major expedition was headed by the Duc de Luynes.

In May 1864, after exploration of northern and central Transjordan
and of the Dead Sea, his party travelled from Jerusalem round the
southern end of the Dead Sea to eṣ-Ṣafi and then south along the
Wadi 'Araba to 'Aqaba. They returned north up the Wadi 'Araba,
turning aside in the usual way to pay a brief visit to Jebel Harun and
Petra before recrossing the 'Araba to el-Weibeh (which they
identified as Kadesh-Barnea of the Old Testament), Kurnub and
beyond. Much of the recording was done by M. Vignes, who noted
among the results of the expedition (de Luynes, 1874: II. 3) first, the
'exploration approfonde' of the Dead Sea; secondly, the establishment
of certain geographical positions on the eastern shore of the Dead
Sea, and thirdly, the study of the course of the Wadi el-Jeib and the
location of the watershed of the Wadi 'Araba (opposite Wadi Abou
Barka (Abu Barqa), north of Wadi Gharandal; cf. de Luynes, 1874: I.
270-71). Robinson's location of Ezion-geber at El-Ghadyan on the
supposition that the shore-line of the Gulf had retreated is dismissed
(*ibid.*, I. 265-69), and Petra's Semitic name is declared to have been
not Sela or Joktheel but Recem (*ibid.*, I. 301). The Duc de Luynes
published the accounts of his expedition in three volumes: the second
contains the account of an important journey from Karak to Shaubak
and back by MM.C. Mauss and H. Sauvaire (the latter chancellor of
the French embassy at Beirut, a photographer and a fluent Arabic
speaker). Mauss and Sauvaire travelled south from Karak by El
Mouteh (Mauta), Djafar, and Zat Ras (Dhat Ras) to Qal'at el-Ḥasā
and 'Uneiza on the *haj* route (the modern Desert Highway) before
turning west to reach Shaubak from the east. They returned via
Dusaq, where they turned north onto the now well-known road to
Twaneh (Thuwana), and so over the Wadi el-Ḥasā past el-'Aina to
Dhat Ras and Karak. Their particular contribution was to measure
barometric pressure at select points along the route in order to
determine their height above sea level, and to collect and publish a
number of Arabic inscriptions. The third volume of the Duc's
Voyages d'Exploration was the work of the geologist Louis Lartet;
this was the first serious study of the geology of the Jordan valley and
Transjordan regions (1876). Lartet was followed in 1883 by Edward
Hull, whose *Memoir on the Geology and Geography of Arabia
Petraea, Palestine and adjoining districts* was published in 1889 for
the Palestine Exploration Fund. In 1891 the Fund published H.
Chichester Hart's *Some account of the fauna and flora of Sinai, Petra
and Wadi 'Arabah.*

The Palestine Exploration Fund had been founded in 1865, and its interest in the Transjordan and Sinai regions began early in its history. In 1870 E.H. Palmer, having explored Sinai as a member of the Ordnance Survey expedition of 1868-69, returned to Palestine on behalf of the P.E.F. to explore the region between Sinai and Judaea. He took the opportunity to cross the Wadi 'Araba and ascend the Naqb er-Rubā'i to Mount Hor and Petra; his party spent one night there, leaving the next morning via the Siq and Elji for a brief visit to Khirbet D'haah (Dḥaḥa, up the valley to the south of Wadi Musa). After a return visit to Petra itself, they left by the fort of 'Aireh, leaving Dibdibeh (Badibda) and Bannoureh to the east, and passing through Wadi Beida, where they visited Beida and el-Barîd. From here Palmer climbed the Wadi Sumra to the Naqb eshkart Emsa'ad and thence to the now well known Naqb Namala, and so north along the Wadi 'Araba, leaving the Samrat Fiddan (Hamra el-Fidān) to the west, descending the Wadi el-Weibeh, and crossing Wadi Salaman and Seil Dhalal to reach Wadi Talah and finally the Ghor (Palmer, 1871: II. 429-59). In 1872 W.C. Maughan approached Petra from 'Aqaba via the eastern route of Wadi Yutm, El Quweira, and Humeima, departing via el-Weibeh and Hebron. He was told that no western traveller had been to Petra for three years past; his predecessor may have been Palmer (Maughan, 1873: 158-239 [188]).

It is remarkable that, though some sixty years had passed since Burckhardt's journey and over fifty since that of Irby and Mangles, very few travellers seem to have reached Petra by the route from Amman south through Moab and across the Wadi el-Ḥasā. Most travellers had reached Petra via the Wadi 'Araba and one of the wadis leading off it eastward past Jebel Harun, and most had departed by a route westward across the Wadi 'Araba towards el-Weibeh and Hebron. This is undoubtedly because the difficulties of the northern approach were well known, the chief of them being the hostility and rapaciousness of the local tribesmen, the Bne Sakhr, and of the rulers of Karak, the Mejelli family. The American Lieutenant Lynch, visiting Karak from the Dead Sea in 1848, felt under threat in Karak and noted that the Muslim Arabs there 'were the only Arabs from whom we had experienced rudeness' (Lynch, 1849: 367), and H.B. Tristram, visiting Moab in 1872, suffered several days' virtual imprisonment in Karak castle (Tristram, 1873: 83-97). Edom was thus virtually inaccessible from the north through much of the nineteenth century. Charles Doughty solved the problem of inaccessibility as Burckhardt had by living and travelling in native style. In 1876 he travelled with the pilgrims' caravan from Damascus south towards Mecca, but he had visited parts of Edom the previous summer, in May-June 1875 (Doughty, 1888: I. 28-49). Doughty began from Maʿan and travelled 'over the moorland' towards Shaubak. Fifteen miles from Maʿan he passed the ruins of Utherah (Udhruh), visited by Wallin thirty years earlier, and then the villages of Mottehma and Hetigy before reaching the ruins of Nejjel (Nijil). A little further on he looked over the cliffs into the Wadi ʿAraba below, with Shaubak 'over the next bent'. Doughty does not say that he entered Shaubak, but goes on to describe his journey south from this point toward Petra, past the ruins of Bir Khidad. Doughty appears to have entered Petra from the north, and to have left it past the theatre and the Khazneh through the Siq, so coming to Elji and the spring ʿAin Harun. From here he made an excursion southwards up into the hills to an ancient site Merbrak (Mabrak?), returning the next day for another visit to Petra before returning to Maʿan the following day. Doughty thus made a circular journey from Maʿan via Shaubak and Petra back to Maʿan; from Shaubak to Mabrak he was covering ground already known and described, but east of the Shaubak-Mabrak line he was on territory less well known to Europeans. It was not until the Arab rebellion of 1916-17 and the exploits of T.E. Lawrence that this area came to the notice of a wider public, and when Doughty's book (first published in 1888) was republished in a new edition in 1921, it was T.E. Lawrence who wrote the introduction.

Doughty was a keen observer of the social and domestic behaviour of his fellow travellers and of those among whom they travelled, and so also was Alois Musil, who travelled through Edom on various occasions in 1896-98 and 1900-1902, noting carefully the topography of his routes. But he was equally concerned with ethnography; volume III of his *Arabia Petraea*, published in 1908, is entitled *Ethnologischer Reisebericht*, and 'presents, as it were, a mosaic, a strictly faithful picture of the life today in Arabia Petraea. Musil describes the life of no less than 48 different tribes' (review in *GJ* 30.2 [Aug. 1907], 210-11). For archaeological and historical purposes, however, Musil's work is less useful than that of his contemporaries in the field, R.E. Brünnow and A. von Domaszewski, whose *Die Provincia Arabia auf Grund zweier in den Jahren 1897 und 1898 unternommenen Reisen und die Berichte früheren Reisender* appears from Strasbourg in 1904-1906. Musil was criticised for writing as though the work of Brünnow and Domaszewski did not exist, referring to it only in his preface and adding little to it (review, *GJ* 30.6 (Dec. 1907), 648-49). In Edom, Brünnow and Domaszewski followed both routes from Dhat Ras into Edom, first exploring the Roman road past el-'Aina and along the Wadi Ja'is to Thuwana and 'Ain et-Tarik, and then the road past El-Akkusa, Rujm Karaka, el-Mismal, Tafila, Buseira, Gharandal, Dana and Bir es-Saba'a to meet the Roman road, which then continues to Dusaq. Here they turned west to Shaubak, and south via 'Ain Nijil and Beida to Petra, then east past Elji and 'Ain Musa to Udhruh. The last section of their route lay south past Basta to 'Ain Sadaqa, the Zadagatta of the Peutinger Table. They did not follow the route from 'Ain Sadaqa to 'Aqaba, referring the reader to the reports of de Laborde (1828), Morris (1840), Maughan (1872), Doughty (1875), and Jaussen (1902) (Brünnow and Domaszewski, 1904: I. 80-100, 108-19, 429-35). The importance of Brünnow and Domaszewski lies in their use of the earlier travellers, in their thorough recording of every milestone, cistern, or building of note, and above all in their published plans and drawings of ancient ruins. Musil, Brünnow, and Domaszewski have left a remarkable record of what was to be seen on the ground at the turn of the century, and much of what they recorded has since disappeared. (A number of other travellers from the last decade of the nineteenth century and the first decade of the twentieth deserve mention: Gray Hill, who reached Petra on his fourth attempt, in 1896 (*PEFQS* 1896: 24-26; *PEFQS* 1897: 35-44, 134-44); C.A. Hornstein, Sept. 1895 (*PEFQS* 1898: 94-103); C.W. Wilson, 1898 (*PEFQS* 1899: 304-16); William Libbey and Franklin E. Hoskins, 1902 (Libbey and Hoskins, 1905); F. Jeremias, 1906 (*PJB* 3 [1907]: 135-76).)

The events of the first World War (1914-1918) in general and the 'Desert Revolt' of the Arabs against the dying Ottoman Empire in particular brought a temporary halt to the scholarly exploration of Transjordan, though T.E. Lawrence's account of the revolt, *Seven Pillars of Wisdom* (1935), made many English readers familiar with the areas of 'Aqaba and Wadi Ram. Tafila, in the mountains of Edom, became known as the site of a minor battle. (For an account of the campaign, see *Palestine and Transjordan* [B.R. 514, Geographical Handbook Series, Naval Intelligence Division, 1943], 455-60.) After the war, however, exploration soon resumed. In 1924 W.F. Albright of the American Schools of Oriental Research led a party south of the Dead Sea into Moab, and followed this in 1933 with an excavation at Adir near Karak (Albright, 1924: 2-12; 1934: 14). His lead was followed by one of his students, Nelson Glueck, who in 1933 began a series of 'Explorations in Eastern Palestine' with a survey of ancient sites in Moab and Edom, published in *AASOR* 14, 15, and 18-19.

Nelson Glueck and his Successors

Noting that this work 'was really commenced by Albright', Glueck started by exploring 150 sites between Amman and Shaubak, mostly in the region of biblical Moab. Between 17 May and 21 May, 1933, Glueck visited northern Edom; he drove from the Hejaz railway line west to Shaubak, then north along the usual road to Tafila, where he turned east again to rejoin the railway at Jurf ed-Derawish (Glueck, 1934: 85, sites 9-33; map, Pl.I, p. 57). The following year, Glueck attempted to cover the whole of Edom (1935). He began with a camel ride through the Wadi 'Araba from the Ghor eṣ-Ṣafi to 'Aqaba (1935: 144, sites 3-22; 19 March—6 April, 1934). At 'Aqaba he endorsed F. Frank's recent discovery and identification of Tell el-Kheleifeh with the biblical Ezion-geber (1935: 48), noting there the presence of Edomite sherds of Early Iron Age I-II (Frank, 1934: 191-280 (243-45); Frank had commented, 'Die Keramik scheint mir sehr alt zu sein; römische Scherben bemerkte ich nicht' (p. 243); see Glueck, 1935: 48; 1939a; 3-7). Glueck then turned to motor transport to explore the Wadi Yutm, the Wadi Ḥismā, and Naqb esh-Shtar (sites 26-43; 6-11 April). From 14-16 April he explored the Wadi Dilagha (sites 87-104). A fortnight later Glueck began a second trip, starting with the Buseira region (sites 186-92; 6-7 May), moving on to the sites around Udhruh (sites 105-107; 8 May), then the central mountains between Udhruh and Petra (sites 108-51; 9-13 May), and then south to the hills west of Naqb esh-Shtar (sites 152-85; 16-19 May). Glueck then moved back north to the Shaubak region (sites 152-85; 21-26 May). A third trip (10-22 June) covered the region immediately south of the Wadi el-Ḥasā (sites 193-235) and completed Glueck's study of Edom.

Glueck's work differed from that of his predecessors such as Musil in that it made use of recent developments in the study of pottery in order to date the occupation of the sites visited. In his introductory pages in *EEP* I 1934, Glueck notes that

> From the surface finds of pottery or fragments of pottery alone, it is now possible to determine with a considerable degree of accuracy the age to which a particular place belongs, even when all other indications are missing. The new study of pottery has been placed on a scientific basis in recent years by the work of several scholars, particularly Père H. Vincent and Professor William F. Albright (p. 3).

On this basis, Glueck classified the sites he explored as Early Bronze, Middle Bronze, Early Iron, Nabataean, and later. In the case of the Iron Age sites, Glueck distinguished between Early Iron I and II, though listing many sites under the inclusive heading EI I-II. In *EEP* II, 1935: 123-37 he discussed 'Edomite pottery' in some detail. He noted the use of the spatulate bar handle and the button handle (Plate 26A), the distinctive painted decoration consisting of parallel vertical bars of dark brown or black paint, or of one or more horizontal bars of paint, or a combination of the two, often in conjunction with hand-burnishing. The problem for Glueck was the accurate dating of this Edomite pottery, and he was well aware of the need of stratigraphic excavation. He thought that the decorated pottery described above belonged to Early Iron I 'to judge from the shape of the vessels' (when compared with pottery from Western Palestine). He noted also the frequent use of a painted checker or trellis design on the rims of Early Iron I vessels, a type 'common in Palestine in LB' and occurring there also in Early Iron I (Glueck, 1935: 129). In addition to the painted pottery, Glueck noted the unpainted storage jars, plain bowls, cooking pots, loop-handled jugs, which he related to similar types in Moab and Palestine. With this material, Glueck made available important new evidence for the history of Edom, and on the basis of it published a number of conclusions which have been extremely influential, finding their way into many text books. They may be summarized, in Glueck's words, as follows:

1. 'Edom and Moab were occupied simultaneously, their histories running parallel courses.'

2. 'An advanced civilization flourished in Edom from the twenty-third to the eighteenth century B.C. when it completely disappeared.'
3. 'Between the eighteenth and the thirteenth centuries B.C. there is a complete gap in the history of settled communities in all of Edom. Not a site was discovered nor a sherd found which could be ascribed to Middle Bronze II or to Late Bronze.'
4. 'There was a highly developed Edomite civilization, which flourished especially between the thirteenth and the eighth centuries B.C. .... During their heyday... the Edomites could compare favourably with any of their neighbours. Their pottery is well made and artistically and distinctively decorated. They engaged extensively not only in trade and agriculture but also in industry, which included mining and smelting the ores in the 'Arabah. Their boundaries were well protected with a system of border fortresses in sight of each other...No records have as yet been discovered, but they certainly will be found if excavations are ever undertaken. The civilization of Esau was certainly not inferior to that of Jacob.'
5. 'From about the end of EI II in general, but in many sites from about the eighth century on, there is another gap in the history of settled communities in Edom. It lasted until the appearance of the Nabataeans' (Glueck, 1935: 138-39).

Glueck's survey work (which was later extended into the Negev) was followed by his excavations at Tell el-Kheleifeh (1938-40), where Glueck at first claimed to have revealed Solomon's seaport of Ezion-geber and his copper refinery (Glueck, 1938b, 1938c, 1939b, 1940b), and at Jebel eṭ-Ṭannur (1937), just south of the Wadi el-Ḥasā, where Glueck excavated a Nabataean temple on a mountain top whose cultic associations may very well have had a long pre-Nabataean history (Glueck, 1966; 1937a, 1937b, 1938a). But subsequent excavations, surveys, and historical research have brought considerable modifications to Glueck's synthesis. His thesis of an occupation gap from the eighteenth to the thirteenth centuries BCE will not hold for northern and central Transjordan, where MB and LB occupied sites and tombs are now well attested (Sauer, 1986: 1-26 [4-8]), though it remains the case that MB and LB remains are much less well attested further south and are rare in southern Moab and Edom (*ibid.*, 8). Glueck's thesis of a fully developed political kingdom of Edom between the thirteenth and the eighth centuries BCE, followed by a period of decline from about 800 BCE, needs to be revised and almost reversed in the light of the results of C.-M. Bennett's excavations at Umm el-Biyara, Tawilan, and Buseira, which demonstrated that these settlements (a small domestic settlement, a country village, and a royal acropolis respectively) flourished only in Iron II B and C rather than in Iron I (Bartlett, 1972: 26-37; 1973: 229-58). Similarly, G. Pratico's reassessment of Glueck's material and reports from Tell el-Kheleifeh has shown that this too belonged mainly to Iron II (and that consequently the frequent identification of Tell el-Kheleifeh with Solomon's Ezion-geber also needs reconsideration) (Pratico, 1985: 1-32). In particular it has been shown that most of the painted pottery from Edom belongs to Iron II, possibly beginning in Late Iron I under Cypro-Phoenician influence (Sauer, 1986: 1-26 [14]). The nature and extent of Iron I occupation and settlement in Edom is not yet clear. M. Weippert and B. MacDonald in recent fieldwork south of the Wadi el-Ḥasā have found Iron Age I pottery at a number of sites (Weippert, 1982: 153-62; MacDonald, Banning and Pavlish, 1980: 169-83; MacDonald, 1982c: 35-52; MacDonald, Rollefson and Roller, 1982: 117-31; MacDonald, Rollefson and Banning, 1983: 311-23), and Sauer points to some possible Iron I sherds published from Buseira (Sauer, 1986: 1-26 [10]); Bennett *et al.*, 1975: 1-19, fig. 8. 7-8; Bennett, 1983:13). Such evidence as exists, however, suggests little more than a thinly spread agricultural community for Edom in Iron Age I; it does not suggest the centrally organized, highly developed kingdom postulated by Glueck. Close examination of the biblical evidence similarly indicates that Edom did not become a centralized or politically developed state until the mid-ninth century BCE and the subsequent eighth-seventh century BCE period of vassaldom to Assyria.

In the last few years, further surveys over the land of Edom have been carried out: in the north between the Wadi el-Ḥasā and Tafila and in the northern 'Araba, by B. MacDonald (see above); in the central region from Tafila to Naqb esh-Shtar, by S. Hart (Hart, 1986a, 1986c; Hart and Falkner, 1985); in the Wadi Ḥismā and surrounding regions, by W. Jobling (Jobling, 1981: 105-12, and further reports in *ADAJ* 26 (1982) 199-209; 27 (1983), 185-96; 28

(1984), 191-202; 29 (1986), 211-20); and in the Ghor and Wadi 'Araba by W.E. Rast and T. Schaub (Rast and Schaub, 1974: 5-53; 1980; 21-61). These recent surveys have examined the ground much more thoroughly than their predecessors for all signs of human activity; previous surveys are criticized for limiting themselves to the more obviously visible remains. Modern exploratory work is also much more concerned with questions of ethno-archaeology, and a number of recent studies have focused on the apparently continual processes of sedentarization and nomadization in Jordan, and the relationship between the pastoral nomad and the agricultural community (e.g., Geraty and LaBianca, 1985: 323-30; Geraty, 1986: 117-44). The ancient industries of the region are also receiving attention; since Frank and Glueck drew attention to the mining activities in the Wadi 'Araba, Andreas Hauptmann and others have examined the mining sites of the eastern side of the Wadi 'Araba and attempted to date them more closely, paying particular attention to the ancient technology (their work adds further support for the view that Edom was at its most active in the eighth-seventh centuries BCE) (Hauptmann, 1986: 236-38). And lastly, there has been much recent study of environmental factors in the history of Jordan and the region of ancient Edom (cf. *SHAJ* II, 1985).

In spite of all the exploratory work of the last two centuries, it is clear that scholarly study of the antiquities and history of Edom is still only just beginning. None of the sites so far excavated has received more than preliminary publication. In spite of Glueck's confident hope, no excavation so far has revealed inscriptional evidence for the political history of Edom. Few attempts have been made at writing a history of Edom, apart from short articles in biblical dictionaries and unpublished theses. F. Buhl's monograph, *Geschichte der Edomiter* (Leipzig, 1893), remains a monument in the field.

Chapter 2

THE LAND OF EDOM

The Land, Routes and Settlements

The Edomites lived in a mountainous country; according to their Judaean neighbours, they lived in the clefts of the rock, and soared aloft like eagles (Jer. 49.16; Obad. 4). From the standpoint of Judah, this was an accurate picture, for the Edomite mountain plateau averaged some 4000 ft above sea level, rising to over 5000 ft near Rashadiya. Their land was generally higher than that of their neighbours to the north and west. The reason for this lay in the geological history of the area. The regions of modern Israel and Jordan are founded on the pre-Cambrian granite platform of the northern edge of the former continental mass of Gondwanaland, the basis of the present continents of Africa and Asia. On top of this granite platform was laid a succession of sandstone and limestone deposits by the ebb and flow of the sea of Tephys over the edge of Gondwanaland through the Cambrian, Jurassic, Cretacean and Eocene eras. The pre-Cambrian granite base can be seen at the southern end of Edom, in the Wadi 'Araba and the Wadi Yutm north of the Gulf of 'Aqaba. The first major covering of sandstone can be seen at Quweira and Petra. In the Cretacean and Eocene periods the whole country was covered over from the northwest by a thick layer of Cenomanian limestone, thinning out towards Ma'an in the southeast. Major faulting and cracking followed in the Pliocene era, creating the rift valley of which the Dead Sea and the Wadi 'Araba form a part. The mountains of Edom and Moab now lay on the raised western edge of a large land mass which tilted down eastwards towards the Persian Gulf. The faulting and tilting left the Edomite mountain range raised a little higher than the land to the west from which it had been fractured. Further transverse fracturing and some volcanic activity left their traces in a number of faults and in the hot springs found along the eastern side of the rift valley, as at Callirrhoe on the east side of the Dead Sea, or in the Wadi 'Afra near its confluence with the Wadi el-Ḥasā. (These may be the 'hot springs in the wilderness' mentioned in Gen. 36.24.) The water run-off westwards from the mountains into the rift valley eroded deep gorges such as the Wadi el-Mūjib and the Wadi el-Ḥasā; this latter, generally identified with the biblical Zered (Num. 21.12), became the border between the Moabites to its north and the Edomites to its south. (Burdon, 1959; Baly, 1974; 15-42; 226-40; Karmon, 1971: 7-20; Vita-Finzi, 1982: 23-27.)

In this way the land known to the writers of the Old Testament as Edom received its basic shaping. It consisted of a high plateau, separated from Moab by the deep-cut Wadi el-Ḥasā. The plateau fell abruptly 4000-5000 ft into the Wadi 'Araba to the west, and sloped away gently to the North Arabian desert on the east. From this quarter, Edom was easy of access, and the mountains appeared far less formidable than to the traveller from the Wadi 'Araba. The plateau can be further divided into a northern and a southern region. 'In the north, from the Wadi el-Ḥasa to a line between Kalat Aneiza on the Hejaz railway and Jebel Dana, it is volcanic country, broken by valleys and extinct craters' (*Palestine and Transjordan*, 1943: 418). This region is known as el-Jibal. The region to its south is known as esh-Shera; its limestine hills curve away towards Ma'an and the southeast, overlooking the Wadi Hismā and the eroded sandstone peaks of Jebel Ramm to the south. Beyond the esh-Shera to the southwest lie the granite mountains of Midian, pierced by the deep gorge of the Wadi Yutm through which runs the main road from Ma'an to 'Aqaba.

Though the power of Edom extended at one period as far as the Gulf of 'Aqaba, the heart of ancient Edom was the plateau between the Wadi el-Ḥasā and Ras en-Naqb overlooking the Wadi Ḥismā, together with the westward facing slopes overlooking the Wadi 'Araba. It is in these regions that most of the Iron Age sites or settlements are located, for here the rainfall is highest (the eastern slopes of the mountains lie in the rain shadow), and here on the western cliffs, at the junction of the Cenomanian limestone strata with the underlying Nubian sandstone, the springs break through to provide water for flocks and crops alike.

The landscape also determines the major routes, which ran along the western edge of the plateau, skirting the heads of the deeply cut wadis, or along the bottom of the eastern slopes of the mountains where they flatten out into the desert. These routes have hardly changed over the millennia; along the edge of the desert runs the modern 'Desert Highway' (the former Darb el-Haj, the pilgrim's route to Mecca) and the Hejaz railway, now rebuilt to carry phosphates to 'Aqaba. Along the western edge of the plateau runs the route now popularly known as 'The King's Highway', though whether this road is precisely identifiable with the King's Highway of Num. 20.17 is not clear, for there is little in the Old Testament account to show for certain which route across Edom the author had in mind. The exploration of the nineteenth century revealed the remains of more than one north-south route through Edom. From the Wadi el-Ḥasā there was more than one way up to the plateau. Burckhardt climbed up the Wadi 'Afra to 'Eima, while Irby and Mangles followed the Wadi La'ban past Jebel eṭ-Ṭannur (Burckhardt, 1822: 401-2; Irby and Mangles, 1844: 114). Brünnow and Domaszewski traced the line of Trajan's Roman road further east, up the Wadi Jā'īs to Thuwana (Brünnow, 1898: 33-39 [36]; Brünnow and Domaszewski, 1904: I. 80-91; cf. Glueck, 1934: 81). The first two routes joined shortly before meeting the third south of Dana; the road then continued south towards Dusaq and Shaubak. From Shaubak there are three possible ways south; one goes to Petra via 'Ain Nijil, el-Barīd and Beida; a second takes a more easterly course over high ground to Elji; and a third goes south-southeast to Udhruh and thence either to Ma'an or to 'Ain Sadaqa. From Ma'an or 'Ain Sadaqa roads led over Naqb esh-Shtar past Humeima and Quweira through the Wadi Yutm to 'Aqaba. Other roads or trails certainly existed connecting the plateau with the Wadi 'Araba, probably, for example, from Tafila, Buseira and Dana down to Feinān and Khirbet en-Nahas, and from the region of Petra to the Wadi 'Araba, either south past Jebel Harun and Sabra or north through the Wadi Namala. Communications between major Iron Age sites must be presumed to have existed, and closer search on the ground may reveal them, as similar roads have been revealed by survey in Moab (Mittmann, 1982: 175-80; Worschech and Knauf, 1985: 128-33; Worschech, 1985: 161-73 [172-73]). Ancient roads noted by Irby and Mangles have already been mentioned (above, p. 18).

The explorations of Glueck, MacDonald and Hart have revealed a large number of Iron Age sites in Edom, but much further work needs to be done before we have a sufficient understanding of their nature and relationship. The limited amount of excavation in Edom so far has shown clearly that, as we might expect, there were several different types of settlement in Edom in the Iron Age; Buseira had an acropolis, with major public buildings; Tawilan was a large village; and the houses on the top of Umm el-Biyara constituted a small and fairly short-lived domestic settlement. Tell el-Kheleifeh on the Gulf of 'Aqaba was probably a fortified caravanserai. Glueck's exploration of the Wadi 'Araba located copper-smelting sites at Feinān, Khirbet en-Nahas, Khirbet el-Ghuweiba and Khirbet el-Jariya (Glueck, 1935: sites 14, 10, 11, 12), with ruined buildings, smelters and slag heaps; a galleried mine was found at Umm el 'Amad in the cliffs west of Shaubak. Guarding the region was Khirbet Hamr Ifdān (site 9), described by Glueck as an acropolis rising some 30 metres above the Wadi 'Araba (Glueck, 1935: 20-35). More recent work has shown that smelting at Feinān and Khirbet en-Nahas is evidenced for the Chalcolithic, Early Bronze and Middle Bronze periods, and that the enormous Iron IIC (8th–5th centuries BCE) slag heaps, totalling over 100,000 tons, suggest a dramatic advance in smelting techniques in the Iron Age (Hauptmann, Weisgerber and Knauf, 1985: 163-95). Further slag heaps have been found in the Wadi Abū Khusheiba, the Wadi Abū Qurdiya, and Sabra near Petra (Hauptmann, 1986a: 31-43), where Glueck reported large deposits of iron ore (1935: 49). Glueck noted two more smelting sites near Umm Rashrash on the Gulf of 'Aqaba (*ibid.*, 42-48), and an acropolis guarding the southern 'Araba at Mene'iyyeh (*ibid.*, site 20).

The great majority of Edomite sites, however, lie on the plateau. Here Glueck stressed the importance of border fortresses (1935: sites 31, 34, 183, 184, 185, 217, 233), especially along the heights above the Wadi el-Ḥasā, along the hills overlooking the desert to the east, and above the Wadi Ḥismā in the south. MacDonald has examined the evidence for the dating of Glueck's proposed Iron Age fortresses in northern Edom, and accepts Khirbet Karaka, Rujm Karaka and Rujm Jā'īs as possible Iron II fortresses or watchtowers along the south bank of the Wadi el-Ḥasā, and suggests five other possible ones (MacDonald, 1984: 113-28). At the southern end of the plateau, at the head of Wadi Dilagha and just north of Ras en-Naqb, Hart in a thorough survey identified three large fortresses or walled villages, seven smaller fortresses or walled villages, two probable forts, two unwalled villages, two hamlets, one isolated building, and twenty-three further sherd find-spots (Hart, 1986: 51-58). This certainly suggests a strong preoccupation in this region with the need for defence. Hart notes also that the area is lacking in water, and cold in winter, and thus hardly suitable for citrus fruit, olives, grapes, wheat and barley, and was thus hardly a major agricultural area. This suggests an emphasis on pastoral rather than agricultural activities in this area. Glueck in his survey noted 'open country villages' (1935: 72; sites 85, 86), an 'agricultural centre' (*ibid.*, 70; site 77), a 'farm centre' (Khirbet Ghanam, *ibid.*, 67; site 53), 'in which the Edomite fellahin lived and stored their crops'. MacDonald in northern Edom noted evidence of ancient agriculture (he does not say what) around Rujm Jāʿīs (MacDonald, Rollefson, Roller, 1982: 126), and identified site 615 as a village, and sites 624, 648, and 654 as Iron Age farms (MacDonald, Rollefson, Banning, 1983: 319). More research is needed on the nature of these farming sites and activities and on what L.T. Geraty has called the 'food system' (Geraty and LaBianca, 1985: 323-30). It seems likely, however, that the farming community, whether raising crops or minding flocks, needed to protect itself; a large number of Glueck's sites are described as walled hilltop sites set in cultivated areas, apparently guarding fields (1935: sites 49, 52, 57, 60, 63, 65, 73, 76, 80, 88, 98, 130, 140, 141, 163, 164, 167, 204, 209, 215, 230, 231). Some of these sites may be what Finkelstein has called farm courtyards (Finkelstein, 1984: 189-209).

Edom and its Regions

So much may be known from modern exploration and scientific study of the land over the last two centuries. The Old Testament writers, to whom we are mostly indebted for our knowledge of the Iron Age kingdom of Edom, say very little about its geography and topography. We are nowhere given any full description of Edom's boundaries, or of her cities, towns and villages. In spite of G.A. Smith's comment that 'Edom is properly the name of the people,... and is doubtfully applied to their land, and certainly not till later writers' (G.A. Smith, 1966: 356), the earliest known reference to Edom (in *Pap. Anastasi vi*, referring to an event in the late thirteenth century BCE) shows that it is the land which was called Edom, and

not the people, who were called *shōsu* (bedouin) from the land of
Edom (Caminos, 1954: 293; *ANET*[3] 259; Giveon, 1971: 131-34). The
Old Testament frequently refers to Edom as a land (e.g., 2 Sam. 8.14;
1 Kgs 11.15; 22.47; Jer. 40.11), but can also use the term in a derived
ethnic sense (e.g., Gen. 36.1, 8, 19; Num. 20.18, 20, 21; 2 Kgs 8.20,
22; Amos 1.11), or comprehensively to denote both land and people
(e.g., Ps. 60.8; Ezek. 25.12-14). It is generally agreed that the name
probably derives from the red Nubian sandstone which is so
prominent a feature of southern Edom and parts of northern Edom.
The land is usually called simply 'Edom', and sometimes 'the land of
Edom' (Gen. 36.16, 17, 21, 31; Num. 20.23; 21.4; 33.37; 1 Kgs 9.26;
Isa. 34.6). Twice we read of the 'field of Edom' (Gen. 32.4; Judg. 5.4),
and once of the 'wilderness of Edom' (2 Kgs 3.8), apparently a
waterless plain (though the topography of this particular story is
largely invention; see below, p. 121). In Num. 20.17, the Israelites,
asking leave to traverse Edom, promise that

> we will not pass through field or vineyard, neither will we drink
> water from a well; we will go along the King's Highway, we will not
> turn aside to the right hand or to the left, until we have passed
> through your territory.

The general reference to fields, vineyards and wells is not unexpected;
the naming of the 'King's Highway' in Num. 20.17; Num. 21.22 is
more interesting. It has been suggested that the origin of the name
lies in the Assyrian period, the name indicating the adoption of the
road by the Assyrian king as it was strategically important for the
Assyrian control of the whole of the Transjordanian region in the
face of the Arab tribes to the east (Oded, 1970: 177-86 [182, n. 41]).
This 'King's Highway' probably includes the main north-south route
through Edom from the Wadi el-Ḥasā to Ras en-Naqb; Num. 21.22
refers to a more northerly section of it in Sihon's territory. In Num.
20.17, however, the narrator appears to be thinking also of a route
from Kadesh west of Edom eastwards into Edom, perhaps the route
described in the list of stations in Num. 33.41-49: Mount Hor,
Zalmonah, Punon, Oboth, Iye-abarim in the territory of Moab,
Dibon-Gad, Almon-Diblathaim, the mountains of Abarim before
Nebo, and the plains of Moab (Aharoni, 1979: 55, 201-2). This cross-
route connecting the region of Petra with the Negev and the
Mediterranean coast must always have been important; it was

perhaps the route by which the people of Gaza 'carried into exile a whole people to deliver them up to Edom' (Amos 1.6). Another important route is mentioned in Deut. 2.8, where the narrator pictures the Israelites journeying from Kadesh to the Red Sea, and then 'away from our brethren the sons of Esau who live in Seir, away from the Arabah road from Elath and Ezion-geber' in the direction of the wilderness of Moab. The 'Arabah road' is presumably the route along the Wadi 'Araba, much used by European explorers in the nineteenth century. It ran north from Elath and Ezion-geber, connecting them with Judah, and probably did not come under Edomite control (though doubtless threatened by Edom) until the late eighth or seventh century BCE. The mining activities of the Wadi 'Araba were well known to the Israelites; reference is probably made to them in Deut. 8.9, 'a land whose stones are iron, and out of whose hills you can dig copper'. Deuteronomy refers only to Israelite mining, and no particular site is mentioned; but ore deposits are found on both sides of the Wadi 'Araba, and the mining and smelting carried on at Umm el-'Amad and Feinān in Iron IIC at least were probably Edomite. Feinān may be identified with Pinon (Gen. 36.41 = Punon, Num. 33.42; Glueck, 1935: 32-36; Abel, 1938: II. 216-17; Hauptmann, Weisgerber, Knauf, 1985: 163-95 [164]). The Edomite mountains rising east of the Wadi 'Araba were well known to the biblical writers. In Jer. 49.16 the Edomites are addressed directly as

> you who live in the clefts of the rock,
> who hold the height of the hill.
> though you make your nest as high as the eagle's,
> I will bring you down from there, says the LORD.

The land of Edom could be divided into several distinct regions geographically, and their names may have been preserved in the Old Testament and elsewhere. The northern region of Edom, between the Wadi el-Ḥasā and Shaubak, now called el-Jibal, and known to Eusebius as Gebalene and to Josephus as Gobolitis (a name perhaps going back to the Ptolemaic administration), may appear in the Old Testament as Gebal. Ps. 83.7 incorporates a list of Israel's enemies, naming Edom and the Ishmaelites, Moab and the Hagrites, Gebal, Ammon and Amalek, Philistia and the inhabitants of Tyre. In this context, Gebal could be understood as referring to the northern region of Edom, but as elsewhere in the Old Testament the name

Gebal appears to indicate Byblos on the Lebanese coast north of modern Beirut (1 Kgs 5.18; Ezek. 27.9; Josh. 13.5), and as a reference to Byblos in Ps. 83.7, which also mentions Philistia and Tyre, would not be out of place, it is far from certain that northern Edom is meant in this Psalm, though it remains a possibility (Wiener, 1928: 180-86; *contra* Dahood, 1968: 274). A second regional name has been found in 'the land of the Temanites' (Gen. 36.34), from which presumably came Eliphaz the Temanite, one of Job's friends (Job 2.11). (Gen. 36.11, 15, 42 express the connection by making Teman a son of Eliphaz.) The place-name Teman occurs elsewhere in Jer. 49.20, where 'the inhabitants of Teman' appear in parallelism with 'Edom'; in Hab. 3.3, where Teman appears in parallelism with Mount Paran as a place from which God comes in glory; in Obad. 9, where Teman is mentioned in parallelism with Mount Esau; in Jer. 49.7-8 and Ezek. 25.12-14, where Teman is mentioned along with Dedan (El-'Ula in the Hejaz region of northern Arabia; cf. Isa. 21.13-14; Jer. 25.23). Glueck identified Teman with Tawilan, 'the largest Edomite centre in the Petra area', and Lagrange with Shaubak (Glueck, 1935: 82-83; Lagrange, 1897: 208-30 [217]; Simons, 1959; 90 § 253), but de Vaux has persuasively argued that Teman was not a city but a region, and in particular the southern region of Edom (de Vaux, 1969: 379-85). In this he follows the lead of Eusebius, who in his *Onomasticon* calls Teman a *chōra* (translated by Jerome as *regio*) and notes that in Hebrew the word *têmā* indicates the south. The reference of Ezek. 25.12-14 ('from Teman even to Dedan they shall fall by the sword') might suggest the Wadi Ḥismā region south of Ras en-Naqb, with which Clermont-Ganneau connected the name of Husham of the land of the Temanites (Gen. 36.34; Clermont-Ganneau, 1906: 464-71 [467, n. 3]).

Another region in some way related to Edom is 'the land of Uz', for in Lam. 4.21 the 'daughter of Edom' is further described in poetic parallelism as 'dweller in the land of Uz'. The land of Uz was the home of Job (Job 1.1), and the kings of the land of Uz are mentioned in a long list of the kings of the nations who are to drink the cup of the Lord (Jer. 25.17-26); here the MT lists the kings of the land of Uz between Pharaoh king of Egypt and the king of the land of the Philistines, but the Septuagint does not include them, and in view of the other associations of Uz, the kings of the land of Uz may be out of place at this point, as Simons supposes (Simons, 1959: 445 §1337).

However, Gen. 36.28 connects Uz with the clans of Seir, and so perhaps with much the same region as that implied by Jer. 25.20 (MT). The problem is further complicated by the direct association of Uz with Aram in Gen. 10.23 (cf. 1 Chron. 1.17) and 22.21, if this is not a completely different Uz (Simons, 1959: 8 §19). The solution to this puzzle perhaps depends upon one's starting point. If we start with the Job story, which assumes that the land of Uz lies within range of a raid by the Sabeans (Job 1.15), we may look for the land of Uz on the borders of northern Arabia, with which the Sabeans are clearly connected (Eph'al, 1982: 227-29). This would agree well enough with the references of Jer. 25.20 and Lam. 4.21. Exactly where the land of Uz was, however, and how it related to Teman and Edom, remain uncertain. One must perhaps think of the region south and east of Teman. Simons' proposal to link it with the hamlet el-'is near Buseirah seems unlikely (Simons, 1959: 25 §68).

In the Old Testament, the land of Edom is often closely connected with the land of Seir or Mount Seir. Scholars have often equated the two places, or claimed that the two names describe different aspects of the land, Seir (meaning 'rough', 'hairy') referring to the wooded eastern slopes of the Wadi 'Araba and Edom (meaning 'red') to the Nubian sandstone cliffs (cf. Abel, 1933: I. 283; Musil, 1926: 252-53). Some have related the name Seir directly to the modern region esh-Shera, in spite of the difference of consonants (Robinson and Smith, 1841: II. 552). Others have distinguished Seir from Edom by referring Seir to the southern Negeb region west of the Wadi 'Araba (Abel, 1933: I. 282-83; Bartlett, 1969: 1-20; Axelsson, 1987: 70). Weippert has identified Seir with the rough steppe and desert land on both sides of the Wadi 'Araba, and Edom with the sandstone region east of the 'Araba (Weippert, 1981: 291).

Our earliest evidence for both names comes from Egypt. In Amarna letter no. 88, from the first half of the fourteenth century BCE, Abdi-hiba of Jerusalem writes to Pharaoh that

> The land of the king is lost; in its entirety it is taken from me; there is war against me, as far as the lands of Seir (and) as far as Gath-carmel! All the governors are at peace, but there is war against me (*ANET*[3] 488).

In the thirteenth century, Rameses II is described as

> a fierce raging lion, who has laid waste to the land of the Shosu,

who has plundered Mount Seir with his valiant arm (Montet, 1933: 70-72; Albright, 1944: 228; Giveon, 1971: 100).

In the eleventh century, Rameses III boasts that

> I brought about the destruction of Seir [determinative, 'foreign people'] among the Shosu tribes. I laid waste their tents with their people, their belongings, and likewise their cattle without number. (Pap. Harris I. 76.9-11; *ANET*[3] 262; Albright, 1944: 207-33 (229); Giveon, 1971: 134-37).

These three passages refer to Seir, with no mention of Edom. From the end of the thirteenth century, however, we have the well-known message of an Egyptian frontier official, informing his superior that

> We have finished letting the Shōsu tribes of Edom pass the fortress of Merneptah-ḥotpḥimā-ĕ (l.p.h.), which is in Tjeku, to the pools of Pi-Tum ... (Caminos, 1954: 293; *ANET*[3] 259; Giveon, 1971: 131-34)

This Egyptian evidence nowhere connects or identifies Edom with the land of Seir, Mount Seir or the people of Seir, except in that both regions are peopled by *shōsu*, and it seems most natural to suppose that the two names referred to different, though perhaps neighbouring, places. Reference to Seir seems comparatively frequent, perhaps because Seir and its inhabitants were slightly nearer to Egypt than Edom was, and so more frequently attacked

It is the Old Testament which connects Seir and Edom. Most obviously, the names appear in parallel in the oracle of Num. 24.18, where Balaam promises that

> Edom shall be dispossessed,
> Seir also, his enemies, shall be dispossessed,

and in Judg. 5.4, where Deborah and Barak sing

> LORD, when thou didst go forth from Seir,
> when thou didst march from the region of Edom ...

Such parallelism does not necessarily indicate identity, as is demonstrated by the similar theophanic description of Deut. 33.2:

> The LORD came from Sinai,
> and dawned from Seir upon us;
> he shone forth from Mount Paran,

he came from the ten thousands of holy ones,
with flaming fire at his right hand.

This verse links Seir with Sinai and Mount Paran, and perhaps also
with Kadesh (cf. Burney, 1918:109-10), all places west or southwest
of the Wadi 'Araba and Edom. Seir is certainly not to be identified
simply with Sinai, and equally is probably not to be identified simply
with Edom.

That Seir was felt to be distinct from Edom, but came to be more
or less identified with Edom, is suggested by the way the two names
are related in a number of passages. In Gen. 32.3 the reference to the
land of Seir has clearly been explained at some stage in the history of
its transmission by the added phrase 'the country of Edom' (the
Hebrew phrase is *sedēh 'edôm*, which appears elsewhere only at Judg.
5.4, from which it probably derives). In Gen. 36, the redactional
linking of Esau who dwelt in the hill country of Seir with Edom is
evident, and will be discussed in another context (see below, Chapter
10). In Ezekiel 35, which is an oracle addressed to Mount Seir, an
explanatory phrase 'and all Edom' has been added to verse 15. The
enigmatic oracle 'concerning Dumah' in Isa. 21.11 ('One is calling to
me from Seir, "Watchman, what of the night?".') is the only other
prophetic reference to Seir, and this makes no explicit reference to
Edom at all; explanatory reference to Edom is conspicuous by its
absence, and clearly Seir could be mentioned independently (on this
text, see Macintosh, 1980: 131-43). In the post-exilic Chronicler,
however, Seir's identity with Edom is taken for granted (2 Chron.
20.10, 22-24; 25.5-20). In Ecclus. 50.26, Seir is one of three detested
nations, and is probably to be identifed with the people of Idumaea;
the other two are the Philistines and the Samaritans.

Some biblical passages suggest that the name Seir might have been
connected particularly with the region west of the Wadi 'Araba
rather than with Edom east of it. In Gen. 36, Esau is presented as
dwelling in the hill country of Seir (Gen. 36.8; cf. Deut. 2.4; Josh.
24.4), and the Horite clans are presented as being descended from
Seir and living in the land of Seir (Gen. 36.20-21, 30; cf. Deut. 2.12,
22). It has long been a matter for comment that the clans of Esau and
of the Horites appear to be closely related to various clans of
southern Judah and its borders (see further below, pp. 88-89). The
narrative of Deut. 1 in particular uses the name Seir with reference
to the territory west of the Wadi 'Araba. Thus Deut. 1.2, 19 envisages

an eleven days journey through the wilderness from Horeb to Kadesh-barnea by way of Mount Seir (the narrator is hardly thinking of a route through Edom east of the 'Araba, unless he locates Horeb in Midian), and Deut. 1.44-45 records an attempted journey from Kadesh 'into the wilderness in the direction of the Red Sea' in which the Israelites are routed by the Amorites (in Num. 14.45, by the Amalekites, who belong to the Negev, and by the Canaanites) 'in Seir' (LXX, 'from Seir') 'as far as Hormah' (i.e., Tell el-Meshash = Tel Masos, near Beersheba). They return to Kadesh, before journeying again in the direction of the Red Sea and 'for many days we went about Mount Seir' (Deut. 2.1). They then travel through the territory of the sons of Esau who live in Seir (Deut. 2.4), apparently via the 'Araba road (2.8) before turning away towards the wilderness of Moab. Other passages which might indicate that Seir could be used of the land west of the Wadi 'Araba are Josh. 11.17 and 12.7, which mention as the southernmost limits of Joshua's conquests Mount Halak 'that rises towards Seir', and 1 Chron. 4.42, which describes how some Simeonites (who belonged to the Negev) went to Mount Seir, destroyed the remnant of the Amalekites, and settled there. (For a more detailed examination of this material, see Bartlett, 1969: 1-20).

This limited evidence is unsatisfactory, but it does tend to support the view that, while the biblical tradition came to identify Seir with Edom (just as it identified Esau as the Edomite ancestor), Seir was not originally identical with Edom. Seir perhaps denoted the wilder, scrubby land south of Judah and Mount Halak and between Kadesh and the Gulf of 'Aqaba. This region was never claimed by Judah as its own, and its borders were never very clearly defined. It belonged to the south, with Sinai and Paran (Deut. 33.2), lying between them and Judah to the north, and Edom to the east.

Edomite Cities and Other Sites Named in the Old Testament

If the biblical writers were somewhat vague about the extent of Edom and its relationship with such places as the land of Teman, the land of Uz, and the land of Seir, they were equally limited in their knowledge of the cities, towns and villages of Edom. The best known places were Bozrah and Elath (which became Edomite only in the second half of the eighth century BCE). Most other places are little more than names preserved in lists or archival records. The following sites are associated with Edom in the Old Testament:

1. AVITH (Gen. 36.35; MT *'āwît*, LXX *Geththaim*; 1 Chron. 1.46; MT *'āyī(w)t*).(On the basis of the LXX, *BH* suggests *'ttym*; Marquart (1896:11) related this name to the epithet *'tym* attached to Cushan in Judg. 3.8, i.e., 'Cushan, head of 'Athaim', but the identification of Cushan (*kwsn*) with Husham (*ḥsm*) of the land of the Temanites will not stand). The name Avith has not been identified with any particular location in Edom, but has been connected with some hills called el-Ghoweythe noted by Burckhardt east of the upper course of the Wadi Mujib (Burckhardt, 1822: 374; Gunkel, 1922:394). This would place Avith east of Moab. The connection is far from certain but it is not inconsistent with the information given in Gen. 36.35, that Avith was the city of Hadad, the son of Bedad, 'who smote Midian in the field of Moab'. For this and other reasons, Hadad and Avith may originally have belonged to Moab, not Edom (Bartlett, 1965: 301-14).

2. BOZRAH (Gen. 36.33; Isa. 34.6; 63.1; Jer. 49.13,22; Amos 1.12: MT *boṣrâ*; LXX *Bosorra* (Gen. 36.33), *Bosor* (Isa. 34.6; 63.1). Bozrah seems to have been the most important city in Edom, as the mention of its 'strongholds' in Amos 1.12 suggests (though as the word is used in Amos ch.1 with reference to Damascus, Gaza, Tyre, Kerioth in Moab, and Jerusalem, it may not imply particular knowledge but only a general idea of what a capital city ought to have). In Amos 1.12 Bozrah is named in parallel with Teman, and in Isa. 34.6, 63.1, Jer. 49.22 with the land of Edom itself. Jer. 49.13 speaks of Bozrah and her cities. The LXX at Amos 1.12 replaces the name Bozrah by *themelia teicheōn* ('foundations of walls') and at Jer. 30.7,16 (= MT 49.13,22) by *polin periochēs* ('city of fortification'), which suggests that the translator no longer understood Bozrah as a place name, and strengthens the possibility that similarly the name Bozrah may also be concealed under the 'fortified city' of Psalms 60.9, 108.10 (MT, *'îr māsûr*, *'ir mibṣār*) (in each case the parallel is supplied by 'Edom') and the Mibzar of Gen. 36.42 (see below, no. 8). There is no mention of Bozrah in the historical writings, but it was clearly an important place, and its identification with the modern Buseira some 35 km southeast of the Dead Sea is generally agreed (the identification goes

back to Seetzen, 1854-59: III. 19). Excavations there by C.-M. Bennett have revealed an acropolis area with evidence of occupation from the eighth to the fifth century BCE with a surrounding wall succeeded by a casemate wall, and a major building, destroyed probably by the Babylonians, partially built over by another public building destroyed in the Persian period (Bennett, 1977: 1-10; 1983: 9-17).

3. DINHABAH (Gen. 36.32. MT _dinhābâ_, LXX _Dennaba_). Dinhabah is said to be the city of Bela, the son of Beor. According to Eusebius and Jerome, Dinhabah is to be identified either with Dannaia, 13 km north of Areopolis (Er-Rabba) toward the Arnon, or with Danaba, 11 km west of Heshbon, north of the Arnon (see Mittmann, 1971: 92-94). Neither of these places is in Edom, but in Moab. Moritz suggested that Dinhabah was a name compounded from _d_ (Old Arabic dialect for Hebrew _min_) as a prefix to the place name _nhbh_, but offered no identification (Moritz, 1937: 102-22 [104]).

4. ELATH (Deut. 2.8; 2 Kgs 16.5; MT _'ēlat_, LXX _'Ailon_; 1 Kgs 9.26, MT _'ēlōt_, LXX _Ailath_; cf. 2 Chron. 8.17; 26.2). This place name may lie behind the personal name Elah in Gen. 36.41. Elath or Eloth ('palm tree[s]') was clearly located at the head of the Gulf of 'Aqaba (Deut. 2.8; 1 Kgs 9.26; 2 Chron. 8.17), and Solomon built Ezion-geber near it (see below, no. 5). Uzziah (or Amaziah; cf. Montgomery and Gehman, 1951:443) built (or rebuilt) Elath, and restored it to Judah (2 Kgs 14.22; 2 Chron. 26.2), presumably after the destruction which may have taken place when Edom rebelled from Judah in Jehoram's reign (2 Kgs 8.20-22). According to 2 Kgs 16.6 (if 'Aram' may be emended to 'Edom' [Montgomery and Gehman, 1951: 458; Gray, 1980, 632]), the king of Edom recovered Elath for Edom in 735 BCE or soon after. F. Frank located Elath at a ruined site 1 km north of modern 'Aqaba (Frank, 1934: 191-280 [243]), but Elath may perhaps be identified with the site of Tell el-Kheleifeh which Frank discovered in 1932 and Glueck excavated in 1938-40. However, the classical Aelana or Aila is probably to be located at modern 'Aqaba. Strabo (_Geog._ xvi. 2.30) notes that it was 1260 stades from Gaza, and the Peutinger Table marks it 50 Roman miles from Phara(n) (on the Peutinger Table, see Finkelstein, 1979: 27-34; the Phara(n)—Haila section is shown on Finkelstein's Pl. II). Eusebius says that Ailath

was in his day called Aila, and was the base camp of the Tenth Legion (Klostermann, 1904: 6-8).

5. EZION-GEBER (Num. 33.35; Deut. 2.8; 1 Kgs 9.26; 22.49; 2 Chron. 8.17; 20.36; MT *'eṣyōn-geber*, LXX *Gasiongaber*). Ezion-geber seems to have been distinct from Elath, for Deut. 2.8 mentions both places side by side, apparently at the head of the Gulf of 'Aqaba, and 1 Kings 9.26 says that Solomon built ships at Ezion-geber 'which is near Eloth on the shore of the Red Sea'. According to 1 Kings 22.48 Jehoshaphat's ships were wrecked there. The distinction between Ezion-geber and Elath is underlined by the fact that Ezion-geber was a port, where ships could be built and might be wrecked, which is not said of Elath; and perhaps also by the fact that whereas Elath was recaptured by Edom, we are not told that Ezion-geber was. Ezion-geber was probably not an Edomite possession, and should not be counted among Edom's cities.

The location of Ezion-geber and Elath has been much debated. Until recently, only one suitable site with evidence of Iron Age occupation was known at the head of the Gulf of 'Aqaba. This was Tell el-Kheleifeh, which Frank, followed by Sellin, identified with Ezion-geber (Frank, 1934: 243; Sellin, 1936: 123-28). (Sellin rejected earlier attempts to locate Ezion-geber at Ghadyan [e.g., by Robinson and Smith, 1841: I, 250-51] on the grounds that, first, the prepositions used in the ancient sources to relate Ezion-geber and Elath [1 Kgs 9.26, *'et*; Eusebius, *para*; Jerome, *iuxta*] indicated closer proximity, and, second, that the distance between Ghadyan and Elath was too great to have become silted up between Solomon's time and the building of Elath.) Sellin suggested that originally Tell el-Kheleifeh, now some 600 metres from the shore, was lapped by a small channel extending north from the gulf; when this sanded up, the port was transferred to Elath, which he tentatively located at a ruined site 1 km north of 'Aqaba (though Sellin recognised that evidence of Iron Age presence there had not yet been found). Glueck agreed that Tell el-Kheleifeh could be identified with Ezion-geber, but denied that it was ever directly on the shore (because of the danger of storms) or that the port ever needed to be moved. Glueck argued that Ezion-geber (Tell el-Kheleifeh) was built in Solomon's time, west of Elath; both cities existed side by side until the destruction of Tell el-Kheleifeh in Jehoram's reign. When Uzziah built Elath and restored it to Judah (2 Chron. 26.2) two generations later, he rebuilt the ruins of Tell el-Kheleifeh which had meantime acquired the name Elath from the nearby town, which now fell into decay (Glueck, 1938c: 2-13; 1965: 70-87).

This complicated theory was unsatisfactory on several counts. In particular, it depended on Glueck's interpretation of the stratigraphy of Tell el-Kheleifeh and his dating of its strata; this has recently been reexamined, and Tell el-Kheleifeh's origins may be no earlier than the eighth century BCE. If Tell el-Kheleifeh was Ezion-geber, the site of the supposed Elath remained without evidence of Iron Age occupion. Tell el-Kheleifeh was not an obvious port; there were no signs of harbour installations. The thesis required that Uzziah rebuilt rather than built (*bnh*) Elath, and proposed an unlikely transference of name from one site to another.

These complications may now have been resolved by the discovery of Iron Age occupation at the island of Jezirat Fara'un some 12 km south of modern Eilat down the west coast of the Gulf of 'Aqaba. In 1961 B. Rothenberg argued that this was the site of the port and harbour of Solomon's Ezion-geber (Rothenberg, 1961: 86-92, 185-89; 1965: 18-28; 1972: 202-7), but the suggestion had been made earlier by Léon de Laborde and by G.H. von Schubert (de Laborde, 1836: 290; von Schubert, 1839: II. 379). Robinson had objected (1841: I. 251, n. 1) that Jezirat Fara'un was 'merely a small rock in the sea, 300 years long', which misses the point of the sheltered harbour facilities, and the potential for defence. If Jezirat Fara'un turns out to be the site of the Ezion-geber, there remains the question of the identification of Tell el-Kheleifeh. Mazar (1975: 46-48; 119-20) suggests identifying it with Abronah (Num. 33.34), between Jotbathah (Wadi et-Taba) and Ezion-geber (which he locates near 'Aqaba). It seems more likely, however, that Tell el-Kheleifeh is to be identified with the Elath built in the eighth century by Uzziah and taken by Edom c. 735 BCE. After the site's decay or destruction in the fifth-fourth centuries BCE, a new settlement arose at Aelana/Aila near modern 'Aqaba.

6. MAGDIEL (Gen. 36.43; 1 Chron. 1.54. MT *magdî'el*, LXX *Megediel*). If a place name lies behind this personal name, it is otherwise unknown. Eusebius sets it without further comment in the region of Gebalene (Klostermann, 1904: 124).

7. MASREKAH (Gen. 36.36; 1 Chron. 1.47; MT *maśrēqâ*; LXX *Masekka*). E. Meyer connected the name of this city with the word *śorēq*, vine, and thought of some vine-growing area in northern Edom, following Eusebius, who put Masrekah in Gebalene (Meyer, 1906: 373; Klostermann, 1904: 124). B. Moritz suggested that Masrekah must be somewhere in the land of the *sorqîm*, whom he identified with the Greek *Sarakēnoi*, who according to Ptolemaeus (*Geog.*V.16.3; VI.7.21; cf. Ammianus Marcellinus, *Rerum Gestarum Libri* XXIII.6.13) dwelt 'to the south of the mountains in the north (*sc.* of Arabia)', that is, in Edom or on its southern borders, together with the Skenitai, Thaditai, and Thamudenoi. The Sarakēnoi dwelt between these last two peoples, and according to Moritz this puts them south-east of 'Aqaba, or perhaps a little further north (Moritz, 1937: 114-15). Simons finds Masrekah in the modern Jebel Mushrāq about half way between Ma'an and 'Aqaba, which is more or less where Moritz suggested, and may be right (Simons, 1959: 221 §390). Recent exploration by W.J. Jobling has produced a limited amount of evidence of Iron Age sites in this region (Jobling, 1981: 105-12 [110, and 393, Pl. 31]).

8. MIBZAH (Gen. 36.42; 1 Chron. 1.53; MT *mibṣār*, LXX *Mazar*). Simons connects this name with the *'îr mibṣār* ('fortified city') of Ps. 108.10 (MT, Ps. 108.11), which might be a description of Bozrah (Simons, 1959: 221 §393). Eusebius identifies Mibzah with a large village of his own day, Mabsara, in Gebalene (Klostermann, 1904: 124).

9. PAU (Gen. 36.39; MT *pā'û*, LXX *Phogor*; 1 Chron. 1.50, MT *pā'î*, LXX *Phogor*). Eusebius names the place Phogor (Klostermann, 1904: 168), which is also the Greek version of the Hebrew Peor in Moab (Num. 23.28; 25.18; 31.16; Josh. 22.17). It is tempting to think of Pau as deriving from the well known Peor by error; it is otherwise unknown.

10. OBOTH (Num. 21.10; 33.43; MT *'ōbōt*, LXX *Oboth*). According to Num. 21.10, Oboth lies between the unnamed place where Moses erected the bronze serpent and 'Iye-abarim, in the wilderness which is opposite Moab, towards the sunrise'; according to Num. 33.44, Oboth lay between Punon and 'Iye-abarim, in the territory of Moab'.

Simons finds Oboth, surprisingly, at the oasis of el-Weibeh on the west side of the Wadi 'Araba (Simons, 1959: 259 §439). Seetzen suggested Katrabba in Moab, southwest of Karak (Seetzen, 1854-59: IV. 228, 230). The name Oboth ('water skins'), however, suggests a source of water, perhaps a spring or a well, and the context in each case suggests a site between Punon or somewhere in the Wadi 'Araba and Moab. Possibly we should locate Oboth at one of the springs in northern Edom between Dana (where the road from Feinān meets the main north-south highway through Edom) and the Wadi el-Ḥasā. Possibly el-'Aina itself, in the Wadi el-Ḥasā, might fit the description, in which case Oboth was in Moabite rather than in Edomite territory.

11. PINON or PUNON (Gen. 36.41; 1 Chron. 1.52; MT *pinon*; LXX *Phinon*; Num. 33.42-43, MT *punon*, LXX *Phino*). Pinon/Punon is generally (since Seetzen, 1854-1859: III. 17) identified with the copper-smelting site of Feinān on the east side of the Wadi 'Araba. The event described in Num. 21.4-9 may belong to this region. The Septuagintal form *Phino(n)*, the later Greek form *Phaino*, and the Arabic forms *Fenān or Feinān* perhaps suggest that the underlying form is Pinon rather than Punon, though the name may appear as a district name *Pwnw* in a topographic list of Rameses II from 'Amara West (Görg, 1982: 15-21 [16f., no. 45]). Pottery from the Late Bronze Age, Iron Age I, and Iron IIC has been found at Feinān (Hauptmann, Weisgerber, Knauf, 1985: 164).

12. REHOBOTH OF THE RIVER (Gen. 36.37; 1 Chron. 1.47: MT *rĕhobôt hannāhār*; LXX *Rooboth tēs para potamon*). The RSV translates this name as 'Rehoboth on the Euphrates', but while it is true that the Hebrew *hannāhār* by itself may indicate the Euphrates in the Old Testament, the Euphrates seems unlikely in the context of Gen. 36.31-39, and most commentators have preferred to seek Rehoboth by the Wadi el-Ḥasā. No convincing site close enough to this wadi to justify the epithet has been discovered, but Glueck noted a Khirbet Riḥāb (1935: 104, no. 212) which he described as 'a small Arabic ruin with 'Ain Riḥāb below it to the north-west'. This prompted Simons to decry Khirbet Riḥāb as 'too insignificant' and to point 'to the more important site of *ḫirbet musrab*' five km to the west (Simons, 1959: 221 §391), but this identification is hardly compelling. B. MacDonald,

however, found Iron Age and Byzantine pottery at Ras er-Rḥab (= Glueck's Khirbet Riḥâb) (MacDonald, 1982: 35-52 (42, site 178); cf. Zwickel, 1985: 28-34), and Riḥâb might therefore stand as a possibility, the 'river' presumably being the seil Riḥâb. The *Palastina historische-archäologische Karte* of Reicke and Rost (1979) place Rehoboth at Ḥirbet 'En Riḥâb, though locating this site on the Wadi 'Afrā, a few kilometres east of its real position. This map suggests an alternative site at Ḥirbet Ṭw. Ifğēğ, southeast towards the desert road.

Eusebius says that Rehoboth is 'now a military garrison in Gebalene', perhaps identifying it with the Roman military station Robatha near Zoara, known from Byzantine sources (Klostermann, 1904: 142). Other sites have been suggested for Robatha, however; e.g., Ruwatha, 3 km southeast of Buseira (Hartmann, 1913: 110-12, 180-98 [183-84]; Graf, 1979b: 121-27 [124-25]). Thus whether Rehoboth is identified with Robatha or not, its site remains doubtful.

13. REKEM (Num. 31.8; Josh. 13.21; 18.27; 1 Chron. 2.43-44: MT *reqem*; LXX *Rokom* [*Rekem*, Josh. 18.27; *Rekom*, 1 Chron. 2.43]). Rekem appears in the Old Testament as the name of a Midianite prince (Num. 31.8; Josh. 13.21), as a city of the tribe of Benjamin (Josh. 18.27), and as a son of Hebron in the tribe of Judah (1 Chron. 2.43-44). That it was also the Semitic name for Petra appears from Josephus (*Ant.* IV.4.7 [82]; IV.7.1 [161]), from Eusebius' *Onomasticon* (Klostermann, 1904: 144), and from a Nabataean inscription from Petra found in 1964 (Starcky, 1965: 95-97). However, it is doubtful whether Petra is mentioned under this name (or any other) in the Old Testament (Cf. G.A. Smith, 1966: 369; Buhl, 1893: 36; Hartmann, 1910: 143-51 [148]). See under Sela below.

14. SELA (2 Kgs 14.7: MT *hassela'*; LXX *Petra*. Cf. Num. 24.21; Judg. 1.36; Isa. 16.1; 42.11; Obad. 3). According to 2 Kgs 14.7, Amaziah king of Judah 'killed ten thousand Edomites in the Valley of Salt and took Sela by storm, and called it Joktheel, which is its name to this day'. The version of this incident given in 2 Chron. 25.11-12 omits the reference to the capture of Sela, but notes that 'The men of Judah captured another ten thousand alive, but took them to the top of a rock and threw them down from the top of the rock'. Many

commentators have identified Sela (meaning 'rock') and the rock
mentioned in 2 Chron. with Umm el-Biyara or el-Habis in Petra
(Glueck, 1935: 49, 82; Simons, 1959: 364 §923; Horsfield and
Conway, 1930: 369-88 [377]). Since Bennett's excavations on Umm
el-Biyara, this site has been ruled out by a number of scholars on the
grounds that it was not occupied before the seventh century BCE.
Sela has therefore increasingly been identified with Khirbet Sil' a few
miles north of Buseira, partly on the ground that this lies much
nearer to the Valley of Salt (identified as the Ghor south of the Dead
Sea) than does Umm el-Biyara. S. Hart has recently shown,
however, after a pottery survey of Khirbet Sil', that 'archaeologically
speaking, Sela' is no more, or no less, likely to be the Rock of Edom
than Umm el-Biyara' (Hart, 1966b: 91-95 [93]). (The proposed
identification of Sela with Kh. Sil' was made by Hartmann [1910:
143-51 [150], but goes back to Seetzen [1854-59: I. 425; III.19]). The
map prepared for the publication of Seetzen's work (dated 1859),
however, shows El Szilla, identified with Sela, a few miles south of
Bzéra (i.e., Buseira), and it looks as if the two names have been
inadvertently reversed in the position on the map (Hartmann, 1910:
143-51 [150]; Seetzen, 1854-59: I.425; III.19).

In Judg. 1.36; Isa. 16.1; 42.11, the Hebrew *sela'* is taken by the RSV
as a place name, but it is not clear that 'the rock' in these references
or at Num. 24.21 and Obad. 3 is a proper name, or if it is, that it is the
place referred to in 2 Kgs 14.7. Glueck observes that 'there must have
existed during the Early Iron Age in eastern Palestine numerous sites
built on more or less isolated prominences and known by the name
"Sela"' (Glueck, 1939: 26; Buhl. 1893: 34-35).

The name Joktheel ('God has captured') reappears in Josh. 15.38
as that of a city in the Shephelah of Judah, but it is not heard of again
in Edom, in spite of the historian's comment that it was still used in
his own day.

15. TOPHEL (Deut. 1.1: MT *topel*; LXX *Tophol*. In Deut. 1.1 Moses is
said to have spoken to Israel 'in the Arabah over against Suph,
between Paran and Tophel, Laban, Hazeroth and Di-zahab'. The
meaning and geographical reference of this passage is far from clear.
The reference to Suph may conceal an original reference to the Yam
Suph, i.e., the Red Sea and the Gulf of 'Aqaba, and the remaining
names may indicate a topographical procession from Paran through

the 'Araba to Tophel and other places. Some have therefore identified Tophel with Tafila in Edom. But Laban and Hazeroth have been connected with Libnah and Hazeroth of the list in Num. 33 (see Num. 33.17-21), and probably belong to Sinai. The identification of Tophel with Tafila remains speculative. Cazelles (1959: 412-15) connects Tophel with a region (not a town) in Moab.

16. VALLEY OF ZERED (Num. 21.12; cf. 'the brook Zered', Deut. 2.13-14: MT *nahal zered*, LXX *pharanx Zaret*). Simons (1959: 260, §266) identifies the Zered with the Wadi el-Ḥasā, noting that 'The parallelism between the crossing of the *nahal* Zered (Deut. 2.9-13) and that of *nahal Arnon* (Deut 2.18-24) is by itself a sufficient reason to identify the former with no smaller a stream than Wadi el-Ḥasā, the 'river' (*nahar*) of Gen. 36.37 // 1 Chron. 1.49 (§391), which Isa. 15.7 (and very probably also Amos 6.14) calls 'the brook of the willows' (§266)'. Most scholars have identified the Zered with the Wadi el-Ḥasā, with or without a bracketed question-mark. Simons' point is less applicable to the account in Num. 21.12, where the Valley of Zered is not described as the boundary between Edom and Moab (as the Arnon is in the next verse described as the boundary between the Moabites and Amorites), and indeed the position of the Valley of Zered, after Oboth and Iye-abarim, suggests that the Wadi el-Ḥasā already lies behind the Israelites. The Valley of Zered might possibly be the upper end of the Wadi el-Ḥasā where it leaves the desert at Qal'at el-Ḥasā to cut through the mountains, or perhaps the upper reaches of the Wadi en-Nukheila as it flows north along the east side of Moab to join the Wadi el-Mūjib. The identity of the Valley of Zered must remain uncertain.

From all this it is clear that the Old Testament historians and prophets had little first hand knowledge of the topography and cities of Edom. Bozrah was known as important; Elath was known, but Elath had been a Judaean possession. Edom's mountains were her best known feature, and a particular place called 'the rock' might have been accepted knowledge, even if its whereabouts were not precisely known; later Diodorus Siculus XIX.95, quoting Hecataeus, can similarly refer to a well known rock in the desert, to which the Nabataeans retreated in time of danger. Pinon/Punon, as an important smelting centre, was known and its whereabouts fairly accurately indicated. But places like Avith, Dinhabah, Magdiel, Mibzar, Pau, Oboth, Rehoboth Hannahar, and Tophel seem to have been little more than names. Some may not have been in Edom at all (Avith, Dinhabah, Oboth, Pau, Tophel); some may not be genuine place names (Magdiel, Mibzar; this last is perhaps a literary creation from a poetic phrase describing Bozrah). Reqem is not connected with Edom by the Old Testament, though as the Semitic name for Petra it may be of some antiquity. The land of Edom remained largely unknown to the peoples of Judah and Israel. This is hardly surprising, in view of the centuries of hostility that began with David's subjugation of Edom.

Chapter 3

SETTLEMENT AND OCCUPATION

Prehistoric Settlement from the Middle Pleistocene to the Middle Bronze Age

What became known in Old Testament times as the land of Edom was inhabited long before history began to be recorded (Stekelis, 1960: Anati, 1963: 59-60). It may help to get the Iron Age occupation of Edom in better perspective if we first note what we can of the earlier occupants of the land; what follows is little more than a list of the results of various surveys and excavations, but it reveals in particular the importance of the environment, and its changes, in the history of settlement. There is evidence for human activity at Ubaidiya in the Jordan valley as far back as the Middle Pleistocene period (c. 300,000—200,000 years BP) (Stekelis, 1960: Anati, 1963: 59-60). A Lower Palaeolithic site with Late Acheulian artifacts was recently discovered near Shaubak; the artifacts seem to have been the deposit of hunters who exploited the annual migration of game, ambushing the animals as they returned each spring to the plateau for their summer grazing from their winter quarters in the Wadi 'Araba (Rollefson, 1981: 151-68; 1985:103-107). In 1979, a survey of Palaeolithic sites in a region of 12 square kilometres around and below Ras en-Naqb found evidence at 57 sites of human activity in the late Pleistocene and Holocene periods, and a further three sites were found near Quweira and on the edge of the Jafr depression (Henry, 1979: 79-85; 1982: 417-44; Henry, Hassan, Jones and Henry, 1981: 113-46; 1983: 1-24; Henry and Turnbull, 1985: 45-64). This evidence corresponds well with what is known from other contemporary sites in the Levant. Sometime about 100,000 years ago the basin of Wadi Judaiyid below Ras en-Naqb was eroded and filled with alluvial fans, which were then covered by dunes of blown sand. On these,

Lower Palaeolothic Mousterian artifacts were found. Moister conditions followed, during which the Lisan lake was formed in what is now the Jordan valley, and there was Middle Palaeolithic Mousterian occupation of the higher ground above the edge of Ras en-Naqb. This period may be dated to about 75,000 to 60,000 years ago. There followed a drier period of some 20,000 years, in which, however, human activity is evidenced by the Mousterian site of Tor Sabiha (J8). During the following period, from 40,000 to 30,000 years ago, there seems to have been an improvement in the area, evidenced by six Upper Palaeolithic sites, but this period was in turn followed by a lengthy more arid period, beginning c. 35,000 BCE. It ended with another moister period, which soon created a new set of alluvial fans, sometime before c. 11,000 BCE on which some twenty Epipalaeolithic sites were found. On the drift sand overlying the fans were found two Natufian sites (J2, J14), dated on C-14 evidence to the eleventh millennium BCE. These were soon covered by blown sand, and moisture again seems to have declined until the ninth millennium BCE when a Pre-Pottery Neolithic site was established on sand dunes overlying the alluvial fan. Surprisingly, no Pottery Neolithic sites were found in this area ('probably more an expression of bias in the survey or geologic exposures than a real lack of occupation by PPNB groups'), but no less than 25% of the 57 sites discovered had a Chalcolithic component; site J24 has a C-14 dating of 3770 +/− 149 BCE (uncalibrated, half-life 5568 years) (Henry, Hassan, Henry, Jones, 1983: 1-24; 1981: 113-45 [143]).

The results of this survey of 12 sq. kilometres around Ras en-Naqb may not be representative of Edom as a whole, for it shows that in the Late Pleistocene and Holocene periods, at any rate, the terraces below the plateau were more suitable for occupation, especially in the drier periods, than the plateau itself. In moister periods the plateau was more attractive, perhaps in part because its savannah-like vegetation was the home of animals that could be hunted for food (though the hunting seems to have taken place at the edge of the plateau). Further north, a survey of the region south of the Wadi el-Ḥasā has revealed lithic evidence of human activity from all periods of the Late Pleistocene for the whole terrain between the western edge of the plateau and the Desert Highway (MacDonald, 1980: 169-83; MacDonald, Rollefson, Roller, 1982: 117-31; MacDonald, Rollefson, Banning, 1983: 311-23). For the region between the western edge of the plateau and the Wadi La'ban, surveyed in 1979, MacDonald noted that all Palaeolithic periods were represented, including Epipalaeolithic (Macdonald, 1980: 169-83; 1982: 35-52). Between the Wadi La'ban and the ridge overlooking the Wadi 'Ali, in 1981 MacDonald recorded the presence of Lower Palaeolithic artifacts (pre-80,000 BCE) at 17 sites, Middle Palaeolithic (80,000—35,000 BCE) at 102 sites, Upper Palaeolithic (35,000—14,000 BCE) at 54 sites, and Epipalaeolithic—Early Neolithic at 36 sites, commenting that Epipalaeolithic was not adequately represented, though it could not always be distinguished from Early Neolithic (MacDonald, Rollefson, Roller, 1982: 117-31 [120]). Further east, in 1982, out of a total of 298 lithic sites surveyed, MacDonald noted 30 Lower Palaeolithic, 50 Lower—Middle Palaeolithic, 188 Middle Palaeolithic, 35 Middle—Upper Palaeolithic, 20 Upper Palaeolithic—Epipalaeolithic, 7 Epipalaeolithic, 17 Epipalaeolithic—Early Neolithic, 48 Early Neolithic, 2 Pottery Neolithic, 1 Chalcolithic, 5 Chalcolithic—Early Bronze (MacDonald, Rollefson, Banning, 1983: 311-23 [314]). MacDonald's statistics for the percentage of sites discovered for each period thus do not entirely correspond with the findings from Ras en-Naqb, where Epipalaeolithic and Chalcolithic sites seem relatively more common than along the Wadi el-Ḥasā.

Further evidence for Epipalaeolithic and Neolithic sites in Edom includes a Kebaran rock-shelter on a ledge above Wadi Madamagh near Petra found by D. Kirkbride (1958: 55-58), and an important Natufian base camp at Tabaqa where the Wadi el-Ahmar joins the Wadi el-Ḥasā. It is probably to be associated with a smaller contemporary site ½ kilometre away on the south bank of the Wadi el-Ḥasā. The two sites are dated to the tenth millennium BCE (Byrd, Rollefson, 1984: 143-50; see MacDonald, Rollefson, Banning, 1983: 311-23 [316]). Natufian occupation is evidenced at Beida near Petra (Kirkbride, 1966: 8-66 [47-51]; 1984: 9-12), and a Natufian crescent was picked up at Wadi Ram (Kirkbride, Harding, 1947: 7-26 [26]) (in the same area lithic evidence of Upper Palaeolithic or Mesolithic was found at Qa' Um Salab and Qa' Abū Qureishi, and Neolithic microliths in Wadi Ram [Zeuner, Kirkbride, Park, 1957: 17-54]). The dating of the Wadi ˙idaiyid Natufian site to the eleventh millennium has led D.O. Henry to suggest that the Natufian culture originated in Jordan and expanded into Palestine (and not *vice versa*) (Henry, 1982: 417-44).

The Natufian period is followed by the Neolithic period. A.M.T. Moore has recently proposed a four-stage sequence for the Levantine Neolithic: (1) Archaic Neolithic, c. 8500—7600 BCE; (2), Neolithic II, 7600—6000 BCE; (3), Developed Neolithic, 6000—5000 BCE; (4), Neolithic IV, 5000—3750 BCE. The Archaic Neolithic is distinguished, *inter alia*, by circular houses with floors below ground level and the under floor burial of bodies from which the heads had been detached. To this period belong Nahal Oren Stratum II and Layers IV, III, II, Mureybat IB, II, III, and Jericho PN and PPNA (Moore, 1982: 1-34). So far there is no certain evidence of sites from this period in southern Jordan (though some of MacDonald's Early Neolithic sites [8000-6000 BCE] might qualify). Moore's Neolithic II (7600-6000 BCE), however, with its rectilinear houses, coloured plaster, and plastered skulls (Jericho PPNB, Beisamun, Tell Ramad, Abu Hureyra, Ras Shamra, Tell Labweh, and Munhatta) is evidenced at Beida (Kirkbride, 1966: 8-66; 1984: 9-12), and Kirkbride notes other possibly contemporary sites in the same region at Shaqaret M'Siad 6 kilometres north, at 'Ain Abu Alleqa in Petra, at el-Thughara southwest of Petra, and at Adh Dhaman south of Sabra (Kirkbride, 1966: 8-66 [53-57]; 1985: 117-24). Another PPNB site has been identified at Khirbet Hammam on the Wadi el-Ḥasā (Rollefson, Zafafi, 1985: 63-69).

The following millennium (Moore's Developed Neolithic, 6000—5000 BCE) remains unevidenced in southern Jordan. MacDonald notes that no definite Middle Neolithic ceramic sites (6000—4750 BCE) have been found in Jordan (MacDonald, Rollefson, Banning, 1983: 311-23 [318]). C.-M. Bennett, however, has excavated a Pottery Neolithic A site with pit dwellings 5 kilometres east of Bab edh-Dhra', and Jobling noted Pottery Neolithic sherds in the Wadi Rummān and Wadi Ishrin (Bennett, 1980: 30-39; Jobling, 1981: 105-112); he also noted a number of probably Chalcolithic sites between Ma'ān and 'Aqaba (Jobling, 1981: 105-12; 1982: 199-209; 1983: 185-96; 1984: 191-202; 1985: 211-20). Price and Garrard (1975: 91-93) noted a site in the Ram area of the Wadi Ḥismā which they dated to the Neolithic/Chalcolithic period, though it was apparently without pottery, which begins to appear in the Levant in the sixth-fifth millennia BCE. V.A. Clark (1979: 57-77) investigated a necropolis near Bab edh-Dhra' with cairn burials and pre-Ghassulian Neolithic pottery. MacDonald found Late Neolithic pottery at two sites in

1982 (sites 857, 870) (MacDonald, Rollefson, Banning, 1983: 311-23 [318]). He found no recognisable Chalcolithic in 1979, though further east in 1981 he noted two sites (308, 346), and in 1982 in the Wadi 'Ali five more (616, 647, 858, 915, 939) (MacDonald, Banning, Pavlish, 1980: 169-83; MacDonald, Rollefson, Roller, 1982: 117-31 [121]; MacDonald, Rollefson, Banning, 1983: 311-23 [318]). Chalcolithic artifacts were found in the Ḥismā region at Al-Nakhila by Kirkbride and Harding (1947: 7-26 [26]). An important Chalcolithic site was excavated by D.O. Henry at Jebel el-Jill near Ras en-Naqb; on C-14 evidence this was dated to the early fourth millennium BCE (Henry Turnbull, 1985: 45-64). The evidence for copper mining at Timna in the Chalcolithic period has recently been strongly challenged by J.D. Muhly, who points to the absence of metal objects or published flints or C-14 datings that might evidence the Chalcolithic dating of the important site 39 at Timna (Muhly, 1984: 276-92).

For the following Early Bronze period, MacDonald notes that south of Wadi el-Ḥasā in 1979, 'Several Early Bronze I—III period (3300—2400 BCE) sites were surveyed; some of these are nothing more than sherd scatters, some are now the sites of modern farms and have been partially or completely destroyed, while others are major architectural sites. Early Bronze IVA-B (2400—2100 BCE) pottery was found in small quantities at several sites, the most important of which was Mashmil (MacDonald, 1982c: 35-52 [38]). D. Graf noted the presence of Early Bronze IVA sherds at Ruwatha near Buseira in 1979 (Graf, 1979a: 72; 1979b: 121-27). MacDonald's 1981 survey further east revealed three or four 'Late Chalc.—EB I' (3750—2900 BCE) sites, six or eight EB I sites (3300—2900 BCE), but nothing for EB II-IV (MacDonald, Rollefson, Roller, 1982: 117-31 [126]). His 1982 survey noted five Chalc.-EB sites, and fifteen EB I sites, which included terrace walls, camps, hamlets, and stone enclosures along the south bank of the Wadi el-Ḥasā and on the ridges above the minor wadis (MacDonald, Rollefson, Banning, 1983: 311-23 [318-19]). In a survey of the southeastern shores of the Dead Sea, Rast and Schaub noted several EB sites: Bab edh-Dhra', eṣ-Ṣafi and Feifeh from EB I-III, and Numeira and Khanazir from EB III-IV (Rast, Schaub, 1974: 5-61). Glueck (*EEP* II, 1935: 148) lists only three EB III—MB I sites for Edom: eṣ-Ṣāfi, Feinān, and Khirbet Mashmil; his map IIb in *EEP* III (1939) adds 'Ain Nijil. It is not irrelevant to add at this point the evidence from Moab immediately to the north. Glueck listed sixteen EB III—MB I sites in *EEP* II (p. 148), and showed twenty-four sites between Wadi Ḥisban and Wadi el-Ḥasā on his maps IIa, IIb in *EEP* III. Miller's survey in central and southern Moab has indicated nine sites with slight evidence of EB I pottery, fifteen with EB II—III pottery, and eighteen with EB IV pottery (though three of these had only one attributable sherd) (Mattingly, 1983: 481-89).

To this evidence, however, we can add at least for Moab the evidence of several excavated sites: Adir, 'Arā'ir, Bab edh-Dhra', Tell Iktanu, and Khirbet Iskander (Cleveland, 1960: 79-97; Olavarri, 1965: 77-94; 1969: 230-59; Lapp, 1966: 104-11; Rast, Schaub, 1976: 1-32; Prag, 1974: 69-116; 1986: 61-72; Parr, 1960: 128-33; Richard, Boraas, 1984: 63-87; Richard, 1982: 289-99; 1983: 45-53). As Suzanne Richard has pointed out, all these sites present two clear occupational levels or building phases, whose material culture is closely related to EB III, and the 'classic' MB I (Richard, 1980: 5-34 [27, n. 3]). Kay Prag (1985: 81-880 and S. Richard (1980: 5-34; 1984: 63-87) have demonstrated that this material (which Prag identifies as EB-MB and Richard as EB IV) shows development from and continuity with the traditions of EB III, and does not necessarily indicate new immigrant groups or even a non-sedentary society in which pastoral and agricultural groups coexist. While Richard underlines internal development (without any occupation gap) from EB III, with some intermingling of Syro-Palestinian traditions, Prag 'pursues a mid course between invasion and indigenous continuity', referring to

> the infiltration of pastoralist-cultivators, who did not blot out the preceding population, but were absorbed by it, and contributed, by a process of nomadization, to the end of urban life; bringing not a complete new ceramic industry but traceable innovations and some brand new customs (Prag, 1985: 81-88 [81, 87]).

This EB IV/EB-MB period is dated c. 2350—1900 BCE; Suzanne Richard has little doubt that at Iskander EB IV was preceded by EB III occupation (Richard, 1983: 45-53), but the available evidence suggests that (apart from the southeastern plain of the Dead Sea) EB III is less well attested in southern Jordan than is EB IV.

The Middle Bronze period is poorly evidenced. MacDonald noted that in 1979 the Wadi el-Ḥasā survey found sherds, in small quantities, at two sites (64 and 172). In 1981, further east, one possible MB sherd was picked up at site 362: in 1982, no MB sherds were found (MacDonald, Banning, Pavlish, 1980: 169-83 [173]; MacDonald, Rollefson, Roller, 1982: 117-31 [126]; MacDonald, Rollefson, Banning, 1983: 311-23 [319]). As is well known, Glueck postulated an occupation gap between the eighteenth and thirteenth centuries BCE.

All this evidence needs careful assessment. Clearly the Old Testament Edomites (and their shadowy predecessors, the Horites) were not the first people to live in this region. Signs of human activity and occupation span the millennia from the Middle Pleistocene until the present day, though the limited evidence suggests heavier occupation at some times than at others. It is important, however, first to relate the human activities on the land to the general environment prevailing at any one time, and secondly, to see the occupation of the land in the context of the occupation of the adjacent areas. It is clear from what has already been said that the occupants of this region were at no time living or developing in complete independence of their neighbours. Their life-style at any given period relates more or less closely to that of the surrounding peoples of the Levant. From earliest times there was contact between the occupants of southern Jordan and their neighbours, as the presence at Beida of obsidian originating from central Anatolia and of sea shells from the Mediterranean or perhaps the Gulf of 'Aqaba shows.

Environment and Population

The question of the climatic environment has received much attention in recent years. It has long been argued that climatic fluctuations in areas of limited rainfall can make all the difference between the possibilities and the impossibility of survival. D.O. Henry has related the evidence for human activity in the Ras en-Naqb area in the Late Pleistocene to the climatic conditions (Henry, Hassan, Henry, Jones, 1983: 1-24). Thus Middle Palaeolithic man took advantage of moister conditions some 75,000—60,000 years ago to occupy the Ras en-Naqb uplands, and Upper Palaeolithic man took equal advantage of moister conditions 37,000—32,000 years ago to occupy the Negev and Sinai. Another moist phase is associated with the late Geometric Kebaran some 13,000 years ago, and, similarly, a wetter phase allowed the Mesolithic and Neolithic cultures to flourish, before slightly drier conditions began with the Chalcolithic period. D. Kirkbride noted that to sustain the vegetation evidenced for PPNB Beida, 300-350 mm p.a. of rain were needed (the present rainfall is an irregular 170—220 mm), and more groundwater than is currently available (Kirkbride, 1985: 127-124 [120]). According to N. Shehadeh (1985: 25-37), the urban EB period c. 2850—2650 BCE was the last period of abundant rainfall in southern Jordan, leading to a drier period which became positively arid between c. 1800 and 1300 BCE.

The conditions of the EB—MB periods have been of particular interest since Glueck published his findings half a century ago. Glueck argued (1935: 137) that for Edom and Moab

> Recurrent phases of extensive settlement belie the theory made popular by Ellsworth Huntington of an increasing diminution of rainfall and corresponding desiccation of Arabia and related parts of the Near East. The abandonment and reoccupation of entire countries such as Moab and Edom cannot be explained by popular theories of precipitation cycles rendering human habitation of these areas progressively impossible. Although all the variables which make for the development and disappearance of population cannot be established for Moab and Edom, the explanation both for the periods of intensive settlement and for those of extended abandonment of their countries is to be found rather in strictly human and particularly in political and economic factors than in climatic changes. Increasingly large areas of southern Jordan are today being occupied by a sedentary population because of the newly established public security and improved economic conditions there. The Negev of Palestine, for instance, could be made as habitable today as it was in the Byzantine period.

That the population of Edom and Moab has fluctuated and continues to fluctuate (and since Glueck's words were written, the population has expanded greatly) is clear. The relative importance of climatic and human factors is still a matter for debate, but it is becoming clearer that human activity and the environment can interact, sometimes with disastrous long-term results for human and animal and plant life. L.T. Geraty and J.R. Harlan have recently drawn on the changes observed in southern Jordan over the last century to illustrate earlier changes. Geraty takes as a typical example the history and currently observed economic situation of Hisban (Geraty, LaBianca, 1985: 323-30; Geraty, 1986: 117-44). Excavation of Tell Hisban has suggested that it was settled in the twelfth century BCE and flourished for the next five hundred years; it declined, was abandoned, and not resettled until c. 200 BCE. It flourished again until c. 750 CE, when it once again declined and was abandoned until c. 1200 CE. It revived under the Mamluks, but suffered another decline from the fifteenth century until it began to be rebuilt in the twentieth. Geraty asks, 'Why the oscillation?', and answers this question by pointing to the history of food production and population development over the last century. Since 1880, the population of the area has risen from about 2,000 to over 40,000 (greatly helped by an influx of Palestinian refugees after 1947). In this period there has been a transition in land use from sheep and goat farming via mixed pastoral and agricultural farming to intensive food production (greatly aided by the skills of the incoming refugees). The country has been policed and pacified; the older fortified houses have become barns, while their owners have built for themselves new, modern houses and villages have expanded. Poultry and even pig-rearing have replaced sheep and goat farming, and pasturage has thus been freed for food production. Roads, reservoirs, market places and various public buildings have appeared to serve the modern agricultural community. It is at this point, when an expanding urban economy is making high demands of the food-producing farmers, that the system is most at risk. Over-exploitation of poor soil and limited water resources leads to exhaustion of the land, and the economy begins a new cycle of decline. Geraty suggests that this pattern has been repeated several times in the last three millennia. His picture supports Glueck's emphasis on the human, political and economic factors over against the theory of climatic change. However, exhaustion of the soil, and the resultant decline of vegetation, lead to a lower rainfall and to a drop in the water table, and restoration of fertility may take many generations. J.R. Harlan (1985: 125-29) notes that the twentieth century has seen a resumption of the urban trend, which last collapsed in the thirteenth century. But he points back to the apparently near paradisal nature of the land as described by western travellers in the nineteenth century: the land was not heavily populated, the rivers were full of fish, the air was full of birds, the Jordan valley was covered with trees and shrubs, and teemed with game, and the plateau above was well grassed. In this century, much of the cover and accompanying wild life has gone, the thickets have been cleared for fields and orchards and vineyards, and the plateau ploughed for crops. Water run-off has increased, and soil erosion with it. Harlan compares the present situation, the result of growing urbanism, with the situation at the end of the Early Bronze age, when writers in Egypt were lamenting a sharp climatic and economic crisis. Harlan quotes (*ibid.*, 127, with references) from the Lament of Ipuwer:

> Grain hath perished everywhere . . .the storehouse is bare, and he that hath kept it lieth stretched out upon the ground,

and from Neferly,

> The whole land has perished . . .the river of Egypt is empty . . .men cross over the water on foot . . .the south wind drives away the north wind.

This brief survey of what is known of the prehistoric predecessors of the Edomites inevitably leads to consideration of the origins of the Edomite people. It has often been assumed that the Edomites, like their neighbours and contemporaries the Ammonites, the Moabites and the Israelites, were to be associated in some way with the Aramaean peoples, who, it was thought, entered and occupied Syria and other parts of the Levant in the thirteenth century BCE as latter day successors of the Amorites. Certainly such evidence as we have indicates that the Israelites, Ammonites, Moabites and Edomites spoke a local variant of North West Semitic, but they did not speak Aramaic, and it was not until the mid-first millennium BCE that their languages began to be affected by or even replaced by Aramaic. But positive evidence for the origins of the Ammonites, Moabites and Edomites is not easy to find. As we have seen, the urban population of EB IV in Transjordan seems to have developed from the population of EB III, perhaps with the help of external influence from Syria and possibly with the help of some newcomers. The ensuing Middle Bronze period seems to have seen a serious population decline. In view of the evidence of the Early Bronze occupation and settlement of Transjordan, perhaps we should apply much the same model to the resettlement of Transjordan at the end of the second millennium BCE in the Late Bronze—Early Iron age, and suppose that the recovery of the population had less to do with the invasion of peoples from Syria or the North Arabian desert than with the kind of economic and environmental factors sketched above. In the absence of any clear evidence that Edom was resettled by the invasion of foreign groups with new and distinctive ways of life, it is easier to believe that the indigenous, if limited, population expanded with improving economic circumstances. Thanks to various surveys of the area, we have more evidence than was available to Glueck fifty years ago, and to this we must now turn.

Chapter 4

EDOM IN THE LATE SECOND MILLENNIUM BCE
THE ARCHAEOLOGICAL AND EGYPTIAN EVIDENCE

Archaeological Evidence from Transjordan

It is quite clear that the early Israelites knew very little about Edom and its history. Their first opportunity of exploring Edom probably came when David conquered and garrisoned 'all Edom' at the beginning of the tenth century BCE (2 Sam. 8.14). Though there are references in the Old Testament to Edom at the time of the Exodus and in the period of the Israelite judges and in the reign of Saul, these references are far from being contemporary witnesses, and they generally reflect knowledge and experience of Edom deriving from the monarchic period, and can give us no reliable information of the history, geography or society of Edom in the period before David's conquest. As we have no extant Edomite texts to lighten our darkness, we are left dependent on two important, if limited, resources. The first is archaeological evidence, and the second is the existence of a few possible allusions to southern Transjordan in the Egyptian records.

We may begin with the archaeological evidence. As we have already seen, human occupation of the southern Transjordan had a long history prior to the second millennium BCE. In this chapter, we are particularly concerned with the population of southern Transjordan in the Late Bronze and Iron I ages. In the 1930s Nelson Glueck, on the basis of his brief, energetic and valuable if slightly unsystematic surveys, argued that there was a gap in the settled occupation of southern Transjordan during the Middle and Late Bronze ages until the thirteenth century BCE when a developed and formidable Edomite kingdom appeared (alongside similar kingdoms in Moab and Ammon). However, Glueck's methods, assumptions and results met criticism: his explorations were not systematic or comprehensive enough, his negative evidence was given too much weight, and his assumption of an antithesis between the desert and the sown, the desert nomad and the settled agriculturalist, has been challenged by research which has demonstrated rather the interdependence of the planter and the herdsman. More recent surveys and excavation have shown that Transjordan was not so thinly populated in the middle of the second millennium BCE as was thought. It is true that most of the evidence—particularly for the Middle Bronze age—comes from northern and central Transjordan, but evidence for human presence and activity in southern Transjordan is growing (Sauer, 1986:1-26).

Before we turn to Edom itself, it is worth summarising briefly what is known of Middle Bronze and Late Bronze age sites further north. Evidence for MB I (Albright's MB IIA) has been found in excavation at Tell el-Hayyat and Tabaqat Fahl in the northern Jordan valley, at Jawa in the desert east of Mafraq, and at Sahab a few kilometres southeast of Amman. Sahāb, Amman itself, and Tell Safūt northwest of Amman seem to have been important fortified sites in MB II-III. Other places occupied at the end of the Middle Bronze age include Tell Deir 'Alla and Tabaqat Fahl. A number of MB tombs are known from central and northern Transjordan, at Tabaqat Fahl, Tell el-Husn, the Beq'ah valley, and Amman; further south, an MB II tomb has been found at Khirbet el-Mukhayyat (by Mount Nebo), and MB sherds have been found on the surface at Jalūl and eṣ-Ṣāfi (Sauer, 1986: 1-26 [4-6]).

The Late Bronze age is better attested, with cities in the north at Tell Irbid and Tell Husn, in the Jordan valley at Tabaqat Fahl, Tell es-Sa'idiyeh, Tell el-Mazar, and Tell Deir 'Alla, and in central Transjordan at Jalūl and Sahāb (*ibid.*, 6-9). Contemporary with these is the building discovered in 1955 at Amman airport, variously interpreted as a temple (Hennessy, 1966: 155-62; G.R.H. Wright, 1966: 350-57; Hankey, 1974: 131-78), a military tower (Fritz, 1971: 140-52), or a mortuary site for Hittite residents (Herr, 1983a: 223-29; 1983b). This building has been compared with similar buildings at Mt Gerizim (Campbell, Wright, 1969: 104-16), Rujm el-Henū (McGovern, 1980: 55-67; 1981: 126-28), Tell Halif (Jacobs, 1984: 197-200); this last is 'a large LB IB building built in the "residency" style, a central room surrounded by smaller rooms on all four sides' (*ibid.*, 198, fig. 1). The Amman airport building has been dated by the

Mycenaean IIA, IIIA and IIIB pottery found in it to the 14th—13th centuries BCE. This pottery, together with Cypriot and Egyptian artifacts, revealed something of the international connections of Transjordan in the Late Bronze age. Mycenaean pottery has been found further north up the Jordan valley at Tell es-Sa'idiyeh and Tabaqat Faḥl, and south of Amman at Madaba (Hankey, 1967: 104-47; 1974: 131-78), but most interestingly at Tell Deir 'Alla at the confluence of the Wadi Zerqa and the Jordan. Excavations here in the 1960s revealed a shrine on a plinth above an 8 metre high artificial mound, dating from the beginning of the Late Bronze age to shortly after 1200 BCE. It had a courtyard and a complex of storage rooms, from which came a group of three inscribed tablets in a still undeciphered script somewhat reminiscent of the Linear B tablets from the Aegean (Franken, 1960: 386-93; 1961: 361-72; 1962: 378-82; 1964: 417-22; Franken, Ibrahim, 1977-78: 57-80).

A few miles from Tell Deir 'Alla, a cemetery at Qataret es-Samra revealed LB local and imported Cypriot base-ring pottery (Leonard, 1979: 53-65), and a survey of the east Jordan valley in 1975 revealed five other LB sites between Wadi Zerka and the river Yarmuk (Ibrahim, Sauer, Yassine, 1976: 41-66). Southeast of Qataret es-Samra, in the Beq'ah valley at Rujm el-Ḥenū, two LB buildings, one with a ground plan like that of the Amman airport building, have been found, with a nearby group of Late Bronze—Early Iron age burial caves; another Late Bronze settlement is being excavated at nearby Umm ed-Dananir (McGovern, 1980: 55-67). There is evidence of a large late Bronze building at Saḥāb, 12 kilometres southeast of Amman (Ibrahim, 1972: 23-26; 1974: 55-61; 1975: 69-82). Further south, in the territory of ancient Moab, Late Bronze—Iron age potters was found at 'Arā'ir just north of the Wadi el-Mūjib (Olavarri, 1965: 77-94; 1969: 230-59), and between the Wadi el-Mūjib and the Wadi el-Ḥasā, Miller's survey identified 75 sites with Late Bronze pottery (compared with only 31 sites with Middle Bronze pottery) (Miller, 1979c: 43-52: 1979b: 79-82: 169-73; Mattingly, 1983: 245-62). A Late Bronze age stamp seal was discovered at er-Rabba in the same region, 10 kilometres north of Karak (Kenna, 1973: 79).

From the same region, and from the end of the Late Bronze age or the beginning of the Iron age, comes the basalt stele found at Balu'a just south of the Wadi el-Mūjib in 1930. The stele shows on the left a god wearing the double crown of Upper and Lower Egypt and an Egyptian kilt, and holding a sceptre. In the middle is a human, royal figure, wearing a headdress which has been identified by some scholars as distinctive of the *shōsu*, a warlike, semi-nomadic people known to us from Egyptian inscriptions. On the right is a goddess wearing the sort of crown worn by the Egyptian god Osiris and holding an *ankh* sign. The faces are not Egyptian, and may perhaps represent local people. The stele, however, shows strong Egyptian influence, and the weathered inscription above it may possibly have been written in a form of Egyptian script. The stele witnesses to Egyptian influence and to some political activity in southern Transjordan in the Late Bronze or early Iron age (Horsfield, Vincent, 1932: 416-44: Drioton, 1933: 343-65; Ward, Martin, 1964: 5-29). Further indications of Egyptian interest in Transjordan in this period can be seen in the 'Job stone' at Sheikh Sa'd (Schumacher, 1891: 142-47; Erman, 1892: 205-11), in a commemorative scarab of Amenophis III found near Petra (Ward, 1973: 45-46), in the Late Bronze II faience vase and cartouche of Queen Twosret found at Tell Deir 'Alla (Franken, 1964b: 73-78; 1961: 361-72, pl. 5; 1962: 464-66), various artifacts from the Amman airport building (Hankey, 1974: 131-78), as well as the Luxor texts describing Rameses II's campaigns in southern Transjordan (Kitchen, 1967: 47-70), and the cartouches of the Nineteenth Dynasty at Timna (Rothenberg, 1972: 163-66). The recent discovery of a broken statuette at Khirbet 'Aṭārūs in Moab, dating perhaps from the 11th—9th centuries BCE and Egyptian in influence, also points the same way (Niemann, 1985: 171-77).

The Evidence of Surveys in Edom

Such evidence as has emerged to date for Transjordan in the mid-second millennium BCE has revealed the presence of cities, fortifications, shrines, foreign trade, connections with the Aegean and with Egypt, buildings, burial caves, inscriptions, sculpture, metal-work, and local pottery. First impressions suggest that the evidence is scantier in the south. It would hardly be surprising to find that population density declined as one travelled south through Moab and Edom into the higher mountains. Assumptions and impressions, however, need to be tested, and in recent years a number of surveys have been conducted in Moab and Edom in order to make a systematic

examination of the evidence of human settlement and occuption in
the region at different historical periods. Thus a team directed by
J.M. Miller explored the plateau between the Wadi el-Mūjib and the
Wadi el-Ḥasā; Burton MacDonald examined the area between the
Wadi el-Ḥasā and Tafila from the western edge of the plateau to the
line of the modern Desert Highway. W.E. Rast and R.T. Schaub
explored the plain around the southeast coast of the Dead Sea. S.
Hart has initiated a survey in the Edomite mountains immediately
north of Ras en-Naqb, and W.J. Jobling has searched the Ḥismā
region between Ras en-Naqb and 'Aqaba (see above, p. 31). These
surveys all had slightly different aims and priorities, and perhaps
some allowance has to be made in assessing the evidence of each for
the fact that aims tend to condition results: a survey party tends to
find what it is looking for rather than what it is not. However, it must
be said that large areas of Edom and Moab have been searched for
indications of human settlement far more thoroughly than ever
before, and from the still limited evidence so far published, we are
beginning to get a more realistic picture of Late Bronze and Iron Age
settlement in Moab and Edom than has previously been available.

Just south of Moab, between the Wadi el-Ḥasā and Tafila, Nelson
Glueck located no Late Bronze sites, and eleven Iron age cities
(Glueck, *EEP* II, 1935] map IIIb). In 1974 and 1978 Manfred
Weippert identified six sites in this region as Iron Age I from surface
sherding (Weippert, 1982: 153-62), to which can be added an Iron I
site at Rujm Khanazir at the northern end of the Wadi 'Araba
discovered by Rast and Schaub (1974: 5-61). (Glueck visited Rujm
Khanazir, but inspite of a careful search was unable to find a single
sherd by which to date it, and suggested it was of mediaeval origin
[*EEP* II, 1935: 10-11]). But a much more comprehensive picture of
the area is now emerging from the results of MacDonald's surveys.
In 1979, MacDonald examined the area between the Wadi el-Ḥasā
and Tafila from the edge of the plateau on the west eastwards to the
Wadi La'ban (MacDonald, 1980: 169-83). In this area four sites (nos
106, 147, 178, 183) appear to have certainly identifiable LB pottery,
and another twelve sites possibly LB pottery. Of these sixteen sites,
Glueck had visited five, finding no trace of LB. Unfortunately, none
of these sites had architectural remains which could be attributed to
the Late Bronze age, but this limited evidence at least suggests that
Edom in the Late Bronze age was not entirely without population.

On the other hand, it must be admitted that the amount of pottery found is small. Of particular importance to us is MacDonald's evidence for Iron I sites. MacDonald distinguished more confidently than Glueck between Iron I and Iron II pottery, and noted twenty-one Iron I sites in the area (at seven of which Glueck had either found no Iron age sherds or had registered what he found more generally as Early Iron I-II). In 1981, working east of the Wadi La'ban, MacDonald noted four sites with Iron I pottery (MacDonald, Rollefson, Roller, 1982: 117-31), and in 1982, one possible Iron I site further east (MacDonald, Rollefson, Banning, 1983: 311-23). It looks as if settlement spots thin out as one advances east from the mountain range towards the Desert Highway.

It is interesting to compare MacDonald's evidence for Iron IA (c. 1200—1000 BCE) or Iron I (c. 1200—900 BCE) material with evidence for the preceding LB and following Iron II periods. McDonald found attributable sherds as follows:

Year	Total sites recorded	MB-LB	LB-Iron IA	Iron IA	Iron I	Iron I-II	Iron II
1979	214	1	16	4	21	8	15
1981	338	1?	-	4	-	-	2
1982	522	-	-	-	1?	-	?
Totals	1074	2?	16	8	22?	8	17?

These findings appear to confirm Glueck's belief that there was settled occupation of some sort between LB and Iron II. It is instructive to consider the question of continuity more closely. Some continuity is clearly evidenced: thus seven of the LB sites appear to continue into Iron I. But, perhaps surprisingly, two major Iron IA sites (147, 212) do not appear to continue into Iron II. MacDonald's 1979 list gives twenty-three sites for Iron IA and Iron (taken together), of which only eight are evidenced for Iron II (out of a total of sixteen possible Iron II sites). These figures suggest that in northern Edom at least there was some continuity and development from LB into Iron I (when there was a significant increase in the number of evidenced sites), and also that only a percentage of Iron I sites survived into Iron II. In Iron II, as we know also from the results of excavation elsewhere in Edom, new sites appear. Buseira, Tawilan, Umm el-Biyara and Tell el-Kheleifeh all seem on present evidence to belong to Iron II. Dornemann has noted that in Transjordan 'the pottery of the 10th century, the end of Iron I, is considerably different from that which preceded it in Iron I: it shows more of a continuity with the pottery of the first centuries of Iron II', and Dornemann argues (1983: 166) that we should consider the Iron age in Transjordan in three divisions, the archaeological material clustering round each: thus (1) 12th—11th centuries, the incipient Iron age assemblage; (2) 10th—8th centuries, the period of local individualism (Edom, Moab, Ammon); (3), 7th—6th centuries, the period of provincial administration under Assyrian control. The first and last of these periods are quite distinct in pottery repertoire, and it is tempting to try to correlate this analysis with that which seems to emerge from MacDonald's evidence by suggesting that MacDonald's LB—Iron IA grouping corresponds with Dornemann's first period, MacDonald's Iron II with Dornemann's third period, and that those Iron I and Iron I-II sites which spanned the gap between the Iron IA and later Iron II sites belonged to the tenth-ninth centuries when Edom was struggling to restore its fortunes after the Davidic conquest.

However, our major concern at this point is with the Late Bronze—Iron IA period. A glance at the nature of the sites explored by MacDonald might tell us a little more about early Edomite society. Unfortunately, he describes very few of them in any detail (MacDonald, 1980: 169-83 [173-76]). Site 64 was a stone structure on a cliff ledge above the Wadi 'Afra with a retaining wall of some 60 metres circumference; the pottery included EB I, MB-LB, Nabataean and Islamic. Site 147 was a platform on a terrace by the Wadi el-Ḥasā, with LB—Iron age pottery. Site 10, Umm er-Riḥ, with Iron IA and II pottery, was a large site, 350 × 125 metres, with many walls, two caves, and possible towers or tombs. Another large site was no. 212, Khirbet Abū Benna, 170 × 70 metres. Here

> the entire site is constructed of large chert blocks. The north, south, east and west walls of some of the ancient buildings are still standing, some to a height of 1-2 metres. . . There is a great deal of evidence of rooms and building foundations.

MacDonald and Weippert claim this site as belonging to Iron IA or I (MacDonald, *ibid.*, 175; Weippert, 1982: 156).

Clearly, such evidence is limited and imprecise. We cannot relate and date the structures and the pottery accurately without excavation and stratigraphy. We should remember also that MacDonald's possible LB sites and most of the Iron I sites yielded very little pottery. Out of the sixteen LB—Iron I sites, only two yielded more than twenty diagnostic sherds collection (sites 61, 183), and out of twenty-two Iron I sites, only four yielded more than forty diagnostic sherds (site 10 [67]; site 18 [95]; site 28 [56]; site 212 [151]). These are the larger sites; the rest are much smaller. Most sites explored were not town or village sites, but perhaps the remains of houses or farm buildings. It looks very much as if during LB and Iron I northern Edom was populated but thinly, with a scatter of small farmers and occasional hamlets or villages. At the southern end of the Edomite mountains, immediately north of Ras en-Naqb, Hart's survey identified two large fortresses (001, 063), one large, defended village (036), and seven smaller fortresses, with two unwalled villages (015, 018), and two 'hamlets' (030, 078). Sherds without building remains were found at about twenty sites in the area. Hart, however, appears to date all these sites to Iron II in the seventh–sixth centuries BCE (Hart, 1986c: 51-58). Further analysis of the pottery found in these two surveys, and the excavation of select sites are needed before we can draw conclusions about settlement in early Iron age Edom with any confidence. In particular we need to know whether the pottery forms which we now attribute to Iron I were in fact limited to use in that period, or whether their use continued into Iron II.

We also need to know precisely how far the territory of Edom extended in any one period. Unfortunately for the early Iron age this is impossible; we simply have not the documentary evidence. However, it may be of importance to note the one Iron I and the one Iron I-II site discovered by W.J. Jobling in Wadi Rummān, between Ras en-Naqb and 'Aqaba (Jobling, 1981: 105-112 [110]), and it is certainly important to note the evidence at Timna in the Wadi 'Araba of mining and religious activities under the control of the Egyptian Nineteenth and Twentieth Dynasties from c. 1300—1150 BCE, at the end of the Late Bronze and the beginning of Iron I (Rothenberg, 1962: 5-65; 1972). Of major interest are the mining areas and smelting camps of the Ramesside period (site 2) and the Hathor sanctuary (site 200). These sites are clearly datable by the inscriptional evidence of Egyptian cartouches bearing the names of the Nineteenth Dynasty Pharaohs Seti I, Rameses II, Merneptah, Seti II, Queen

Twosret (whose cartouche appears also at Tell Deir 'Alla), and the Twentieth Dynasty Rameses III and Rameses IV (Rothenberg, 1972: 163-66). The mining sites and the sanctuary both produced three types of pottery, apparently contemporary with one another: LB—Iron I wheelmade pottery, 'Negev' ware (known from the central Negev, Beersheba and the Wadi 'Araba throughout most of the Late Bronze—Iron age), and what has become known as 'Midianite' pottery, which perhaps originated from Qurayyah in the Hejaz and has since been recognized at a number of sites in Israel and Jordan, either side of the Wadi 'Araba (Rothenberg, 1972: 155-62; Rothenberg, Glass, 1983: 65-124; Parr, Harding, Dayton, 1968/69: 193-242; Parr, 1982: 127-33).

Timna is important to the historian of Edom because it demonstrates, first, Egypt's interests in the Wadi 'Araba on the western borders of Edom at the end of the Late Bronze age, and, secondly, the links and communications that undoubtedly existed at this time between the Wadi 'Araba region and the Negev to the west, and the Hejaz to the south. Jobling's survey found 'Midianite' ware in the Wadi Rummān, and Rothenberg's distribution map notes it at various sites in the 'Araba, the Edomite mountain range, the Negev, and southern Judah (Jobling, 1981: 105-12 [110, pl. 31]; Rothenberg, Glass, 1983: 70, fig. 2). There has been much speculation that the labour force at Timna was Midianite, but as Muhly has pointed out, this idea:

> is really based on nothing more than a possible connection between the Midianites and the Kenites (a connection) based solely upon those confused traditions regarding the father-in-law of Moses. ... The Kenites are in turn metalworkers only by virtue of an assumed etymology, the name being derived from a common Semitic word for 'smith', and an assumed ancestor in the folk-lore figure of Tubal-Cain, the first metalworker. The entire hypothesis hardly deserves serious consideration (Muhly, 1984: cols. 276-92, [col. 278]).

Whether there were Midianites at Timna or not, it is more than likely that the basic labour force was made up of local people as well as prisoners, slaves, or any other unfortunates who could be compelled to work there; the work force might include people from either side of the Wadi 'Araba. Timna was probably of some importance for the economic life of this region in the fourteenth—twelfth centuries BCE.

The Late Bronze—Iron I Inhabitants of Edom

The question is, who were the local people who have left behind them such sparse traces of their occupation of the land in the Late Bronze—Iron I period, and what the nature of their occupation? The author of Deut. 2.10-12 and 20-22 notes that east of the Jordan the Ammonites of his own day had been preceded by the Zamzummim and the Moabites by the Emim (both groups could be called 'Rephaim'), and that the sons of Esau, who lived in Seir, were preceded by the Horites: 'but the sons of Esau dispossessed them, and destroyed them from before them, and settled in their stead; as Israel did to the land of their possession, which the LORD gave to them'. The Deuteronomist is clearly concerned to show that each group had its own God-given inheritance, taken over from legendary predecessors, and can tell us nothing of any historical value about the Horites. He assumes that, just as the Israelites dispossessed the Canaanites, so the peoples of Ammon, Moab, and Edom (whom he identifies as the sons of Esau, living in Seir) ousted their predecessors. The identity of the Horites has been much discussed, as has the origin of the name (Speiser, 1962: 645; de Vaux, 1967: 481-503). Gen. 36.20-30 links the Horites with Seir, and lists two generations of their clans. The names listed are Semitic, but they appear to be at home in the Negev rather than in Edom east of the 'Araba, and their association with Edom is probably secondary (see below, pp. 87-90). Some scholars have connected the name 'Horite' with the Hurrians, a non-Semitic people from northern Mesopotamia (Ginsberg, Maisler, 1934: 243-67 [256-65]; Winckler, 1895, 1900: II.1.6); and identified some of the personal names in Gen. 36.20-29 as Hurrian, though Speiser (1962: 645) denies this identification. It would perhaps not be surprising to find some Hurrian names among those of Horite clans of southern Palestine; other individuals with Hurrian names are known in Palestine from the Late Bronze-Amarna age. R. de Vaux, however, suggested that 'Horite' derived from 'Huru', the Egyptian name for Canaan, and was reapplied by the Israelites to one particular group of pre-Israelite inhabitants of southern Jordan (de Vaux, 1957: 481-503; cf. Meyer, 1906: 329-30; Müller, 1893: 155-56). The Israelites themselves probably understood the word to mean 'cave-dwellers', and perhaps used it as a contemptuous term for the assumed predecessors of the Edomites, who were themselves known to live in caves (Jer. 49.16; Obad. 3).

The biblical writers, compounding assumptions, legends and folk etymology, can tell us little of value about the LB—Iron I inhabitants of southern Transjordan. More helpful are the Egyptian sources, which speak of people called the *shōsu* active in this area. Particularly important is the famous text of Pap. Anastasi VI: 54-56, which is a schoolboy's model copy of a document from a frontier official of the reign of Merneptah:

> We have just finished letting the Shōsu tribes of Edom pass the fortress of Merneptaḥ-ḥotphimā-'ĕ (life, prosperity, health), which is in Tjeku, to the pools of Pi-tūm . . . (Caminos, 1954: 293).

'Edom' here has the determinative 'foreign hill country', and is spelt out carefully with full syllabic orthography, which indicates that 'Edom' is known to the Egyptians as a foreign, non-Egyptian name. Clearly, this particular place name was in use by the late 13th century BCE (and perhaps as early as the 15th century BCE, if *'i-d-ma* on Thutmoses III's list indicates Edom [Helck, 1971: 243]).

The *shōsu* are well known. They appear in Egyptian documents from the time of Thutmoses II (1493-1490 BCE) down to Rameses III (1193-1162 BCE). Thutmoses II took uncountable *shōsu* prisoners (Giveon, 1971:10); Thutmoses III (1490-1436 BCE) defeated them on his fourteenth campaign to Syria (*ibid.*, 10-12); Amenophis II (1436-1413 BCE) employed *shōsu* captives in Egypt; c. 1430 BCE he lists 15,200 *shōsu* captives alongside 36,300 *Kharu* and 3,600 *'Apiru* (*ibid.*, 14). Seti I (1303-1290 BCE) fought the *shōsu* near Gaza (*ibid.*, 39-60). On one text, Rameses II (1290-1224 BCE) is described as:

> a fierce, raging lion, who laid waste to the land of the Shōsu, who has plundered Mount Seir with his valiant arm (*ibid.*, 100).

From Rameses III's reign (1193-1162 BCE) comes this reference in the Papyrus Harris I. 76: 9-11:

> I brought about the destruction of Seir (det., 'foreign people') among the Shōsu tribes. I laid waste their tents with their people, their belongings, and likewise their cattle without number. They were bound and brought as spoil, as tribute of Egypt. I gave them to the divine Ennead as slaves of their temples (*ibid.*, 134-37).

References like these have led many scholars to connect the *shōsu* firmly with the history of southern Palestine and Transjordan. Helck located them in southern Palestine, comparing them with the similar

Habiru further north (Helck, 1968: 472-80). Giveon sees them as 'a group of Asiatic bedouin, half-nomads', located mainly east of the Nile Delta and south of Palestine. Giveon argues that the account of Thutmoses III's campaign suggests that the *shōsu* belong to southern Palestine, where Thutmoses defeated them before going north (Giveon, 1971: 12). M. Görg (1979: 199-292) rejects this as presupposing what it wishes to prove, pointing out that Thutmoses III is more likely to have used the coastal route north than the desert route, that the scene of his campaign might have been Upper Retenu rather than Lower Retenu, that 15,300 prisoners is too large a figure to apply to the thinly populated southern regions of Palestine, and that there is a good deal of evidence locating the *shōsu* in Syria. Whether *shōsu* can be located in Syria or not, clearly there were *shōsu* in Edom and Seir. But that is not to say that all the inhabitants of Seir and Edom were necessarily *shōsu*, and it is not to say that the distribution of *shōsu* people was limited to those regions. There is some evidence to suggest that *shōsu* might be found in Nubia (Ward, 1972: 35-60 [39-41]), and rather more to suggest that *shōsu* might be found further north in Syria. Thus a toponym list from Thebes in Egypt from the reign of Amenophis III (1403-1365 BCE) (Giveon, 1971: 22-24) names a 'spring of the *shōsu*' along with the place names *dw-ty-n3* and *S3-m-ʿw-n3*. (The latter is probably *Samḫuna* of Amarna letter EA 225:4, biblical Shimron [Josh. 11.1; 12.20; 19.15], now Khirbet Sammuniya near Nahalal; *dw-tʿy-n3* is *tw-tʿy-n3* of Thutmoses III's list [no. 9] in the Beqaʿ valley; and *ʿyn Š3św* is probably the *Enišasi* of Amarna letter EA 187:12, *E(ni)šasi* of EA 363:4, *ʿn š3św* of Pap. Anastasi I.19:1, and *ʿn š3(s)w* of Thutmoses III's list (no. 5), to be located also in the southern Beqaʿ [Weippert, 1974: 265-80, 427-33 [273]; Ahitub, 1973: 58-60]). Another toponym list from Soleb in Nubia names *shōsu* together with the places Pella in northern Transjordan, and Arrapha and Qatna in Syria (Giveon, 1971: 24-25). At the battle of Kadesh in Syria (1286 BCE), *shōsu* spies were active on behalf of Rameses II's opponents (Giveon, 1971: 65-69). A particularly tantalising document, copied in the time of Rameses II at 'Amara West from an earlier document of Amenophis III's reign which survives at Soleb (Giveon, 1971: 27), apparently lists a number of *shōsu* tribes. Above each name is a picture of a captive *shōsu*. The document reads (Giveon, 1971: 75-76):

šsw s'rr	Seir (in the land of) Shōsu
šsw rbn	Laban (in the land of) Shōsu
šsw psps	Pyspys (in the land of) Shōsu
šsw smt	Samath (in the land of) Shōsu
šsw yhw	Yahwa (in the land of) Shōsu
šsw wrbwr *	Arbel (?) (in the land of) Shōsu

* at Soleb, the text reads *tr br*

The association here of the *shōsu* with the name *yhw*, so reminiscent of Israel's God, Yahweh, has caused much comment and speculation. Scholars have argued that, as in the Old Testament Yahweh is said to have come from Seir and Edom in the south (cf. Deut. 33.2; Judg. 5.4; Hab. 3.3), so here *s'rr* should be identifed with Seir (in spite of the extra letter *r*) and *rbn* with Laban of Deut. 1.1, and have attempted to identify the other names in the list with places in and around Edom. (Particularly influential has been Grdseloff, 1947: 69-99.) R. Giveon states that *yhw* here is 'sicher eine Form von Beith Yahweh, eine Stadt, deren Tempel Yahweh gewidmet ist', and that this document confirms the origin of the *shōsu* in southern Transjordan (Giveon, 1983: col. 533). But this speculation has been ended by the demonstration that the first two names (*s'rr*, *rbn*) appear on Thutmoses III's list (nos 337, 10), and that the second name (*rbn*) and the last two names (*yhw*, *tr br*) appear on Rameses III's list from Medinet Habu, along with names which can be reasonably identified with places on the Phoenician coast and in Syria, a long way from Edom, and this gives us further evidence of the *shōsu* in Syria (Astour, 1979: 17-34).

The *shōsu*, then, were probably not confined to the regions of southern Palestine and southern Transjordan, but were apparently active further north in Syria and possibly also to the south in Nubia. That they were known from Edom and Seir, however, shows that the Egyptians were well aware of the population to be found there, and indicates how they thought of them. As W.A. Ward has noted, *shōsu* may be a social rather than an ethnic term:

> It is significant that practically all the references to the Shasu in Egyptian records are in a military context. They fight with or against Egyptian armies in Syria or Palestine, or appear as robber bands operating on their own. . . . The Egyptian view of the Shasu would thus seem to be of freebooters, originating in Transjordan, who were encountered predominantly in their dual role of

mercenaries and robber bands serving or preying on towns and caravan routes of Canaan (Ward, 1972: 35-60 [52-53]).

Similarly, Gottwald declares that 'the most striking feature . . . is their militarization' (Gottwald, 1979: 459). Clearly, the Egyptians saw the people of Edom and Seir as bellicose by nature, but also as tent-dwellers, with cattle and other possessions, able to travel to Egypt when necessity arose. The name _shōsu_ itself may derive from the Egyptian root _s3s_, to travel, to wander; or it may derive from a North-west Semitic root evidenced in the Hebrew _šasāh_ and _šasās_, to plunder, to pillage, in _šusume_ of Amarna letter 252: 30, 'despoilers', 'plunderers', and _tšm_, 'plunderers' in the Keret epic from Ugarit. The arguments, which depend on whether the Egyptian _3_ was a root consonant in _š3sw_ or whether the _š3_ is merely group writing for _š_ (so Giveon), seem finely balanced (Ward, 1972: 35-60 [55-59]), with a slight bias in favour of the Egyptian origin. If the word is Egyptian, it is thus probably a generic term for people popularly classed as wanderers, presumably in distinction from the settled people of the towns or the Nile valley as a whole, and also, perhaps, in distinction from other Asiatics such as the Huru and the _'Apiru_. People from Seir and Edom apparently fall into this category, but _shōsu_ was not a name for the national group later known to the Israelites as 'Edomites', for that nation had not yet come into being and acquired a sense of national identity, so far as we can tell, and the name _shōsu_ was used in a much wider sense. It has been suggested that the _shōsu_ can be identified in the Egyptian reliefs by their clothing—by their short cloaks with tassels, and in particular by their headdresses, which appear to be made of a wide, perhaps stiffened band completely enclosing the hair. This is seen on figures contemporary with the Nineteenth Dynasty (1305-1196 BCE) (Giveon, 1971: 251-53, Pl. 17, nos 5,6). However, Ward has shown that such dress is not exclusive to the _shōsu_ on the Egyptian reliefs, but can appear on other foreigners from the north, including the Sea Peoples (Ward, 1972: 35-60 [45-50]). The headband may not have been limited to the _shōsu_, but it is interesting that it appears on the central figure on the Balu'a stele from Moab, who may perhaps be identified as a local ruler of some kind. This stele, probably of local if Egyptianising workmanship, may well present authentic local knowledge of how people dressed in southern Transjordan at this time. If the figure here represented were not a _shōsu_, he might well have been taken for one and described as such in contemporary Egypt.

It must be admitted that it is not easy to draw a clear picture of the state of affairs in Edom at the end of the Bronze Age and the beginning of the Iron Age, in spite of much recent research and exploration. Nevertheless, a picture is emerging. The land was populated, though not densely, with small farmers and herdsmen. In times of difficulty, some at least might migrate to Egypt in search of pasture and food. Here they were known as *shōsu* and thus identified with potentially warlike and dangerous peoples of Palestine, Transjordan, and Syria. This Egyptian term was perhaps somewhat imprecise, and not particularly complimentary. Edom's population perhaps included some who worked as skilled, semi-skilled, or unskilled workers at the mines in the Wadi 'Araba and who worshipped, it may be, at the shrine at Timna. We have as yet no evidence of Late Bronze architecture and building in Edom, though from Iron I there are a number of signs of habitation including what begin to look like larger villages. A little further north, at Balu'a in Moab, we have evidence that local leaders might be commemorated in monumental form, in Egyptianizing style. Nothing similar to this has been found in Edom, perhaps because Edom was a poorer place. Perhaps the scarab of Amenophis III found near Petra belonged to one of the wealthier families, and was handed down as an heirloom, and may be taken as further witness to Edom's contact with Egypt in this period. Indeed, the Late Bronze age, at least, was an age when wide-ranging contacts were possible for Edom. The Mycenaean world of the Mediterranean had access and influence reaching into the Transjordan south at least as far as Madaba; conversely, pottery from the Hejaz spread north to the Wadi 'Araba, the Negev, southern Transjordan, and even to Amman. Clearly, while Edom was on the fringe of a very vital and active Late Bronze world, it was not completely beyond that fringe. In particular, like the rest of Transjordan, Edom lay within the sphere of Egyptian influence and perhaps even administration. The 'Job stone' at Sheikh Sa'd, the LB II faience vase and cartouche of Queen Twosret at Tell Deir 'Allā, artifacts from the Amman airport building, the Luxor texts indicating Rameses II's activity in Moab, the Balu'a stele, and the Timna mines all witness to Egypt's interests and influence. But these probably declined in the twelfth and eleventh centuries BCE, allowing the development of a local sense of nationality which was both suppressed and strengthened by king David's occupation of Transjordan c. 1000 BCE. But this period between the Late Bronze age and the arrival of David and his general Joab remains something of a dark age.

Chapter 5

EDOM IN THE LATE SECOND MILLENNIUM BCE: THE BIBLICAL EVIDENCE

Genesis 25-36

The land of Edom was populated in the Late Bronze and Early Iron ages, but the archaeological evidence alone can give us only a limited picture of its social and political history. The main evidence available for that is to be found in the literature of the Edomites' major enemies, the inhabitants of Judah and Jerusalem, from the pages of the Old Testament. Gen. 25-27, 31 give an account of Esau and Jacob, who are seen as the ancestors of Edom and Israel respectively, and Gen. 36 contains a succession list of the kings 'who reigned in the land of Edom, before any king reigned over the Israelites', together with a group of seven other lists containing names of tribes, chiefs and places attributed to Edom. Exod. 15.15 mentions the 'chiefs' of Edom in parallel with the 'leaders' of Moab. Num. 20.14-21 (cf. Judg. 11.17-18) tells how Edom refused to give the Israelites passage through their territory, forcing the Israelites to turn away, a story which Deut. 2.1-8 presents differently, implying that the Israelites in fact travelled through the Edomite territory, and that the Edomites were afraid of them. Judg. 3.8-11, with some slight emendation, may possibly tell of a local struggle between Israelites and Edomites in southern Judah.

Taken at face value, this material has suggested the following historical sequence. The Edomites were a people closely related to the Israelites, descendants of Jacob's brother Esau. They entered their land at much the same time as, or a little earlier than, the Israelites entered theirs (according to many scholars, as part of the same general Aramaean migration; cf. Noth, 1960: 83). They were hostile to the Israelites, and refused to let them cross Edom as an escape route from Egypt through Transjordan. They developed a monarchy before the Israelites did. However, critical analysis of the biblical narratives over the last century has shown that these narratives give a picture of Edom and her relations with Israel which derive at the earliest from the period of the Israelite and Judahite monarchies, and which reflect the political relationships of that period and perhaps even later. These narratives are far from being contemporary or near-contemporary accounts of events between the fourteenth and the tenth centuries BCE, and they are not impartial witnesses to those political relationships.

A clear case in point is the story of Jacob and Esau as presented in Gen. 25–36. When Rebekah, the wife of Isaac, conceived, she is told in an oracle from the Lord that

> Two nations are in your womb
> and two peoples, born of you, shall be divided;
> the one shall be stronger than the other,
> the elder shall serve the younger (Gen. 25.23).

The first twin to be born is called Esau, who is identified as Edom by two punning references: first, he is said to have come forth 'red' (*'admônî*, Gen. 25.25), and, secondly, he asks to be fed with 'that red pottage' (*min hā'ēdōm hā'ēdōm hazzeh*, Gen. 25.30); 'therefore his name was called Edom'. Esau is throughout portrayed in a poor light; for the sake of satisfying his immediate hunger, he surrenders his birthright (Gen. 25.34); to the grief of his parents, he married Hittite women (Gen. 26.34f.); in contrast to Jacob, who is 'a quiet man, dwelling in tents' and 'a smooth man', Esau is presented as 'a skilful hunter, a man of the field' and 'a hairy man' (Gen. 25.27; 27.11), and he is cheated of his father's blessing by Jacob, the ancestor of Israel. The blessings addressed by Isaac to Jacob and Esau explicitly refer to political relationships. To Jacob, Isaac says,

> See, the smell of my son
> is as the smell of a field which the LORD has blessed!
> May God give you of the dew of heaven,
> and of the fatness of the earth,
> and plenty of grain and wine.
> Let peoples serve you,
> and nations bow down to you.
> Be lord over your brothers,
> and may your mother's sons bow down to you.
> Cursed be every one who curses you,
> and blessed be every one who blesses you! (Gen. 27.27-29)

Jacob is thus promised agricultural prosperity and political dominion. But to Esau Isaac can offer only the reverse:

> Behold, away from the fatness of the earth shall your dwelling be,
> and away from the dew of heaven on high.
> By your sword you shall live,
> and you shall serve your brother:
> but when you break loose
> you shall break his yoke from your neck (Gen. 27.39-40).

Esau's lot is cast, as it were, on stony ground, and he is promised not dominion but the yoke of vassaldom, which he will eventually shake off. The reference here is certainly to the Davidic conquest and rule of Edom, and Edom's subsequent revolt and independence under Jehoram of Judah c. 845 BCE (2 Kgs 8.20). The narrator emphasizes Esau's hatred for Jacob (Gen. 27.41-42) and his dependence on the sword (Gen. 27.40), and it is no accident that Esau's readiness with the sword is emphasized in other Old Testament passages referring to Edom. Thus in Num. 20.14-21, when Moses' messengers ask permission for Israel to pass through Edom, Edom forbids them 'lest I come out with the sword against you'. The oracle in Amos 1.11-12 threatens Edom

> because he pursued his brother with the sword,
> and cast off all pity,
> and his anger tore perpetually,
> and he kept his wrath for ever.

This is probably a reference to Edom's vindictiveness when she rebelled from Judah and regained independence (2 Kgs 8.20), or, as some scholars believe, to Edom's behaviour when the Babylonians captured Jerusalem in 587 BCE (for discussion of the date and authenticity of this passage, see Bartlett, 1977: 2-27 [10-16]; for Edom's behaviour in 587 BCE, see below, Chapter 8). Clearly, Edom had a reputation for readiness with the sword, and this reputation certainly influenced the Israelite presentation of Edom's history. This is particularly clear, as we shall see, when we examine the evidence for Edom's involvement in the events of 587 BCE. And so, to resume our account of the Jacob-Esau story, it is not surprising to read that Jacob, on his return from Haran, is afraid of the outcome of his coming meeting with Esau, and prays to be delivered from the hand of his brother, 'for I fear him, lest he come and slay us all, the

mothers with the children' (Gen. 32.11). These narratives tell us of
the political relationships of the later monarchic period, and one is
reminded of two letters dating from the end of the Judahite
monarchy, c. 600 BCE, found at Arad on Judah's southern border.
One letter orders troops to be moved to Ramath-negeb 'lest the
Edomites go there', and the second refers to some hostile Edomite
activity in the region (see Pardee, 1982: 58-61, 63-65, and see below,
pp. 149-50).

Genesis 36 is a complex chapter, in which the editor has brought
together much genealogical and other material relating primarily to
Esau, the brother of Jacob. Here too Esau is identified as Edom or as
the father of the Edomites. It cannot be assumed without careful
analysis that the names given in this chapter simply represent early
clans or families of the Edomites and their predecessors, or give us
any solid evidence for the early history of the Edomites. Recent study
has shown that the Old Testament authors (and other ancient
writers) used genealogies for a variety of purposes—e.g., to demonstrate
politial or social relationships, to link traditions, to span gaps
between known events, to provide a basis for chronological speculation,
to legitimise office holders or establish hereditary succession (cf.
Johnson, 1969: R.R. Wilson, 1975: 168-69). The main function of the
genealogies in Gen. 36 was apparently to underline both the links
between Esau/Edom and Jacob/Israel, as well as the differences. The
heading of ch. 36.1, 'These are the descendants of Esau' is balanced
by the following heading in Gen. 37.2, 'This is the history of the
family of Jacob'.

Genesis 36 falls easily into seven units:

1.	vv. 1-5:	the descendants of Esau (that is, Edom), with an appendix in vv.6-8 on Esau's separation from Jacob (cf. Lot's separation from Abraham, Gen. 13.6-12)
2.	vv. 9-14:	the descendants of Esau the father of the Edomites
3.	vv. 15-19:	the chiefs of the sons of Esau
4.	vv. 20-28:	the sons of Seir the Horite
5.	vv. 29-30:	the chiefs of the Horites
6.	vv. 31-39:	the kings who reigned in the land of Edom, before any king reigned over the Israelites
7.	vv. 40-43:	the chiefs of Esau, according to their families and their dwelling places, by their names.

The core of this material is surely to be found in section (2) (on which seem to depend sections (1), (3), and (7)) and section (4) (on which depends section (5)). Section (6), the succession list of the kings, is equally important but basically unrelated, and will be considered separately. The first section, vv.1-8, links the following material with the main narrative of Genesis, adjusting the information about Esau's wives in vv.9-14 to harmonize at least to some extent with previous information, and describing by way of introduction Esau's peaceful settlement in Seir in terms closely parallel with the story of Lot in Gen. 13.6-12. It is quite clear that Esau's primary connection is with Seir rather than with Edom, and that he has only secondarily become identified as 'the father of the Edomites' and as 'Edom'. The primary connection with Seir is revealed by the two core lists of the families of Esau and Seir (sections (2) and (4)), which are linked by two important figures, Timna, and Oholibamah. Timna appears in the first as a concubine of Esau's son Eliphaz and mother of Amalek, and in the second as sister of Seir's son Lotan. Oholibamah is Esau's wife in the first, and daughter of Anah, the son of Seir, in the second list. But here we can observe that the editor of the list of vv.9-14 clearly drew upon the list of the sons of Seir (vv.20-28), for he misread it and confused Anah, son of Seir and father of Oholibamah (vv.20,25) with Anah the son of Zibeon, the Anah who found the hot springs in the wilderness (v.24). (The *hapax legomenon yēmîn* has been otherwise variously translated as 'lakes' [Beeston, 1974: 109-10], 'marsh fish' [Driver, 1975: 109-10], or as a proper name [Yellin, 1932: 93-94].) This confusion led the editor to describe Oholibamah wrongly as the daughter of Anah, the daughter of Zibeon (v.14, whence v.2).

The list of the sons of Seir, then, may be the older of the two core lists. The names are as follows:

Seir

Lotan*	Shobal	Zibeon	Anah	Dishon	Ezer	Dishan
Hori	Alvan	Aiah	Dishon	Hemdan	Bilhan	Uz
Heman	Manahath	Anah**	Oholibamah	Eshban	Zaavan	Aran
	Ebal			Ithran	Akan	
	Shepho			Cheran		
	Onam					

* Lotan's sister was Timna
** He is the Anah who found the hot springs in the wilderness as he pastured the asses of Zibeon his father.

We note that this list comprises only three generations (Seir, his sons, and their children). Only two women are mentioned: Timna as Lotan's sister, and Oholibamah as Anah's daughter. Of the 29 names, 13 end in *-an* or *-on*, which suggested a Canaanite background to Albright (1956: 126-28, 210). Moritz, however, noted Arabic associations for most of these names (Moritz, 1926: 81-92; see also Montgomery, 1934, reprint 1969: 47). The name Lotan may be a variant of Lot, who is associated with the Dead Sea region and with the Moabites and Ammonites (Gen. 19.30-38); Shobal appears, according to Moritz (1926: 90, citing Musil), as a place name in northern Edom, but in the Old Testament the name reappears among the Calebite families in 1 Chron. 2.50-52, while Onam similarly reappears as a Jerahmeelite (1 Chron. 2.26), and this connection of Seirite names with southern Judah may be significant (for these connections see Meyer, 1906: 328-54; Wellhausen, 1870: 28-30; Bartlett, 1969: 1-20 [2-5]). Thus also from this list Hori might be linked with Calebite Hur (1 Chron. 2.19, 50; 4.1; Exod. 31.2; cf. Num. 13.5), Manahath with Menuhoth (1 Chron. 2.52 and perhaps with the town Manahath south-west of Jerusalem (Aharoni, 1979: 245), Onam and Aran with Jerahmeel's sons Onam and Oren (1 Chron. 2.25-26), Ithran with Jether (1 Chron. 2.32), the Ithrites (1 Chron. 2.53) and the town Jattir (Josh. 21.14), Akan with Jaakan (1 Chron. 1.42, cf. the Bene-Jaakan of Num. 33.31, Deut. 10.6 between the wilderness of Sinai and Ezion-geber). In short, Seir's sons and grandsons seem to be associated with the clans of the Negev on the southern fringes of Judah, and thus to the region west of the Wadi 'Araba with which the place name Seir itself may be connected (see above, pp. 41-44). The name of Lotan's sister, Timna, may thus similarly be connected with the mining region of Timna on the western side of the Wadi 'Araba. It is not impossible that at the heart of this list of the sons of Seir lies authentic knowledge of the clans of the region of Seir, the first generation, perhaps, representing the major groupings, and the second the sub-groups. The description of Seir as a 'Horite', however, seems less secure, and it is possible that the eponymous Seir has been dubbed 'Horite' as an assumed predecessor of Esau/Edom. In view of all this, it seems unlikely that this list can tell us much about the early history of the occupants of the land of Edom east of the Wadi 'Araba.

The genealogy assigned to Esau needs similar scrutiny. After an expanded *tŏlĕdôt* formula (v.9) in which Esau is described as the father of the Edomites and located in the hill country of Seir, a second formula introduces the list of Esau's sons: Eliphaz the son of Adah, and Reuel the son of Basemath. Then follow the lists of (1) the sons of Eliphaz (Teman, Omar, Zepho, Gatam and Kenaz), to which is appended a note telling how Eliphaz had another son Amalek by his concubine Timna, and (2) the sons of Reuel (Nahath, Zerah, Shammah, Mizzah). Each list has a similar concluding formula: 'these are the sons of Adah, Esau's wife', 'these are the sons of Basemath, Esau's wife' (vv.12b, 13b). Then in v.14 we return to the previous generation and to the sons which Oholibamah bore to Esau (Jeush, Jalam, Korah), but a different form of wording is used from that for Eliphaz and Reuel in v.10, and v.14 looks suspiciously like an editorial addition. As noted above, the editor has drawn the contents of this verse from a misreading of the list of the sons of Seir, and he may be deliberately creating a link between Seir and Esau.

It is instructive to consider the names of Esau's family. Eliphaz, as is well known, appears elsewhere in the Israelite tradition as one of Job's comforters and is described as a Temanite (Job 2.11), and it can hardly be accidental that in the present genealogy Eliphaz' eldest son is given as Teman. Teman is probably the southern region of Edom (see above, p. 40), and Esau is here being linked with an area which seemed appropriate to the editor. Omar appears to be an Arabic name (cf. *emir*, 'prince'), but neither it nor Zepho nor Gatam are attested elsewhere in the Old Testament. Kenaz, however, is presumably the eponymous ancestor of the Kenizzites (Num. 32.12; Josh. 14.6,14; 15.7; Judg. 1.13; 3.9,11) of the Negev. Esau is also seen in this genealogy as related to the Amalekites, well known as inhabitants of the Negev hostile to the Israelites (Exod. 17.8-16; 1 Sam. 30; 2 Sam. 1.8, 13). The Amalekites are here given a somewhat lower status, and the editor may be quietly making the point that Israel's arch-enemy Edom is known by the company it keeps. The other son of Esau is Reuel; the name appears elsewhere in the Old Testament as the father-in-law of Moses, a Midianite (Exod. 2.18). The names of Reuel's sons form two pairs, meaning 'descent', 'rising', and 'here', 'there', which may suggest artificiality. Nahath, however, appears as a Judahite (2 Chron. 31.13), Zerah as a clan of Judah (Gen. 38.30; cf. Num. 26.13; 1 Chron. 6.6,26), and for Shammah compare 1 Sam. 16.9; 2 Sam. 23.11, and the Jerahmeelite

(1 Chron. 2.28, 32) or Calebite (1 Chron. 2.44-45) clan Shammai. There is little in these names, in short, which positively suggests that the writer was drawing on genuinely Edomite material, and much that suggests that he was preparing a list of names appropriate to the much later Edom that he knew, an Edom lying between southern Judah and the Hejaz.

A point of some interest in this chapter is the use of the word *'allûpîm*, apparently of leaders of chiefs. It appears in this sense in Exod. 15.15 in parallel with the *'êlê mō'āb*, 'rams of Moab'. The word may be related to the Ugaritic *'lp*, 'prince', and to the North-west Semitic root *'lp*, 'thousand'. According to Mendenhall (1958: 52-66), in the Old Testament *'elep* refers to the sub-section of a tribe (cf. Judg. 6.10; Mic. 5.1) or to the contingent of troops sent by that sub-section to war on specific occasions; they would be led by *rāšê 'elep* (Num. 1.16; 10.4; Josh. 22.21). Here Mendenhall follows W.M.F. Petrie's suggestion that *'elep* meant a tent-group or family (Petrie, 1911: 43). However, if we may trust Exod. 15.15 and Gen. 36, a by-form of the word with a doubled second root consonant has taken on a new meaning and was used in Edom as the equivalent of the Israelite *rāšê 'alpê yisrā'ēl* (cf. Cross, Freedman, 1955: 248; de Vaux, 1973: II. 58-59). It is unfortunate that we have no more evidence of this usage.

Num. 20.14-21 and Deut. 2.1-8

Num. 20.14-21 (cf. Judg. 11.17) tells the well-known story of how Moses, leading the Israelites through the wilderness, sent messengers from Kadesh asking the Edomites to grant passage through their country; the Edomites turn out in force and refuse passage, and the Israelites turn away.

> Moses sent messengers from Kadesh to the king of Edom, 'Thus says your brother Israel: You know all the adversity that has befallen us; how our fathers went down to Egypt, and we dwelt in Egypt a long time; and the Egyptians dealt harshly with us and our fathers; and when we cried to the LORD, he heard our voice, and sent an angel and brought us forth out of Egypt; and here we are in Kadesh, a city on the edge of your territory. Now let us pass through your land. We will not pass through field or vineyard, neither will we drink water from a well; we will go along the King's Highway, we will not turn aside to the right hand or to the left,

until we have passed through your territory'. But Edom said to
him, 'You shall not pass through, lest I come out with the sword
against you'. And the people of Israel said to him, 'We will go up by
the highway; and if we drink of your water, I and my cattle, then I
will pay for it; let me only pass through on foot, nothing more'. But
he said, 'You shall not pass through'. And Edom came out against
them with many men, and with a strong force. Thus Edom refused
to give Israel passage through his territory; so Israel turned away
from him.

A similar account appears in Deut. 2.18, where the Lord instructs
Moses to command the people to pass through the territories of the
children of Esau who dwell in Seir, purchasing from them the
necessary provisions; but they are not to settle there, for the land has
been given to Esau for possession. These two accounts appear to
differ on one basic point (among a number of others): Num. 20
explicitly says that the Israelites could not and did not traverse
Edom, while Deut. 2 implies that they did.

Any assessment of the historicity of these accounts must (as
always) depend on the view taken of the origins of this material and
the aims of its compilers and editors. The literary-critical problems
of these passages and their relationship to each other have been
much discussed. Num. 20.14-21 has usually been allocated to J or E,
or JE. It seems clear that Num. 20.14b-16 is either the source for
Deut. 26.5-9 (Carmichael, 1969: 273-89) or derived from that
passage (Mittmann, 1973: 143-49); the latter seems more likely. The
narrative of Num. 20.14, 17-21 is closely related to that of Num.
21.21-23, in which Sihon of Heshbon refuses permission to Israel to
traverse his territory. Both narratives have been thought to derive
from E (though Mittmann argues that the Edom story is a slightly
adapted copy of the original Sihon story); on these two accounts
depend those of Deut. 2.1-8, 26-37. Van Seters would reverse this
dependency, arguing that Num. 20.14-21 is basically dependent on
Deut. 2.26-37 and Judg. 11.19-26 (van Seters, 1972: 182-97; see
further Bartlett, 1978b: 347-51, and van Seters, 1980: 117-24). But
whether we have an E narrative with Deuteronomic expansion, or a
basically Deuteronomic narrative, or refuse to think in such source-
critical terms at all, we must reckon with the probability that this
story belongs essentially to the monarchic or even exilic period, and
there are a number of minor indications that point this way. The

reference to the unnamed king of Edom suggests that the narrator is assuming from his knowledge of contemporary Edom the existence of a monarchy in ancient Edom. The reference to the 'King's Highway' may suggest the Assyrian period and the imperial administration (see above, p. 38). The reference to the boundary Edom, apparently on the borders of Kadesh, probably reflects the situation of the later monarchy when, as we know from both biblical and extra-biblical sources, Edom's border ran alongside Judah's in the Negev (cf. Glueck, 1936a: 145-57; Bartlett, 1969: 1-20 [15-16]; 1982: 13-24 [14-16]; Aharoni, 1979: 69-70; cf. Num. 34.3-6; Josh. 15.1-4; Ezek. 47.19; 48.28). The emphasis on the hostility of Edom and her readiness with the sword reflect the attitude visible in Amos 1.11-12, which probably refers to Edom's struggle for independence under Jehoram (though some refer it to Edom's behaviour in 587 BCE). The description of Israel as Edom's 'brother' (Num. 20.14) also indicates the monarchic period (Bartlett, 1969: 1-20; 1977: 2-27; see below, ch. 10).

The Deuteronomic passage (Deut. 2.1-8), interestingly, reveals a different attitude to Edom. The author plays down Israelite hostility towards Edom. He describes the Edomites as 'your/our brethren the sons of Esau, who live in Seir', and refers to them without rancour or bitterness. In verse 5 he makes the Lord warn Israel not to contend with the sons of Esau, which suggests that he knows of the tradition of hostility and is deliberately countering it. He makes the point that God has given Esau his territory as a possession (just as God will grant Israel her own territory for possession). All this must in some way relate to the attitude expressed in Deut. 23.7: 'You shall not abhor an Edomite, for he is your brother'. To judge by the use of the term 'brother' elsewhere in Deut. (when not used in the limited family sense, it is used mainly to refer to an Israelite as opposed to an alien; cf. Deut. 1.16; 15.2-3,7,9,11,12; 17.15; 23.19f.; see Bartlett, 1977: 2-27 [5-8]), the Deuteronomist is here indicating that Edom is not to be treated as a pagan alien but almost as a fellow Israelite, whose children can in the third generation become accepted members of the Israelite community (Deut. 23.8). As a brother, the Edomite belongs to the Israelite rather than to the Canaanite religious tradition. The Deuteronomist may have some understanding that in matters of religion Edomites and Israelites had much in common. For the future, the Deuteronomist may be saying, Israel and Edom must forget their past hostilities.

The narratives of Israel's contact with Edom in the wilderness thus have important political and theological overtones. Num. 20.14-21 reflects an attitude of political hostility towards Edom, and Deut. 2.1-8 and 23.7 suggest a more positive approach to Edom, based on the Deuteronomistic view of the geographical extent of Israel's inheritance; other nations had their God-given inheritance also. These stories are not told as fragments of antiquarian research, but as political and theological propaganda. They contribute virtually nothing to our knowledge of the land of Edom in the thirteenth-twelfth centuries BCE.

Judges 3.7-11

We are no better off for the period of the Israelite judges, in which Edom is barely mentioned. The court poet of Judges 5 (see note, p. 102) describes Israel's gGod Yahweh as coming from Edom and Seir (v. 4) to aid his people, but this reference (almost certainly from the northern kingdom of Israel in the monarchic period) tells us nothing of the situation in Edom in the 12th—11th centuries BCE. More problematic is the account of the deliverer Othniel in Judg. 3.7-11, which tells how Othniel the son of Kenaz (cf. Gen. 36.11) rescued Israel from Cushan-rishathaim king of Mesopotamia (Aram Naharaim). Mayes has argued that this episode of Othniel was composed as a typical example of how God worked on Israel's behalf through deliverers, in order to provide an introduction to the collection of deliverer stories, and perhaps also to provide a suitable deliverer for the tribe of Judah. 'Any historical basis that there may be to the account will be found only in an investigation of the names of Othniel and his opponent Cushan-rishathaim, "king of Mesopotamia"' (Mayes, 1977: 285-331 [311]). Othniel is associated in Josh. 15.16-19 and Judg. 1.12-15 with Caleb the son of Jephunneh the Kenizzite and with the capture of Debir, formerly Kiriath-sepher (formerly identified with Tell Beit Mirsim and now by many with Kh. Rabūd). Othniel is thus clearly located in southern Judah. Cushan-rishathaim of Aram-naharaim is a more elusive person. In view of Othniel's geographical location, a number of scholars have emended Aram to Edom, and eliminated Naharaim (v.8) as a gloss (for references see Malamat, 1954: 231-42 [232]). Cushan would then have come from Edom. Rishathaim, traditionally interpreted as meaning 'of double wickedness' (*ibid.*, 232, n. 8), has been variously explained. Marquart (1986: 11) proposed *rôš 'ataîm*, 'chief of 'Athaim', a name he took from the LXX version of the Chronicler's version (1 Chron. 1.46) of Hadad's city Avith (Gen. 36.35). A. Klostermann (1896: 119), followed by J. Gray (1967: 214-15, 260-61), proposed *rôš hattěmāni*, 'chief of the Temanites', which would not be inapposite with the name Cushan, which appears in association with Midian in Hab. 3.7, and which, with its final syllable *-an*, is of a form common among the names of the descendants of Seir (Gen. 36.20-27).

However, while it seems likely that Othniel was involved with some more local opponent than one from northern Syria, these suggestions remain speculative, and even if the compiler of the collection of deliverer stories in Judges wrote 'Edom' where 'Aram (-Naharaim)' now stands, he may not have had any reliable information to hand. Further, the emendation remains doubtful; if the story was composed, as Mayes suggests, to give an example of God's saving activity by way of introduction to other such stories of deliverance, the author may have intended Aram, not Edom, in which case we can draw nothing of any significance for 12th—11th century BCE Edom from the story. Accepting Aram-Naharaim, Malamat (1954: 231-42) proposes to identify Cushan-rishathaim with a certain Arsu or Irsu, a Syrian ruler mentioned in Pap. Harris I.75: 1-9 (cf. *ANET³* 260), who, according to Malamat, seized the Egyptian throne in an anarchic period at the end of the Nineteenth Dynasty about 1200 BCE. The identification of Cushan with Irsu, however, seems highly speculative. E. Täubler (1947: 136-42) argued that the name Cushan-rishathaim derives from a literary attempt to associate the Midianite Cushan with Babylon (the home of wickedness) and so to bring Cushan into contempt. More prosaically, R. Boling (1975:81) suggests that the place name Aram-naharaim results from the mistaken re-division of an original *'rmn hrym*, 'fortress of the mountains'; but where was this? The identity of Cushan-rishathaim and his connection, if any, with Edom, remain totally obscure.

The Edomite King-List: Gen. 36.31-39; 1 Chron. 1.43-50

More promising, at first sight, is the list in Gen. 36.31-39 (cf. 1 Chron. 1.43-50), which purports to describe 'the kings who reigned in the land of Edom, before any king reigned over the Israelites'. The list cannot be older than the early monarchic period of Judah and Israel, as the introduction makes clear. The second clause of the introduction has been interpreted to mean either 'before there ruled a king for the sons of Israel (over Edom)' (cf. Buhl, 1893: 47; Skinner, 1912: 434; Simons, 1959: 24, note 9), in which case perhaps David is meant, or, more probably, 'before a king ruled in Israel', in which case perhaps Saul is meant. This second interpretation appears to be that accepted by the Septuagintal tradition; thus Codex Alexandrinus gives 'before a king ruled in Jerusalem', and the Lucianic recension 'before a king ruled in Israel'. The difficulty of accepting this last as the meaning of the Hebrew is that the verb *malak*, in the sense 'to rule over', is usually followed by *bĕ* or *'al* rather than by *lĕ* as in Gen. 36.31; Marquart (1896:73) therefore proposed the insertion of an *'ayin* before the MT *lamed* to give *'al*, but Meyer (1906: 353, n. 2), denied the need to improve the text in this way. The RV, RSV and NEB all adopt the second interpretation. In either case, however, the list in its present form almost certainly derives from later in the monarchic period; the introductory sentence suggests strongly that the author knows he is speaking of the distant past. The more difficult question is, whether any part of this list contains ancient and authentic material about Edom's early monarchy.

The material of the list is not homogeneous. It was pointed out over sixty years ago (Desnoyers, 1922: 71, n. 2) that in the list two different formulas are used to denote the place of rule or origin of the kings:

(1) 'and the name of his city was . . . ' (Bela, Hadad, Hadar)
(2) ' . . . from . . . ' (Jobab, Husham, Samlah, Shaul)

(One person, Baal-hanan the son of Achbor, is not connected with any particular place.) A third formula has been used to connect the different members of the list: ' . . . died, and . . . reigned in his stead'. This formula not only links the names; it gives them a sequence. Without the formula, these names would have no relation to one another, for each king is connected with a different place, and no king is succeeded by his son. If the list represents a genuine sequence of kings, ruling Edom one after another, then the principle of succession was not dynastic; perhaps the succession went to the chief of the strongest tribe. But it seems much more likely that the succession of kings offered in this list is artificial. The list has been put together from a short list of four names (Jobab the son of Zerah of Bozrah, Husham of the land of the Temanites, Samlah of Masrekah, Shaul of Rehoboth by the River), a group of three names given together with the formula 'and the name of his city was . . . ' (Bela, Hadad, Hadar), and one single name (Baal-hanan the son of Achbor) with no note of place attached.

A closer study of this list yields interesting results. The first name, Bela the son of Beor, has often been compared and sometimes identified with Balaam, son of Beor, who was summoned to Balak, the king of Moab (Num. 22.2–24.25) (for references, see Skinner, 1912: 435; Bartlett, 1965: 301-14 [303, n. 3]). The text discovered in 1967 at Tell Deir 'Allā, dating probably from the seventh century BCE, mentions a prophet called Balaam and shows that this figure was known in the middle Jordan valley in the period of the Israelite and Judahite monarchy (Franken, 1967: 480-81; Hoftijzer and van der Kooij, 1976; H. and M. Weippert, 1982: 77-103). In the biblical texts, Balaam is variously said to have come from 'Pethor, which is by the River' (Num. 22.5), Aram (Num. 23.7), the land of Amaw, or, perhaps, the land of the children of Ammon (Num. 22.5), or Midian (Num. 31.8). (In Num. 22.5 the RSV gives 'the land of Amaw', following the Hebrew consonants, but apparently ignoring the inclusion of the word *bne*, 'sons of'; the NEB improves by rendering 'the land of the Amavites', though this land and these people are otherwise unknown.) The RV translates 'to the land of the children of his people'. Some have followed the evidence of the Samaritan, Syriac, Lucianic and vulgate versions and read, adding the letter *nun*, 'the children of Ammon' (cf. Meyer, 1906: 377). There is thus no suggestion that the Balaam of these texts belongs to Edom, unless with some scholars (e.g. Moritz, 1937: 101-22 [106]) Aram in Num. 23.7 is to be emended to 'Edom', but the parallelism of this verse makes the emendation unnecessary, 'the mountains of the east' (*qedem*) providing a better geographical parallel to Aram than to Edom (on *qedem*, see Eph'al, 1982: 10; Simons, 1959: 13 §35). If, then, Bela son of Beor of the Edomite king-list is to be identified with Balaam son of Beor, Bela was not an Edomite. The name Bela occurs twice elsewhere in the Old Testament, once as an alternative name for Zoar at the southern end of the Dead Sea (Gen. 14.2,8), and once of a clan chief from the regions of Moab and Gilead (1 Chron. 5.8).

regions of Bela and Balaam are not necessarily to be identified; there may have been confusion between two well known figures. But the associations of these names appear to have been with Moab and Gilead rather than with Edom, and this makes it all the more noteworthy that Bela's city Dinhabah was connected by Eusebius with Moab (see above, p. 46); Dinhabah has not been connected with any site in Edom.

A second name in the king-list is also firmly associated with Moab. Hadad, son of Bedad, 'defeated Midian in the field of Moab' (Gen. 36.35). No Edomite site has been proposed for Hadad's city, Avith; the name was associated by Burckhardt with a chain of low mountains east of the upper course of the River Arnon (el-Mūjib), though this identification is hardly certain (see above, p. 45). However, unless we simply assume from his presence in the king-list that Hadad was at home in Edom, the only evidence we have for his location is a tradition linking him firmly with Moab.

A third name in the list may also have Moabite connections. Pau (or Pai, 1 Chron. 1.50), the city of Hadar (Hadad, 1 Chron. 1.50) has sometimes been equated with Peor in Moab (Num. 23.28; 25.18; 31.16; Josh. 22.17). The Septuagint renders both Pau and Peor by *Phogor*, and Eusebius follows this (cf. Skinner, 1910: 436; Klostermann, 1904:168; Moritz, 1937:121). Marquart, followed by Meyer (Marquart, 1896:10; Meyer, 1906; 375-76; cf. Skinner, 1910: 436) suggested that the name of Hadar's wife's grandparent Me-zahab was a place name rather than a personal name, and he compared it with the Di-zahab of Deut. 1.1 (which he wished to change to Me-zahab, 'Golden-water') and with the Vaheb in Suphah in Num. 21.14 (which with a slight change could be read as Zahab in Suphah). These two places might be found in Moab. There are far too many hypotheses here, but again it can be said that, apart from the fact that Hadar/Hadad has been included in a list purporting to be of Edomite kings, there is nothing which positively connects him with Edom; such faint evidence as we have suggests Moab.

These three names, Bela, Hadad, and Hadar/Hadad, are precisely those names which are distinguished in the kinglist by the use of the formula 'and the name of his city was . . . '. That they form a group by themselves is perhaps underlined by the evidence of their Moabite connections. One might add that cities seem to have been more common in Moab in the Iron age than in Edom, where very few cities are known. A list of early kings, each with his city, does not correspond with what we know of this early period of Edom's history. Edom was clearly not a land of city-states at this stage.

We may now turn to those names on the list given with the formula '. . . of . . . '. The first two names are reassuring, in that they are associated with two well-known Edomite place names. Bozrah is modern Buseira, some 35 km south of the Dead Sea, occupying a strong position at the head of a wadi which runs northwest into the Wadi 'Araba and controlling the north-south road along the watershed which has become known as the King's Highway. Old Testament references make it clear that Bozrah was known as the most important city of Edom; Amos 1.12 speaks of 'Bozrah and her palaces', and mentions it in parallel with Teman. Other passages mention Bozrah in parallel with Edom itself (Isa. 34.6; 63.1; cf. Jer. 49.22). Jer. 49.13 speaks of Bozrah and 'all her cities'. All our evidence, however, both literary and archaeological, for Bozrah as a place of importance comes from the eighth and following centuries, apart from this reference in the king-list. As yet, no firm archaeological evidence for a ninth, tenth, or eleventh century BCE city has been found (cf. Bennett 1973, 1974a, 1975, 1977, 1983; the suggestion [Milward, 1975: 16-17] that the fragment of an Egyptian faience chalice from Dynasty XXI or XXII 'indicates that there was by then a settlement of some importance, a large trading post perhaps, or, even by the ninth century, the northern capital of the Edomite kingdom' goes far beyond the evidence). What all this probably means is that, if Bozrah existed before the eighth century BCE, it was a comparatively small place, and physical evidence of it has not appeared in the areas excavated so far. The name Jobab son of Zerah is not evidenced elsewhere for Edom, but the names are well enough known; Jobab occurs in Gen. 10.29; Josh. 11.1, and 1 Chron. 8.9, 18 as that of an Arabian tribe, a north Palestinian king, and two Benjaminites. Zerah is a common name, but it occurs as one of Esau's grandsons in Gen. 36.17 and it is just possible that the editor of Gen. 36 had this in mind. Jobab is the only member of the group of four kings presented with the formula ' . . . of . . . ' to have his father named, and the editor may in this way have given the king of the most important place in Edom a connection with the genealogy of Esau.

According to the list, Jobab's successor was Husham of the land of the Temanites. As we have seen, the name Teman probably designated the southern region of Edom (see above, p. 40); the name later came to be used poetically as a synonym for Edom itself. Teman was not a city name. Husham, then, may have ruled over the large southern region of Edom; his name reminded Clermont-Ganneau of the Wadi Ḥismā, which runs in a wide sweep between the southern end of the Edomite central mountain range and the peaks of Jebel Ramm (Clermont-Ganneau, 1906: 464-71). E.A. Knauf, however, believes that the land of the Temanites was the region of the oasis of Teima, much further south in northwest Arabia (Knauf, 1985: 245-53 [249-50]); he appears to base this on the association of Teman with Dedan in Ezek. 25.13. Whether the Hebrew form *temâni* could be used for the inhabitants of Teima, however, is not clear.

With Samlah of Masrekah we are back in the realm of conjecture. As we have seen, Masrekah may belong to the region of Jebel Mishrāq in the Ḥismā region between Maʿan and ʿAqaba. Shaul of Rehoboth by the river, however, perhaps belonged to the northwest corner of Edom (see above, pp. 50-51). The other name on the list, Baal-hanan son of Achbor, is not connected with any place. The fact that Baal-hanan's father's name is given may suggest that he belonged to the group of names which included Bela and Hadad, and that the note of place ('and the name of his city was ... ') has disappeared. We are left with a fragment of information, and we do not know why the compiler of the list included it with the other names.

The analysis of this list, then, suggests that it contains four figures—and perhaps four only—belonging to Edom. They are not connected by any family relationship or principle of succession, and each is associated with a different region. It is not clear whether the region named is intended to denote the birth-place of the king, or his residence, or his place of rule. Probably the editor understood the place names to refer to the kings' birth-places. He clearly thought that these kings ruled over Edom as a whole (cf Gen. 36.31), as Edom's kings did in later times nearer his own day. So far as we know, centralised rule in Edom went back only to the mid-ninth century BCE when 'Edom revolted from the rule of Judah, and set up a king of their own' (2 Kgs 8.20), and was preceded by the centralised government imposed by David in the tenth century (2 Sam. 8.14). If Jobab of Bozrah, Husham of the land of the Temanites, Samlah of

Masrekah, and Shaul of Rehoboth on the River are genuinely pre-Davidic figures, it is possible that we should think of them as local rulers, controlling separate and independent regions, to be compared with the various local rulers mentioned in the books of Joshua and Judges (in which case, the references to Bozrah and the land of the Temanites, not otherwise mentioned before the eighth century BCE, might be anachronistic). But it is also possible that the Israelite editor who formed this list was drawing on names which in reality belonged to the ninth-eighth centuries BCE (a period already sufficiently remote from his own day), and in this case the references to Bozrah and to the land of the Temanites are more likely to be original (cf. Ishida, 1977: 22-23, and review by Tigay, 1981: 251).

The date of the original compilation of the list is clearly important for our assessment of it. Knauf (1985: 245-53) has argued that this list cannot be dated earlier than the end of the sixth century BCE. The picture it presents of Edom ruled by kings from different areas reflects (for Knauf) not the pre-monarchic period in Edom but the post-monarchic period of the early Persian empire, when Bozrah, Teima, Dedan, and Tell el-Kheleifeh were the main centres of government. Certainly this list can hardly pre-date the existence of Bozrah or Teman as important places, and on present evidence Bozrah did not exist as an important urban centre before the eighth century BCE. Amos 1.12 singles out Teman and Bozrah as the objects of Yahweh's punishment for Edom's crimes, and if this oracle is authentic (and not, as some believe, an addition from after 587 BCE), then knowledge of Teman and Bozrah is evidenced in Israel for the mid-eighth century. It is true, however, that other references to Teman and Bozrah are later, probably sixth-century (Teman: Obad. 9; Jer. 49.7; Ezek. 25.13; cf. Job 2.11; Bozrah: Isa. 34.6; 63.1; Jer. 49.13-22). If Amos 1.12 is indeed a later addition to the oracles of the prophet Amos, then Teman and Bozrah are not well evidenced in the literary sources, at least, before the sixth century BCE, and the editor's source for Gen. 36.30-39 may not be so old after all.

However, Amos 1.12 cannot be so easily dismissed as an exilic addition as it used to be (see Bartlett 1977: 2-27 [10-12]), and in any case Bozrah certainly existed as an important urban centre from the eighth century BCE, as excavation there has shown. There is no reason why the editor's material for this list should not derive from the mid-monarchic period at least. But its literary origins appear to be Israelite, not Edomite. The formula of the framework, 'and he died, and ... reigned in his stead' is used in the Deuteronomic history (cf. 1 Kgs 16.22; 2 Kgs 1.17; 8.15; 12.22; 13.24), and it is not impossible that this list belonged to the Deuteronomistic archives before it was incorporated into the collection of material about Edom in Gen. 36. This would also explain why alone of the seven sections of this chapter, Gen. 36.30-39 makes no reference to Edom (apart from its introductory sentence) and does not identify Esau with Edom. The editor took over the list whole, adding only the opening sentence 'These are the kings who reigned in the land of Edom, before any king reigned over the Israelites'. His predecessor had ordered the kings in succession by a standard formula used by the Deuteronomistic historian, drawing perhaps on two groups of material, one of which had some local knowledge of Edom. This material named four different places, two of which were probably known in Israel and Judah by the mid-eighth century BCE. The other two were not important places, and are not mentioned again.

It is fairly clear that the editor who combined the two groups of material into one list had only a fairly scanty knowledge of the geography and history of the regions east of the Dead Sea; thus he could combine into an Edomite list names from both Edom and Moab, names which for the most part no longer meant much to him. But knowledge of these persons and places must have come into Israel or Judah from somewhere. I previously suggested that it came through the contact of Judah with Edom in the reigns of David and Solomon in the tenth century BCE (Bartlett, 1965: 301-14 [314]). In view of the presence of Bozrah in this list, however, the basic list cannot certainly be dated earlier than the eighth century BCE, and may reflect the reign of Uzziah, who 'built Elath' on the Gulf of 'Aqaba 'and restored it to Judah' (2 Kgs 14.22). Edom in this eighth century was an active, independent and hostile kingdom on Judah's borders, and surely of increasing interest and concern to Judah. It is in this century that Bozrah developed and became known in Israelite literature. It seems most likely, then, that the core of this Edomite king-list derives from information which became current in Judah in the eighth century; this was edited, perhaps by a Deuteronomistic hand, in the seventh century and incorporated thereafter into the Pentateuchal history.

The result of this for our historical inquiry is that we still know nothing for certain about the social and political situation in Edom before David's occupation of the land. At best we can point to the possibility of pre-Davidic rule in Edom being exercised on a regional basis, but as the list is clearly a relatively late construction on the basis of fragmentary information, there is little certainty in any historical reconstruction based upon it.

Note: The Song of Deborah

The 'Song of Deborah' (Judg. 5.2-31) has often been thought to have a liturgical or cultic background, and the speaker of verse 3 identified in consequence as a leader in the cult. But though Yahweh is invoked in verses 4 and 31, the Song of Deborah does not convey the sense or mood of worship, even though the speaker announces that he will sing and make melody to the Lord (verse 3). The speaker is in fact addressing himself to the kings and princes of a court, as verse 3a suggests. He is extolling the valour of the tribes of Israel and their leaders in the ancient battle against the kings of Canaan, in the days of Shamgar and Jael. The tribes given honourable mention are the major tribes of the northern kingdom of Israel, and the poet surely proclaimed the triumphs of the Lord and his peasantry in Israel (v.11) at the Israelite court; the absence of any reference to Judah also makes this clear. The poet is concerned to present dramatically to his audience the mustering of the tribes, the battle, and as a climax the escape and death of Sisera at the hands of the heroine Jael. The speaker is not leading worship; he is the Israelite equivalent of Homer's bard Demodocus, who sang at the Phaeacian court of the loves of the gods and of the battles of the Trojan War (Od. 8.266ff.; 521ff.).

Chapter 6

EDOM UNDER DAVID AND SOLOMON

The Conquest of Edom under David

The evidence for the state of affairs in Edom before the time of the
Israelite monarchy is, as we have seen, far from satisfactory, the
biblical evidence, at least, deriving from much later, tendentious
sources. The first clear reference to any historical event appears in
the brief notice of the exploits of king Saul of Israel in the years just
before the beginning of the first millennium BCE. According to
1 Sam. 14.47-48,

> When Saul had taken the kingship over Israel, he fought against all
> his enemies of every side, against Moab, against the Ammonites,
> against Edom, against the kings of Zobah, and against the
> Philistines; wherever he turned he put them to the worse. And he
> did valiantly, and smote the Amalekites, and delivered Israel out of
> the hands of those who plundered them.

This summary of Saul's achievements is full of Deuteronomic
expressions and is similar to the Deuteronomic historian's summary
of David's wars in 2 Sam. 8.1-14. Saul is here presented as a
successful figure who 'delivered Israel' in the manner of the earlier
judges. But whereas fuller accounts of his wars with the Ammonites
and Philistines are preserved in 1 Sam. 11 and 1 Sam. 13-14, we have
no other accounts of his wars against Moab, Edom, and the kings of
Zobah. The war against Edom might be eliminated altogether if we
were to follow the evidence of the LXX and read 'Aram', Syria, for
'Edom' in verse 47. Many scholars, suspicious of the attribution of so
many major military conquests to Saul, have suggested that he has
been credited with what were really David's achievements (cf., e.g.,
Buhl, 1893: 55; see Hertzberg, 1964: 119). However, there are some
reasons for doubting this. The historian was not over-sympathetic

towards Saul or concerned to magnify his exploits at the expense of David's (cf. Thornton, 1967: 413-23), and the reference to the presence of Doeg the Edomite at Saul's court, if historical, at least may confirm that contact between Israel and Edom was possible in Saul's day. While Doeg may be functioning in the story as the archetypal villainous Edomite (Klein, 1983: 212), who alone of Saul's officials was treacherous enough to betray David and massacre the priests of Nob and their families, the original reason for his presence in Israel is less certain. He may have been in Israel as a mercenary or an adventurer or a pilgrim; but his presence, if not merely fictional, makes Saul's contact with Edom the more likely, as does also the note that Saul defeated the Amalekites who lived to the south of Judah, on the borders of Edom.

It is not clear how successful Saul was in his war with Edom. The MT *yaršia'* might be translated 'he put them to the worse' (RSV), or 'he acted wickedly' (Hertzberg, 1964: 119-20); the reading *yiwwāšea'* (*Niph'al*), on the evidence of the LXX, yields the translation 'he was successful' (NEB), while the slight emendation *yōšīa'* would give a more positive assessment, 'he did saving acts' (see Driver, 1913: 120). However one reads and translates this word, there is nothing to suggest that Saul invaded or occupied Edom, which was hardly a threat to his kingdom. But there was almost certainly some growing contact between Edom and her neighbours, which naturally influenced and stimulated the political development of all concerned.

For Edom's sufferings at the hands of David or his generals there is a certain amount of evidence in 2 Sam. 8.13-14, 1 Kgs 11.15-16, the title of Ps. 60, and 1 Chron. 18.12. It is possible to date David's war against Edom c. 990 BCE. The beginning of David's reign in Jerusalem may be dated to 1004/3, or perhaps 996/5 BCE (Bartlett, 1976: 205-6 [218, n. 42]; Thiele, 1966: 52; but note also Hayes, Miller, 1979: 679). In 2 Sam. 8 the war against Edom appears as the last of David's wars, and this is probably correct. Edom was not the most pressing threat to David's kingdom. David inherited the Philistine struggle from the days of Saul, and this was therefore probably his first task (2 Sam. 8.1). Next, perhaps, came the Moabites, and then the Ammonites and Aramaeans (2 Sam. 8.2-12). The place of the Ammonite war in David's reign can perhaps be roughly fixed by the fact that Solomon's birth happened in the course of this war. David reigned for thirty-three years in Jerusalem (2 Sam.

5.5), and Solomon succeeded him as a fairly young man, to reign for forty years (1 Kgs 11.42). If Solomon on accession was aged between twenty and thirty, which seems a reasonable guess, his birth and the Ammonite war would have taken place between the third and thirteenth years of David's reign in Jerusalem. Only after this, and perhaps after the campaigns against the Amalekites, which may also belong to the earlier part of David's reign, can we date the invasion of Edom, which would thus fall either between c. 1000—990 BCE or between c. 992—982 BCE; the later alternative seems more likely, as it allows more time for the previous campaigns (see Bartlett, 1976: 205-26 [218-20]). At David's motives we can only surmise. He presumably wished to secure the southeastern borders of Judah, and perhaps also control the trade route north from the Gulf of 'Aqaba.

Reconstructing the details of David's campaign is not easy. According to the MT of 2 Sam. 8.13-14,

> David made a name for himself when he returned from smiting Edom (MT, Aram) in the Valley of Salt, eighteen thousand men. And he put garrisons in Edom; throughout all Edom he put garrisons, and all the Edomites became David's servants.

If the figure of those killed is trustworthy (Ps. 60, title, gives twelve thousand), we might guess at an Edomite population at this time of about 100,000, which seems too high. Comparison of this text with 1 Chron. 18.12 raises further questions. The text of 2 Sam. 8.13 appears to credit this campaign to David in person, making no mention of his general Joab, but as this chapter is a summary of David's achievements abroad, the absence of the general's name here is probably not significant. 1 Chron. 18.12 (followed by Jos. *Ant.* VII.5.4 [109]) credits the campaign to Abishai the son of Zeruiah; McCarter (1984: 243,246) follows this, reconstructing 2 Sam. 8.13 to read, 'Also, Abishai son of Zeruiah defeated the Edomites in the Valley of Salt—eighteen thousands'. According to 1 Kgs 11.15, however, the campaign was conducted by Abishai's brother Joab (cf. the title of Ps. 60). Joab's treatment of Edom after the battle was ruthless. He spent six months in Edom 'until he had cut off every male in Edom'. This would have been no easy task in such difficult terrain, and such determined extermination would have created lasting hatred of Judah in Edom. Amos 1.11 later reveals the spirit in which Edom took her revenge:

> For three transgressions of Edom, and for four,
>   I will not revoke the punishment;
> because he pursued his brother with the sword,
>   and cast off all pity.

Part of Joab's work was the establishment of Judah's military control of Edom. According to 2 Sam. 8.14, David—probably acting through Joab—'put garrisons in Edom; throughout all Edom he put garrisons'. The reduplication is slightly surprising, and may be a conflation of two versions of the account. The word translated 'garrisons' (*nĕṣîbîm*) might also be translated 'governors', and McCarter (1984: 246) has suggested that one of the two conflated texts read 'and he stationed in Edom a prefect' (*neṣîb*). Whether McCarter's view of the text is right or not, such an action at least seems highly probable, and that a prefect or governor was appointed over Edom at some stage is confirmed by 1 Kgs 22.47, where such an officer is mentioned as being in control in Jehoshaphat's day. That the Edomites became David's servants probably means that they were compelled to pay tribute in some form, as did the Moabites (2 Sam. 8.2), but this is not specifically mentioned. What is emphasised both in 1 Sam. 8.13-14 and in 1 Kgs 11.15-16 is the thoroughness of Joab's work; he put garrisons (or governors) through all Edom, and all the Edomites became David's servants, and he slew every male in Edom. This emphasis is interesting. The historian seems to be aware that the conquest of Edom was brutally thorough (or perhaps the historian is indicating that Judah's most hated enemy naturally deserved such treatment). Such thorough occupation would suggest also that Judah had recognised the full potential of Edom as a hostile nation, and it allowed Judah to explore, perhaps for the first time, the full extent of Edom's territory. Conversely, the experience probably helped the development of national self-consciousness in Edom itself. The Edomites now began to known themselves to be a nation, with interests that differed sharply from Judah's. But so thoroughly did Joab do his work that it was a century and a half before Edom could become an independent nation.

It has recently been argued (Miller and Hayes, 1986: 182) that 'the Edom that David subjected and secured with garrisons was most likely the area southwest of the Dead Sea, along his own kingdom's southern frontier, inhabited by "Edomite" tribes such as the Kenizzites and the Amalekites'. On this view, David and Joab did not penetrate Edom proper to the east of the Wadi 'Araba, where lay the later Edomite capital of Bozrah: but only the region of Seir; but if this is right, the emphasis of 2 Sam. 8.14 that David put garrisons 'throughout all Edom' and that 'all the Edomites' became his servants is strange. Miller and Hayes' view is largely dependent on the identification of the Valley of Salt, where the Edomites were defeated, with the Wadi el-milh east of Beersheba. Noth (1960: 196), however, locates it east of the Wadi 'Araba, and others in the region of the Ghor at the southern end of the Dead Sea. It is difficult to argue from any of these uncertainties. The primary question here must be, what territory had the author of 2 Sam. 8 (the Deuteronomistic Historian?) in mind when he used the name 'Edom' (especially when he used it alongside 'Moab' and 'the Ammonites', 2 Sam. 8.12)? If the text derives as is likely from the later monarchic period, the author may indeed have had in mind an Edom which extended westwards to the borders of Judah described in Num. 34.3, Josh. 15.1-4, but equally he knew that Edom (with its capital Bozrah) was located in the mountains east of the Wadi 'Araba, and he stresses that David conquered all Edom. Perhaps this is his expression of what he thought must have been the case; and here we reach a secondary question: what are the historical probabilities of the matter? Miller and Hayes clearly take a minimalist view of David's achievements in the south-east, and think it unlikely that he needed to subject and garrison the mountains east of the Wadi 'Araba. This is possible; but our analysis of the archaeological evidence has shown that settlement east of the 'Araba is developing by this time, and David may have felt that control of the route to the Gulf of 'Aqaba through the 'Araba involved control of the mountains to the east of it. On balance it is likely that David did conquer the land east of the Wadi 'Araba; the subsequent history of Edom makes better sense on this assumption. One further point might be added: if the tradition that David conquered Edom is ancient and reliable, then the territory meant is likely to be that east of the 'Araba rather than the land west of it, which was known in earlier times as the land of Seir.

The Story of Hadad (1 Kgs 11.14-22)

Joab's massacre, however, was not total. We are told that Hadad the

Edomite, of the royal house of Edom, still only a child, escaped to Egypt with certain Edomites of his father's servants (1 Kgs 11.14-17). Hadad later married into the Egyptian royal house, had a son, Genubath, and after David's death returned to Edom, apparently against Pharaoh's will, and became an adversary to Solomon (1 Kgs 11.14-22). Far reaching conclusions about Edom's history have been drawn from this account; in particular, it has often been taken to demonstrate that Edom in David's time had an hereditary monarchy, and that in Solomon's time Edom was lost to Judah through Hadad's successful opposition (cf., e.g., Noth, 1960: 205-206). But too much has been read into this acount. The phrase *mizzera' hammelek* ('of the royal house', RSV, NEB) need not mean that Hadad was the son and heir of his father the king. Ishmael (2 Kgs 25.25; Jer. 41.1) is similarly described, but he was not the direct heir to the throne of Judah, and Hadad may have been no more than a prince, the sole remaining member of the king's family. Equally, the 'servants' are not necessarily to be understood as royal officials; they may have been simply the staff of a land-owning member of the royal family. Unless we assume that Hadad's father was the king of Edom, and the son of a king, there is no evidence that Edom had an hereditary monarchy at this time. We may also note that there is no suggestion that Hadad's son Genubath followed him in any royal position in Edom. However, it is clear that if, as seems likely, the historian is following authentic tradition here, the family of the king counted for something in Edom at this time, and we may probably accept that there was a king or ruler in Edom when David attacked, though we do not know his name or where he ruled. (Hadad has sometimes been identified with Hadar/Hadad of Gen. 36.39, his two predecessors in the king-list (Baal-hanan and Shaul) being then identified with El-hanan (2 Sam. 21.19, the slayer of Goliath and so further identified with David) and Saul the king of Israel (Honeyman, 1948: 13-25 [24]; cf. earlier, Cannon 1927: 129-40 [137]). These identifications, however, are hazardous in the extreme. David's conquest of Edom seems to have come just at the moment when Edom was attempting to establish a monarchy, and to have set back its establishment by a century and a half.

The Hebrew text of the account of Hadad's flight into Egypt presents a number of minor difficulties—one notices, for example, that verse 18 relates the departure of Hadad's party from Midian without noting his arrival there—but the idea of a flight through the wilder regions south of Edom, and then west through Paran to the northern region of the Sinai peninsula to Egypt, makes good sense. Joab's attack presumably came from the north via the Valley of Salt at the southern end of the Dead Sea, and Midian, and ultimately Egypt, were the natural places of refuge for the defeated Edomites. Egypt's earlier interest in Transjordan has been noted. What is more surprising, in view of Egypt's known unwillingness to allow members of its royal family to marry abroad, is Hadad's subsequent marriage to the queen's sister (see Malamat, 1963: 9-17; Schulman, 1979: 177-93; 1986: 122-35). But if Egypt had political ambitions in Edom and its neighbouring territories, such a political marriage may have been acceptable. There is reason to doubt the similar, perhaps dependent, story of the marriage of the Ephraimite adventurer Jeroboam to a daughter of Pharaoh which has been added to the account of Jeroboam in the Septuagint, but no reason to doubt that Solomon was given a daughter of Pharaoh in marriage for political reasons. Through the tenth century BCE Egypt had a growing interest in Palestine, and under Shishak, c. 925 BCE, actually invaded Judah.

It is likely that Hadad arrived in Egypt as a small boy in the reign of Amenemope (c. 993-984 BCE) and grew up under Osochor (c. 984-978 BCE) and Siamun (c. 978-959 BCE). The account in 1 Kgs 11 suggests that by the time of David's death Hadad had married and that his son Genubath was already weaned. Hadad's marriage, then, probably took place early in Siamun's reign and towards the end of David's reign (Bartlett, 1976: 218-23; Schulman, 1986: 122-35 [128]), when Egypt's natural policy was that of supporting an obvious enemy of the Davidic regime. David's death might be considered a ripe moment for Egypt to regain, through Hadad, influence or even control in Edom. But Egyptian policy seems to have changed after the accession of Solomon, presumably because it was seen that, as 1 Kgs 2.46 puts it, 'the kingdom was established in the hand of Solomon', and perhaps in Solomon's third or fourth year he was given Pharaoh's daughter in marriage, with the city of Gezer as her dowry (1 Kgs 3.1; 9.16). Pharaoh's main objective was possibly, as Kitchen (1973: 281-82) has argued, 'to crush Philistine commercial rivalry' and to gain security and commercial advantages in Palestine and Syria.

It is this change in Egyptian policy, from support for Hadad to

support for Solomon, which may explain the dialogue reported in
1 Kgs 11.22 between Pharaoh (Siamun) and Hadad.

> But when Hadad heard in Egypt that David slept with his fathers
> and that Joab the commander of the army was dead, Hadad said to
> Pharaoh, 'Let me depart, that I may go to my own country'. But
> Pharaoh said to him, 'What have you lacked with me that you are
> now seeking to go to your own country?' And he said to him, 'Only
> let me go.'

Pharaoh is unwilling to let Hadad go, because it would be politically
embarrassing for Siamun to appear to be supporting Hadad against
Solomon at that time. Pharaoh preferred to keep Hadad in Egypt, as
a diplomatic card reserved for future use.

The account of Hadad began by saying that the Lord raised up an
adversary against Solomon, and it is followed by the parallel account
of how God raised up another adversary against Solomon in Syria.
This latter account ends by saying that Rezon 'was an adversary of
Israel all the days of Solomon, doing mischief as Hadad did; and he
abhorred Israel, and reigned over Syria' (1 Kgs 11.25). It is thus made
clear that Hadad caused Solomon some trouble, though the Hebrew
text of 1 Kings 11 does not give any details of what that might have
involved at all. The Septuagint, however, completes its version of the
Hadad story with the words, 'And Hader returned to his land. This is
the evil which Hader did. He oppressed Israel, and ruled in the land
of Edom.' This appears to be the equivalent of what the Hebrew text
(reading 'Aram' in place of 'Edom') has at the end of the account of
Rezon in 1 Kgs 11.25, and many scholars have followed the
Septuagint and transposed the final words of the Hebrew of 1 Kgs
11.25 ('and he abhorred Israel, and reigned over Edom') to follow the
Hadad story at 1 Kgs 11.22 (see Bartlett, 1976: 205-26 [213-15] for a
detailed study of this problem).

There are several objections to this reconstruction, however. In
the first place, the Hebrew account of Hadad is artistically complete
without the explicit reference to Hadad's return and subsequent
activity; indeed, the Septuagint ending comes as an anti-climax after
the dialogue between Hadad and Pharaoh. To this subjective
argument we may add that, secondly, though the Hebrew text of 1
Kgs 11.25 contains two serious difficulties, it seems more likely that
it describes the behaviour of Syria towards Solomon than that it
describes the behaviour of Edom. The MT says that the subject of the

verse 'loathed' (RV, JB, NEB footnote) or 'abhorred' (RSV) Israel (*wayyāqoṣ*). The Syriac and the Septuagint suggest rather that one should read the Hebrew *wayyāṣoq*, 'and he oppressed' (NEB, 'maintained a stranglehold upon'). If this is right, the subject of the verb is much more likely to be Rezon of Syria than Hadad of Edom, for at this time Syria was a much greater threat to Solomon that Edom was. Rezon son of Eliada was busy regaining from Israel and rebuilding the former empire of Hadadezer of Zobah. He re-centred the Aramaean empire on Damascus, which was much nearer the border of Solomon's territories than Hadadezer's kingdom of Zobah had been. Continued pressure from Damascus on Israel and Transjordan in the tenth and ninth centuries BCE is clear from the narratives of 2 Sam. 10, 1 Kgs 15.16-22; 1 Kgs 20 and 1 Kgs 22. Hadad of Edom was a much less important enemy, capable of far less damage to Solomon's kingdom. Edom was still recovering from the massacres of Joab's campaign, and there is no suggestion in 1 Kings of any Edomite activity to disrupt Solomon's trading contacts south with Arabia and the Red Sea. According to 1 Kgs 9.26, Solomon 'built a fleet of ships at Ezion-geber, which is near Eloth on the shore of the Red Sea, in the land of Edom', and, with the help of the seamen of Hiram of Tyre, traded with Ophir (cf. 1 Kgs 10.22). The site of Ezion-geber is possibly the island of Jezirat Fara'un; Glueck's earlier identification of Ezion-geber as Tell el-Kheleifeh must be abandoned, for recent re-examination of Glueck's excavations here has shown that there is no evidence that the site existed earlier than the eighth century BCE (see above, pp. 47-48). For this reason, earlier suggestions that Hadad the Edomite was responsible for a late tenth-century destruction of Ezion-geber (Tell el-Kheleifeh) must also be rejected, as must the attribution of this alleged destruction to Shoshenq (Shishak, king of Egypt, 1 Kgs 14.25). This claim had already been dismissed by Kitchen in his re-examination of Shoshenq's topographical list (1973: 296-300, 432-47). Kitchen has shown that though Shoshenq sent a task-force into the Negev, it is unlikely that it reached as far as the Gulf of 'Aqaba, and he dismisses attempts to identify the *sbrt n gbry* of the list with Ezion-geber. There is no evidence that Shoshenq entered Edom.

Schulman (1986: 122-35) has proposed a new solution to the problem of the conclusion of the Hadad story. Noting that the narrative appears to end *in medias res*, Schulman reconstructs the conclusion of the story from a conflation of the versions of the MT, the LXX, and Josephus (*Ant.* VIII.7.6 [199-204]). Thus: Pharaoh at first refused Hadad permission to return to Edom after David's death, but then relented (Josephus). Hadad returned to Edom (LXX, Josephus), and became king (LXX); he failed to stir Edom to revolt because Solomon's control was too strong, and so joined Rezon of Syria, attacked Israel from Syria and ultimately became ruler of part of Syria (Josephus). All three versions end with a statement that this was the mischief he did to Israel. The basis for this reconstruction is Schulman's argument that Josephus was using the Hebrew text rather than the LXX as his source (on the grounds that Josephus' version of the name Tahpenes (Thaphine) is closer to the Hebrew version than the LXX's Thekemeina), and that therefore Josephus' version should be given due credence. Josephus' version appears to take 1 Kgs 11.25 MT to mean that *Hadad* (not Rezon) ruled in *Aram* (Syria: not Edom). Josephus, however, may not have been following the original form of the Hebrew text (on this see Bartlett, 1976: 213-15), and he may perhaps have been influenced by the common association of the name Hadad (in various forms) with Syria. Whether Hadad ended up in Syria or not, however, Schulman rightly recognises that Hadad had no success in Edom.

It is in the period after the end of Solomon's reign (rather than at the beginning of Solomon's reign) that we might expect to find some evidence of Egyptian support for Edom. In the layer of debris from the destruction of Buseira in the sixth century BCE was found a rim fragment of an Egyptian relief chalice (Milward, 1975: 16-18). Such chalices were made between the 11th and the 8th centuries BCE. They were rare and costly items, and the Buseira fragment has been interpreted as an heirloom, perhaps originally brought to Buseira as an object of trade or as a costly gift. The suggestion that Hadad brought it back with him (Bennett, *ibid.*, 18) stretches possibility and coincidence too far, and this fragment is far too slight a piece of evidence from which to demonstrate Egyptian support for Edom in the late tenth century BCE though it might suggest that diplomatic or other links between Edom and Egypt were not entirely lacking in the Third Intermediate Period of Egypt's history. But of Hadad and his son Genubath we hear no more. In spite of Shoshenq's attack on Judah c. 925 BCE, there is no suggestion that Judah's control of Edom weakened, though it is certainly possible; Judahite troops may have been withdrawn from the garrisons in Edom to meet the crisis.

David conquered Edom at the beginning of the tenth century BCE, and from then until the revolt of Edom in the reign of Jehoram of Judah in the mid-ninth century BCE we hear very little indeed of conditions in the country. Edom was probably ruled by a governor, appointed by David and his successors, and the system seems to have continued until at least Jehoshaphat's time (1 Kgs 22.47). The land was probably garrisoned, and the Edomites, like the Moabites and the Syrians, 'became David's servants' (2 Sam. 8.14). In the case of the Syrians, this statement is followed by the further statement that they brought tribute, but this is not said in the case of Edom, though a general summary refers to 'the silver and gold which he (David) dedicated from all the nations he subdued, from Edom, Moab, the Ammonites, the Philistines, Amalek, and from the spoil of Hadadezer the son of Rehob, king of Zobah' (2 Sam. 8.11-12). It is unlikely that David got much gold from Edom, which was poorer than the other countries listed. Solomon, according to 1 Kgs 11.1, included Edomite women among his wives. His sea-trading activities from Ezion-geber have already been mentioned; the timber for the ships may have come from Edom (Gray, 1980: 256), but the seamen and shipwrights came from Tyre. After the reign of Solomon, we hear nothing at all of Edom until the reign of Jehoshaphat (c. 868-847 BCE). Judah seems to have been able to remain in control of Edom, in spite of the revolt of Israel from the rule of Jerusalem, the Egyptian invasion, and Judah's continuing struggles with Israel. But Edom's population, especially her male population, must have been steadily recovering from the damage inflicted by Joab. That any vestige of Hadad's family had survived, or surviving had any influence, we do not know. In Jehoshaphat's time, we are told, 'there was no king in Edom'. It was from this situation that Edom made a new start in the mid-ninth century.

Chapter 7

THE KINGDOM OF EDOM

The Establishment of the Kingdom

Our knowledge of the kingdom of Edom begins with the Deuteronomistic historian's account of the reign of king Jehoshaphat of Judah
(868-847 BCE), when 'There was no king in Edom: a deputy was king'
(1 Kgs 22.47, RSV). If this translation is correct (see below),
Jehoshaphat appears to have continued the form of direct rule over
the province of Edom originally imposed by David. The form of rule
by a governor appointed from Jerusalem was still in operation in the
later years of Jehoshaphat's reign, to judge from the reference in v.49
to the proposed partnership of Ahaziah son of Ahab, king of Israel
(852-1 BCE), in Jehoshaphat's trade with Ophir. However, the text of
verses 47-48 contains some minor difficulties. The Hebrew reads:

> ûmelek êyn bĕ'ĕdôm niṣṣāb melek: yehôšāpaṭ 'aśār ŏnīyyôt taršîš
> lāleket 'ôpîrâ lazzāhāb...

The first problem is how to construe the words *niṣṣāb melek*. We
might take *niṣṣāb* with the preceding words and translate (cf. LXX),
'There was no king appointed in Edom. King Jehoshaphat made
ships....' Alternatively, we might take the words as a separate
phrase and translate (cf. RSV, NEB), 'there was no king in Edom: a
deputy was king'. Another possibility is that we might point *nṣb* to
read *nĕṣîb*, and translate 'a (or, the) deputy of king Jehoshapat made
ships....' (see Stade, 1885: 178). (Donner, 1977: 381-434 [392],
suggests that 'Perhaps Jehoshaphat's shipbuilding was limited to a
makeshift renovation of Solomon's old and now rotted merchant
ships'. If the original ships had survived into Jehoshaphat's reign,
they may have been beyond renovation.) However we construe the
words, the text indicates that there was no king in Edom in the time
of Jehoshaphat, and this is confirmed by 2 Kgs 8.20, which states that

in the days of Jehoshaphat's son Jehoram (847-845 BCE) Edom 'revolted from the rule of Judah, and set up a king of their own'. Possibly an appointee of Jehoshaphat governed in Edom; or possibly the text says only that an appointee of Jehoshaphat made (if *'āśār* may be corrected to *'āśâ*) ships (or a ship) with the aim of trading to Ophir.

A second question may be raised about the destruction of the ships at Ezion-geber (v.48). The wrecking (RSV: MT *nišběrûh*, Q*e*re *nišběrû*) of the ships has often been attributed to one of the squalls that blow across the Gulf of 'Aqaba, and Glueck pictured the ships as having been 'broken on the rocks near Ezion-geber' (Glueck, 1935; 51; 1937-39: 6). The Hebrew text of 1 Kgs 22.48 does not state the means of destruction, and might equally indicate human activity (cf. *CAH III*, 1925: 366). Edom's population had probably by now expanded again to the point at which pressure for home rule was growing, and Ezion-geber, a key point on one of Judah's important trade-routes, was an obvious target for a raid. This would have been one of the more obvious preliminaries to the decisive revolt which took place in the reign of Jehoshaphat's son Jehoram. However we interpret the destruction of the ships, the event was followed, according to 1 Kgs 22.49, by the offer of Ahaziah son of Ahab, king of Israel, to join Jehoshaphat in this seafaring venture, an offer which Jehoshaphat declined. The Chronicler tried to make better sense of the affair by reversing the sequence of events. According to 2 Chron. 20.35-37, Jehoshaphat's shipbuilding was a joint venture with Ahaziah of Israel ('who did wickedly'); Eliezer the son of Dodavahu of Mareshah warned Jehoshaphat of Yahweh's unfavourable reaction, and the fleet was wrecked and unable to sail (for the Chronicler's version, see Williamson, 1982: 302-303). The version in 1 Kings seems more likely; Jehoshaphat was surely unwilling to allow Israelite participation in a trade route which, misfortune apart, was known to be profitable.

Of Jehoram, who reigned in Judah for eight years (variously dated between 852 and 842 BCE), the two main details recorded by the Old Testament are that in his reign both Edom and Libnah revolted from Edom (2 Kgs 8.20-24). Of Libnah, a city on the edge of the Philistine territory (identified by Albright [1923: 1-17]) with T. Burnât and by Abel (1938: II. 369-70) with T. eṣ-ṣāfi) little is known, but clearly Edom was not alone in seizing a moment of weakness in which to rebel. 2 Chron. 21.16f. notes that the Philistines and the Arabs attacked Judah in Jehoram's reign (after paying tribute to Judah in Jehoshaphat's reign, 2 Chron. 17.11) and were forced to show more deference in Uzziah's reign in the following century (2 Chron. 26.6f.). Edomite and Philistine hostility against Judah coincided again in the reign of Ahaz (2 Chron. 28.16-18). Against Judah, Edom and Philistia had common interest. However, it was in Jehoram's reign that Edom made a decisive and successful bid for independence from Judah: 'In his days Edom revolted from the rule of Judah, and set up a king of their own' (2 Kgs 8.20). This is explicit as far as it goes, but we would like to know much more—in particular, the name of the new Edomite king, and the manner of his choosing, and the social background to the revolt. It is most likely that the new king was a person who had emerged as a natural leader in the period of growing discontent that must have preceded the actual revolt. The Old Testament historian is altogether too laconic, and here we suffer, as so often, from the fact that our only source for these events had no interest in making much of an Edomite success. The continuation of the account in 2 Kgs 8.21 raises further questions: according to the RSV,

> Then Joram passed over to Zair with all his chariots, and rose by night, and he and his chariot commanders smote the Edomites who had surrounded him; but his army fled home. So Edom revolted from the rule of Judah to this day.

If Joram defeated a surrounding army, it is surprising that his army then fled and that Edom's revolt was successful. The difficulty may be alleviated by translating 'smote' (*wayyakkeh*) as 'attacked' or even 'broke through', and by understanding the passage to mean that the king and his chariots managed to break through the surrounding Edomite troops, leaving the infantry to escape as best it could (see Jones, 1984: 448). The historian is perhaps making the best of a disaster for Judah's army. A more radical solution was proposed by B. Stade (1901: 337-40), who by a slight rearrangement of the word order in the Hebrew offered the following translation:

> Then Joram passed over to Zair, and all his chariots with him, and the Edomites which compassed him about rose up by night and smote him and the captains of his chariots, and the people fled to their tents.

However we explain or translate the Hebrew text, the sequel makes it clear that this was an Edomite victory, with permanent consequences. The place of battle, Zair, is otherwise unknown; various emendations have been suggested—Zoar, at the southern end of the Dead Sea, cf. Isa. 15.5; Jer. 48.34 (Montgomery, Gehman, 1951: 396), Zior, i.e. Si'ir, 7 km north of Hebron, Josh. 15.54 (Jones, 1984: 448), and Seir (Simons, 1959: 362, §914). Perhaps the first suggestion is best, though it seems unreasonable to force a possible or plausible identification upon a place-name merely because it is otherwise unknown or unattested. Zoar is tempting because it lay in the Valley of Salt, the scene of a former battle between Judah and Edom (2 Sam. 8.13) and the obvious site for such a confrontation. This battle was presumably the culmination of the revolt, in whose earlier stages the position of the Judahite governor of Edom and the local military garrisons must have been made untenable. Exactly when the revolt began we do not know—the final years or the end of Jehoshaphat's reign are an obvious possibility—but it not surprisingly follows fairly soon after the revolt of Edom's neighbour Moab from Israel after Ahab's death (2 Kgs 1.1; 3.5).

That the new kingdom of Edom began in the reign of Jehoram of Judah seems certain from 1 Kgs 22.47 and 2 Kgs 8.20, but the matter is slightly complicated by the narrative of 2 Kgs 3.4-27, which tells of a campaign of Jehoram of Israel, Jehoshaphat of Judah, and an unnamed king of Edom against king Mesha of Moab. This reference to a king of Edom in the reign of Jehoshaphat conflicts with the two statements of 1 Kgs 22.47 and 2 Kgs 8.20, which say quite clearly that there was no king of Edom in Jehoshaphat's reign, and that the Edomites set up a king of their own in Jehoram's reign. Another difficulty is that the campaign is hard to date, for while 2 Kgs 1.1 and 3.5 say that Mesha of Moab rebelled after the death of Ahab of Israel, Mesha himself on his stele implies that he freed himself, or at least the region of Madaba, from Israelite control during Ahab's reign (Mesha stele, lines 5-9; see Ullendorff, 1958: 195-98, Miller, 1974: 9-18). This apparent contradiction, however, is perhaps met by the suggestion that Mesha rebelled at the end of Ahab's reign in 853 BCE, and that Jehoram of Israel and his associates campaigned in 849 BCE when Syria's involvement with the invading Assyrians removed Syrian pressure from Israel (Liver, 1967: 14-31 [26]). But this does not solve our basic problem. One solution might be to suppose, with many scholars, that there was a co-regency of Jehoshaphat and Jehoram, and that, not long after Edom had revolted at the beginning of Jehoram's reign, the new king of Edom joined with Judah (led by the senior partner in the reign, Jehoshaphat) and Israel against Moab (Gray, 1980: 66-67, 465). It seems unlikely, however, that the aging Jehoshaphat would lead Judah's army on such an expedition when the younger Jehoram was available and anxious to prove himself.

Another suggestion is that the campaign described in 2 Kgs 3 belongs in fact to the reigns of Jehoram of Israel and Jehoram (or even Ahaziah) of Judah, and that the naming of Jehoshaphat in this connection is a mistake, perhaps due to the compression of the wars against Mesha of Moab into too short a period (Miller, 1967: 276-88 (278-79). There are two pieces of evidence which may point in this direction. First, the Lucianic recension of the Greek translation of 2 Kgs 3.4-27 does not name Jehoshaphat as the king of Judah involved, but Ahaziah, and recent work on the Lucianic recension has demonstrated that it is this recension 'which has best preserved the old Greek chronology in this section of Kings' (Shenkel, 1968: 108). Secondly, though 2 Kgs 3.1 brings Jehoram of Israel to the throne in the 18th year of Jehoshaphat, 2 Kgs 1.17 brings him to the throne in the second year of king Jehoram the son of Jehoshaphat, king of Judah. If this is right, then by the time of Jehoram of Israel's campaign against Moab, Jehoram of Judah could have reached the throne, and Edom could have rebelled and set up a king for herself, particularly if, as is likely, Edom's revolt took place early in the reign of Jehoram of Judah.

In spite of all this, however, there is another possibility to be considered. Examination of the narrative of 2 Kings 3 has shown its similarity to and its dependence upon the narrative of 1 Kings 22 (de Vries, 1978, Bartlett, 1983: 135-46: Jones, 1984: 390-92). In each case the king of Israel (Ahab/Jehoram) invites Jehoshaphat of Judah to campaign with him (against Syria/Moab). Jehoshaphat responds in the same terms; a prophet of the Lord (contrasted with the court prophets) makes his pronouncement; and disaster comes upon Israel. The historian is using accounts of Israel's military failures to demonstrate that the political aims of the kings of Israel were not always in accord with the word of the Lord as spoken by his prophets. It is important for our present purpose to note the conclusion of several recent scholars, that the campaigns of 1 Kings

20 and 22.1-38 must be dated later than Ahab's reign (for Ahab was on friendly terms with the Syrians, and died peacefully); it was Jehoram of Israel, not Ahab, who was wounded at Ramoth-gilead and died of an arrow wound in his chariot (inflicted by Jehu) (2 Kgs 9.24; cf. 1 Kgs 22.34f.), and it is hard to resist the conclusion that the narrative of 1 Kings 22 'has been developed from the historical background of the events recorded in 2 Kgs 8.28ff.' (de Vries, 1978: 99; Miller (1986: 441-54), however, argues that the battles in 1 Kings 20, 22, and 2 Kings 3 refer to the reign of Jehoahaz the son of Jehu: see Bartlett, 1983: 143-44). In 1 Kings 22 the historian has attributed to Jehoshaphat's reign a campaign against Syria which belongs later, to the reign of Jehoram son of Ahab, and much the same thing has happened in the closely related and dependent 2 Kings 3, where Jehoshaphat is portrayed in a very similar manner and given a very similar role in the story. 2 Kings 3 is basically concerned with Jehoram of Israel's response to Mesha's rebellion, which began with the death of Ahab. Ahab's successor Ahaziah had a brief reign (1 Kgs 22.51), but by the time of his death Jehoshaphat had been succeeded by Jehoram of Judah (2 Kgs 1.17). Jehoshaphat can have been involved in the campaign of Jehoram of Israel against Moab only if we work on the basis of a co-regency of Jehoshaphat and Jehoram of Judah, or totally reject the synchronism of 2 Kgs 1.17 in favour of that of 2 Kgs 3.1.

Jehoshaphat's real connection with Jehoram of Israel's campaign against Moab, then, seems insecure, and this leaves us with the chronologically possible position that Jehoram of Israel was associated with a king of Edom in his campaign against Moab. It is chronologically possible because Jehoram of Judah, in whose reign Edom founded a new monarchy, reigned between the fifth and twelfth years of Jehoram of Israel (2 Kgs 8.16, 25). But one cannot help noticing that in the campaign against Moab the king of Edom plays a very minor and shadowy part, and his position demands close scrutiny.

The campaign against Moab begins with Jehoram's mustering of troops, his invitation to the king of Judah to join him, and the king of Judah's response. Jehoram is asked about the route to be taken, and he replies, 'By the way of the wilderness of Edom', which is an unusual phrase, and does not certainly refer to any known region of Edom. This account of the 'circuitous march of seven days' in the wilderness, without water for army or beasts, followed by the prophetic provision of water, is highly reminiscent of Num. 20, in which the story of the Israelites' attempt to pass through Edom is preceded by a wandering in the wilderness (Num. 20.2-13) where there is no water to drink and the people complain that they and their cattle are about to die, until Moses miraculously produces water. The geography of 2 Kings 3 is not real, at least until it reaches Kir-hareseth in v. 25. The location of the march in the wilderness of Edom has as much to do with the literary and theological element in the story as it has with the historical and geographical. In v. 20 the promised water is said to come 'from the direction of Edom' and the Moabites see it, appropriately, as red as 'blood' (*'adummîm kaddam*), a clear punning reference to Edom (cf. Gen. 25.25). It is the land of Edom that is important in this story, not the king of Edom and his military power. There is no reference to the king of Edom in the original planning of the campaign; the reference to the unnamed king of Edom in vv. 9 and 12 is inspired by the immediately previous geographical references. The king of Edom has been brought into the story simply becase the story-teller thought he ought to have been there if the campaign was taking place across Edomite territory.

One other reference to Edom in this story requires consideration. In v. 26, the king of Moab tries to break through 'opposite the king of Edom'. In the context of a story in which the king of Edom is allied with Israel and thus Moab's enemy, the Hebrew phrase *'ēl melek 'ĕdôm* has been taken to mean 'against the king of Edom', with hostile intent, or 'towards the king of Edom', as a possible if unwilling ally, or, as in the RSV, 'opposite the king of Edom', in a merely neutral sense describing where the king tried to escape. Many have followed the Old Latin and read 'Aram' for 'Edom', with the comment that Damascus would have been the Moabite king's naturall ally (see Montgomery, Gehman, 1951: 313; Jones, 1984: 399-400; Bartlett, 1983: 143-44). In this case the reference to the king of Edom disappears; in the former case, the king of Edom is given a role (though a passive one) at the end of the story, but his presence may still be explained along the lines suggested above.

2 Kings 3, then, provides no solid evidence for the presence of the King of Edom in any campaign involving Jehoshaphat of Judah and Jehoram of Israel against Mesha of Moab. The account dates from a time when the existence of the kings of Edom was taken for granted. The king of Edom was brought into the story simply because the

story was associated with the wilderness of Edom where the water appeared, appropriately, red as blood. And the presence of the wilderness of Edom may derive from the comparable account of the waterless wanderings of the Israelites in the wilderness near Edom in Numbers 20. 2 Kings 3 represents the grafting of prophetic legend onto a historical core which was concerned with Jehoram of Israel's response to Mesha's rebellion; neither Jehoshaphat nor the unnamed king of Edom had any part in this original event (Bartlett, 1983: 135-46).

We may therefore confidently accept the record of 2 Kgs 8.20 that it was not until the reign of Jehoram of Judah that monarchy was established, or perhaps re-established, in Edom. We may probably date this event somewhere in the mid-840s BCE, the precise year depending upon what date we accept for the beginning of the independent reign of Jehoram. It is interesting that the revolt of Edom against Judah should follow so closely on the revolt of Moab against Israel. Clearly, both Moab and Edom were becoming stronger in the ninth century BCE, and Israel and Judah were under pressure from Assyria and Syria. Moab's revolt perhaps encouraged similar action in Edom. The new king of Edom may not have been displeased to see the growing strength of Syria to the north; and the king of Israel may have welcomed Edomite resurgence, for a stronger Israel on the southern borders of Moab and Judah was much to Israel's advantage.

Edom in the First Half of the Eighth Century BCE

We hear nothing at all of Edom for another half-century, during which time we must suppose that the new king and his successor or successors were establishing the kingdom. Edom had the advantage that Moab was recovering from her wars with Israel and presumably concerned to establish her own internal affairs, that Israel was occupied with Syrian and Assyrian attacks, and that both Israel and Judah were suffering from internal revolutions. It is not until the reign of Amaziah of Judah (c. 801-787 BCE) that Edom again comes into conflict with Judah. According to 2 Kgs 14.27, Amaziah

> killed ten thousand Edomites in the Valley of Salt and took Sela by storm (or 'took possession of' [Gray, 190: 604, note c]), and called it Joktheel, which is its name to this day.

The motive for this attack is not clear. It has been suggested that when Hazael king of Syria took Gath and threatened Jerusalem (2 Kgs 12.17), Edom profited from Judah's difficulties to attack Judahite settlements in the Negev. This is a guess, based, perhaps upon other examples of the readiness of both Edom and Philistia to attack the south-western and south-eastern borders of Judah (cf. 2 Chron. 28.16-18). More probably, Amaziah wished to win glory for himself by recovering Edom for Judah; this would explain why he called the place he captured 'Joktheel' ('El has destroyed [it]) (Starcky, 1966: cols 886-1017 [891-92]), and it would explain the taunt of the king of Israel recorded in 2 Kgs 14.10 ('You have indeed smitten Edom, and your heart has lifted you up. Be content with your glory, and stay at home. . . '). Amaziah's battle took place, like others before it, in the valley at the southern end of the Dead Sea. The place Sela has often been identified with the height of Umm el-biyara in Petra, though there is no evidence for a settlement there as early as Amaziah's time. Sela has also been identified with the equally precipitous Khirbet Sil', a few kilometres north of Buseira. This latter site is perhaps a more likely candidate for Sela, for it is much nearer the Valley of Salt and more accessible to Amaziah's attack. The identification of Sela/Joktheel remains uncertain (see above, pp. 51-52); but wherever Sela was, and in spite of the historian's remark that Sela was called Joktheel until his own day, it is very unlikely that Amaziah's success was lasting, for there is no evidence that Judah's rule over Edom was restored, even temporarily. 2 Chron. 25.12 adds that the Judahite soldiers, in addition to the ten thousand Edomites killed in battle, killed a further ten thousand by throwing them from the top of a rock, which may be no more than an elaboration of the reference to Sela ('rock'), and at best the exaggeration of some quite possible brutality of war. More interesting is the Chronicler's story (2 Chron. 24.5-13) that Amaziah discharged a number of Ephraimite recruits that he had mustered for the campaign. If there is any truth in the story, the troops may have been dismissed because their loyalty of Judah in a campaign against Edom was suspected. According to the Chronicler, the dismissed soldiers retaliated by attacking towns on Judah's northern borders, killing and looting. This behaviour might explain Amaziah's subsequent challenge to the king of Israel (2 Kgs 14.8).

Even if the number of Edomites killed in battle was not as high as the historians of 2 Kings and 2 Chronicles suggest, this invasion by Judah must have been a serious set-back for the kingdom of Edom coming at a time when Edom had just about established herself as a kingdom. It would have meant not only the loss of manpower and pride, but also, in all probability, the weakening of whatever central government and administration had been established over the last half-century. The power and authority of the king in particular may have been weakened. We still do not know the name of the king of Edom at this time; we do not hear of any Edomite king by name until Tiglath-pileser III's records, half a century or more later, and there can be little doubt that this first half of the eighth century BCE was a period of relative weakness for Edom. A second contributory factor to this was perhaps the tribute now demanded from Edom by Assyria. In 805-3 BCE and again in 796 BCE, Adad-nirari III (810-783 BCE) campaigned in the west; on an inscription found at Calah he describes himself as conquering

> as far as the Great Sea of the Rising Sun (and) from the banks of the Euphrates, the country of the Hittites, Amurru-country in its full extent, Tyre, Sidon, Israel (^{Mat}Hu-um-ri), Edom (^{mat}U-du-mu), Palestine (*Pa-la-as-tu*), as far as the shore of the Great Sea of the Setting Sun, I made them submit all to my feet, imposing upon them tribute (*ANET^3* 281; Luckenbill, 1926: I §§739-40).

It is perhaps a little odd that Edom in the far south should be mentioned when Ammon and Moab are not, and it is unlikely that Assyria gained any real control over Edom at this stage. Adad-nirari did not campaign in southern Jordan, and the words 'imposing upon them tribute' may have meant, in Edom's case at least, no more than that Edom sent some token of respect and submission to Damascus when Adad-nirari appeared on the horizon. That Edom's name appears unaccompanied by Ammon and Moab may suggest that Edom volunteered some form of tribute (much as Ahaz of Judah did later when threatened by Syria and Israel) in order to gain Assyrian diplomatic support against the contemporary threat from Amaziah's invasion of Edom. Whether Edom continued paying tribute we may doubt. Assyria appears to take no further interest in Edom until Tiglath-pileser III's reign.

A sign of Edom's weakness in the first half of the eighth century BCE is Judah's revived interest in the route through the Gulf of 'Aqaba. 2 Kgs 14.22 says that Azariah (Uzziah) of Judah 'built Elath and restored it to Judah, after the king slept with his fathers'. The reference to Amaziah's death perhaps suggests that for the first few years of his reign Uzziah was co-regent with his father. The date of Amaziah's death is variously given between 783 and 767 BCE (see Hayes, Miller, 1977: 682) and the building of Elath (Tell el-Kheleifeh; for this identification see above pp. 46-48) thus perhaps belongs to the decade 770-760 BCE. This still leaves an important problem to be resolved, however, for Tell el-Kheleifeh now appears to have had two major architectural phases (Pratico, 1982: 120-21; 1985: 1-32). The later phase, the fortified settlement with the offset/inset wall, is clearly dated by the associated wheel-made pottery forms to the period of the 8th-6th centuries BCE. The earlier phase, the casemate fortress, is harder to date because the associated pottery was not isolated in excavation, and though some 'Negevite' pottery can be assigned to it, these forms have too wide an attestation through the Iron Age to be used on their own as a precise chronological tool. This Negevite ware appears in both phases of Tell el-Kheleifeh. Architecturally, Tell el-Kheleifeh's casemate fortress may be compared with the central Negev fortresses, currently dated on the evidence of the wheel-made pottery forms to Iron I. However, there is no sign of Iron I wheel-made pottery from Tell el-Kheleifeh, and, apart from some fifth–fourth century material to be discussed later,

> the pottery evidence indicates that Tell el-Kheleifeh was occupied between the 8th and the early 6th century BCE. While acknowledging the presence of forms that can be dated earlier, these are the horizons presented by the site's pottery as a whole (Pratico, 1985: 1-32 [26]).

On this evidence, Tell el-Kheleifeh could be the foundation of Uzziah referred to in 2 Kgs 14.22, but the identification remains uncertain.

One of Glueck's finds from what is now seen as the second architectural phase of Tell el-Kheleifeh was a signet-ring and seal with the inscription 'belonging to Jotham' (Glueck, 1940b: 2-18; Avigad, 1961: 18-22; Galling 1967: 131-34; see below pp. 211-12). Glueck believed that the reference was to Uzziah's successor, Jotham king of Judah, and that the seal therefore might have belonged to Jotham's official representative at Elath. More recently, however, the seal has been dated to the early or mid-seventh century BCE on epigraphic grounds, making the attribution to Jotham of Judah less likely (Herr, 1978: 163; caution was earlier expressed by Diringer, 1969: 224-25, and Galling, 1967: 131-34). The seal also showed a horned ram below the inscription with another object to its left; Avigad (1961: 18-22) suggested that the ram (Heb. *'yl*) was a pictorial representation of the town's name, *'ylt*, and that the object engraved in front of the ram was either a pair of bellows or a copper ingot, symbolizing metallurgical activity. However, Glueck's interpretation of Tell el-Kheleifeh as a smeltery was revised (Rothenberg 1962: 5-71 [44-56]; Glueck, 1970: 111-18), and the object on the seal reinterpreted as a scarab (Galling, 1967: 131-34). The Jotham seal thus cannot bear the weight of interpretation formerly put upon it. Indeed the interest of Uzziah and Jotham in this region is not positively indicated by the Old Testament apart from the reference to the building of Elath and perhaps to the building of towers in the wilderness (2 Chron. 26.10), if the wilderness here refers to the Negev. There is no suggestion that Uzziah had any military or political contact with Edom. Judah was probably content to keep a firm hold on the route south to the Gulf of 'Aqaba: Edom for its part was probably content to avoid direct contact with the well-trained and maintained army of Uzziah (2 Chron. 26.11-15).

One might also suppose, however, that this period of peace and prosperity for Judah and Israel saw also the slow recovery of the Edomite kingdom. The prophet Amos, shortly after 760 BCE, criticizes the city of Gaza 'because they carried into exile a whole people to deliver them up to Edom' (Amos 1.6), which has suggested to some that Edom was an important stage on a slave-trading route with connections to Arabia and Syria. This reference does not tell us much, however, about the state of Edom at this time, and the allusion in this verse to Edom has been denied. M. Haran has argued that Edom was never a slave-trading centre, and that in Amos 1.6 the original recipient of the exiled people was not Edom but Aram, Syria (Haran, 1968: 201-12). If the oracle in Amos 1.11-12 is authentic, it is evidence for Amos' knowledge (and for his contemporaries' knowledge) of the region of Teman and of 'the strongholds of Bozrah'. Even without Amos' reference, the existence of Bozrah by this time seems more than likely, though the archaeological evidence is limited and of uncertain interpretation. The Assyrian evidence from Tiglath-pileser III's reign, however, for the kingdom of Edom and its king Qosmalak, added to the biblical evidence that Edom had a king from the mid-ninth century, makes it probable that a palace or stronghold of some sort now existed as the centre of Edomite rule and administration, and Bozrah is by far the likeliest place. Again, if Amos' oracle against Edom is authentic, it probably refers to Edom's quite understandable behaviour at the time of her rebellion from Judah (Bartlett, 1977: 2-27 [10-16], but its very presence among Amos' oracles in the mid-eighth century BCE witnesses to his knowledge of the warlike character of Edom. In the eighth century BCE the Edomites were seen by their neighbours as a fierce people.

Judah's difficulties at the end of Jotham's reign and the beginning of Ahaz' reign seem to have given Edom a new opportunity to assert itself at Judah's expense. Judah was under pressure from the kings of Syria and Israel, who wished to replace the new king Ahaz with a certain son of Tabeel and to bring Judah into their revolt against their new Assyrian overlord (cf. 2 Kgs 16.1-5; Isa. 7.1-9). According to 2 Kgs 16.6,

> At that time the king of Edom recovered Elath for Edom and drove the men of Judah from Elath, where they dwell to this day.

(The MT reads, 'Rezin king of Syria recovered Elath for Syria'. Rezin was probably added when Aram was read by mistake for Edom [Montgomery, Gehman, 1951: 458; Jones, 1984: 535-36; Gray, 1980: 632, note *e*]. Syrian occupation of Elath seems unlikely.). The parallel account in 2 Chron. 28.16-18 says nothing about Elath, but states:

> At that time Ahaz sent to the king of Assyria for help. For the Edomites had again invaded and defeated Judah, and carried away captives. And the Philistines had made raids on the cities in the Shephelah and the Negeb of Judah, and had taken Beth-shemesh, Aijalon, Gederoth, Soco with its villages, Timnah with its villages; and they settled there.

The Chronicler makes the Edomite and Philistine raids the reason for Ahaz' appeal to Assyria (and certainly Edom and Philistia might be natural allies against Judah), but 2 Kgs 16.7 and Isa. 7.3ff. suggest that more compelling was the attack by Syria and Israel. However, the capture of Elath must be regarded as an important development for the kingdom of Edom, both politically and economically. From now on, Edom, not Judah, could derive the benefit of trade passing between Arabia and Damascus through the Gulf of 'Aqaba, and from now on Edom, not Judah, could control the southern region of the

Wadi 'Araba. This made it easier for Edomites to extend their influence into the southern regions of Judah, as they did over the next two centuries. It has been suggested that Stratum IX of Arad, which the excavator assigned to the period of Uzziah, was destroyed by an Edomite raid at the same time as the capture of Elath (*EAEHL*: I. 84). If so, we have more evidence of Edom's early interest in the Negev. But Arad, unlike Elath, did not become Edomite at this time, and Judah remained firmly in control of Arad until the beginning of the sixth century BCE.

Edom under the Assyrian Empire

The immediate result of the Syro-Ephraimite rebellion against Assyria was that in 732 BCE Tiglath-pileser III took Damascus, and the revolt collapsed. It was probably on this occasion (if not in 734 BCE after the suppression of the revolt of Ashkelon and Gaza) that Tiglath-pileser

> received the tribute of . . . Sanipu of Bit-Ammon, Salamanu of Moab, . . . Mitinti of Ashkelon, Jehoahaz (*Iaú-ha-zi*) of Judah, Kaushmalaku of Edom (*Udu-mu-a-a-*), Muzr. [. . .], Hanno (*Ha-a-nu-u-nu*) of Gaza (*Ha-za-at-a-a*), (consisting of) gold, silver, tin, iron, antimony, linen garments with multi-colored trimmings, garments of their native (industries) (being made of) dark purple wool, . . . all kinds of costly objects be they products of the sea or of the continent (*ANET³* 282; Luckenbill, 1926: I. §§800-801,803).

This probably indicates that Edom became Assyria's vassal, with the obligation of paying regular tribute and perhaps also, among other things, of giving Assyria whatever military assistance might be required from time to time. Whether Assyrian officials were posted in Edom we do not know. We hear nothing from the Old Testament of the presence of Assyrian officials stationed in Jerusalem, but it is not unlikely that there were such officials here and in other vassal countries like Edom to look after Assyrian interests, to report back, and to supervise arrangements for sending regular tribute. A late eighth-century letter found at Nimrud is a report to the Assyrian king from Qurdi-Aššur, perhaps a senior Assyrian official in Syria or Palestine (Saggs, 1955: 126-54 [131-33, Letter XIV]). He reports that a document concerning the slaughter of the men of a Moabite city by the men of Gidir-land is being brought to the king by 'the messenger of Aia-nuri, a Dabilite, Ezazu by name'. Aianuri was perhaps another Assyrian official; Ezazu was perhaps the Assyrian form of the West Semitic name *'azaz* (the sole Azaz in the Old Testament [1 Chron. 5.8] appears to belong to Moab); and the gentilic form 'Dabilite' has been interpreted by Saggs as an Assyrian scribe's mistake for 'Dibonite'. Mittman (1972: 15-25) interprets the term to mean 'a man from Tafila'; modern Tafila, perhaps the Tophel of Deut. 1.1, lies between the Wadi el-Ḥasā and Buseira, and if Mittmann is right, Ezazu may have been an Edomite. Cazelles (1959: 412-15), however, denies that Tophel is to be identified with Tafila, on the ground that the initial consonants differ, and identifies Tophel of Deut. 1.1 with the Dabilu of the Nimrud letter, locating it in Moab, not Edom. This communication, then, perhaps witnesses to three strata of Assyrian officialdom in the west: Qurdi-Aššur (a regional governor?), Aianuri (a more local figure? but still Assyrian), and his messenger Ezazu, perhaps recruited from among the local population. Neo-Assyrian influence has been seen in the architecture of the acropolis at Buseira (Bennett, 1978: 165-71 [169]). It has also been suggested that the important road which ran from north to south through Transjordan, from Damascus through Rabbath-Ammon, Heshbon, Dibon, Aroer, Kir-haresheth, and Bozrah, received its name, 'the King's Highway' (Num. 20.17) from the Assyrian period when it became a major, guarded route of the imperial administration (see above, p. 38). The Assyrians liked to be well informed about their subjects, and it is noticeable that it is from Assyrian sources, not from Judah or Israel, that we learn the names of a number of Edomite kings.

Tiglath-Pileser names Qosmalak as the Edomite king reigning c. 735 BCE. No other Edomite king is named until the time of Sennacherib (704-681 BCE) and we have no means of knowing Qosmalak's precise dates. Two out of the three Edomite royal names known to us from this period include the divine name *qaus* as an element of their names. The fact that this divine name appears in a royal name suggests that *qws* was not the name of a god that had only just become known in Edom. Unless Qosmalak was the first of a new dynasty, or a religious reformer incorporating the name of a newly adopted deity into his throne name, we must suppose that *qws* appears in his name because *qws* was a—or the—generally accepted principal deity in Edom. Very likely some of Qosmalak's predecessors bore similar theophoric names. It must be admitted, however, that our other evidence for *qws* is later rather than earlier, and that there are some indications that in earlier times the Edomites knew and worshipped the well-known North-west Semitic gods Hadad and El, as well as the Israelite Yahweh (see below, Chapter 11). It may therefore be that the divine name *qws* became accepted and of importance in Edom in the earlier period of Edom's monarchy—indeed, that this deity of Arabian background was introduced by the Edomite dynasty which had its beginnings when Edom gained her independence from Judah c. 845 BC.

The next Assyrian reference to Edom is from the reign of Sargon II (721-705 BCE). When Ashdod rebelled against Assyria in 713 BCE, the Ashdodites deposed the Assyrian-appointed king, put a Greek commoner, *Ia-ma-ni*, in his place, prepared the water supply for a siege and

> Then [to] the rulers of Palestine (*Pi-liš-te*), Judah (*Ia-ú-di*), Ed[om], Moab (and) those who live (on islands) and bring tribute [and] *tâmartu*-gifts to my Lord Ashur—he spread countless evil lies to alienate (them) from me, and (also) sent bribes to Pir'u, king of Musru—a potentate, incapable to save them—and asked him to be an ally (*ANET³* 287; Luckenbill, 1927: II §§193-95).

Clearly Ashdod sought the support of all southern Palestine and Egypt, and the help of Moab and Edom is not despised. We have already noted the common interests of Philistia and Edom (cf. Amos 1.6; 2 Chron. 28.16-18). How far Edom committed herself to helping Ashdod we do not know. As the southernmost and most remote vassal kingdom, her natural inclination would probably be to avoid putting at risk her not too onerous vassaldom. At all events, we do not hear that Edom suffered any reprisals, and she probably continued to pay her tribute to Assyria. A letter discovered at Nimrud in 1952 is probably related to Sargon's campaign of 712 BCE against Ashdod (Saggs, 1955: 126-54 [134-35, Letter XVI]). It appears to describe the delivery of tribute by officials of Egypt, Gaza, Judah, Moab and Ammon. The Edomites, with two other peoples whose identity is not clear, are named at the end of the list, but there is a lacuna in the text at this point, and we cannot tell what is said about the Edomites. From their position in the list, they may have appeared to the Assyrians as less important than the Egyptians, and people of Gaza, Judah, Moab and Ammon, or perhaps as conveying a different or less valuable gift.

When Sennacherib invaded the west eleven years later to punish
Hezekiah of Judah for his rebellion, his appearance brought
submission from a large number of kings:

> As to all the kings of the Amurru—Menahem (*Mi-in-ḫi-im-mu*)
> from Samsimuruna, Tuba'lu from Sidon, Abili'ti from Arvad,
> Urumilki from Byblos, Mitinti from Ashdod, Buduili from Beth-
> Ammon, Kammusunabdi from Moab (and) Aiarammu from Edom,
> they brought sumptuous gifts (*igisû*) and—fourfold—their heavy
> *tâmartu*-presents to me and kissed my feet. Sidqia, however, king
> of Ashkelon, who did not bow to my yoke, I deported and sent to
> Assyria, his family-gods, himself, his wife, his children, his
> brothers, all the male descendants of his family (*ANET³* 287;
> Luckenbill, 1924: 30; 1927: II. §§23ff.; for Aiarammu, Luckenbill
> (1924: 30; 1927: 119) gives Malik-rammu).

Clearly Aiarammu took care to avoid that fate for himself and his
family, but he may have played with the idea of supporting
Hezekiah's rebellion. Hezekiah apparently had the support of Egypt,
of Philistia, and the advantage that Luli, the king of Tyre and Sidon,
and Merodach-Baladan in Babylon, were also rebelling against
Assyria. An ostracon discovered in a room of Stratum VIII at Arad,
whose destruction is associated by the excavator with the campaign
of Sennacherib in 701 BCE, appears to refer to some sort of
communications between the Judahite and Edomite authorities
(Aharoni, 1970: 16-42 [28-32]; 1981: 70-74, n. 40). The ostracon is a
letter from two men, Gemaryahu and Nehemyahu, perhaps in
charge of the military post at Ramath-negeb on the border between
Judah and Edom south of Arad. They write to their superior officer
Malkiyahu in Arad to explain how they have correctly passed on
correspondence from Edom. The letter ends with the statement that
the king of Judah should know that the writers cannot send
(something), and with a reference to the evil that Edom has done.
The evil that Edom has done is perhaps Edom's prompt submission
to Sennacherib as he approaches to suppress the rebellion, but this is
far from certain (A.F. Rainey, in Aharoni, 1981: 74; the king of Judah
would thus be Hezekiah). The date of this letter and its interpretation
are open to much discussion, but it may refer to diplomatic activity
between Edom and Judah on the eve of Sennacherib's invasion of
Judah. There must have been such interchanges between the affected
neighbouring states, and Edom will have had her diplomats and

couriers like the rest. These years of Assyrian vassaldom, when Edom quite suddenly was brought into international politics after several centuries of obscurity, must have been testing years, and Edom did well to be cautious. Judah was devastated in 701 BCE, but Edom seems to have been left alone. From sometime in this period— perhaps from the reign of Sennacherib or his successor Esarhaddon— comes a text listing tribute received from several states, including, probably, Edom: the first side reads:

> Two minas of gold from the inhabitants of Bit-Ammon (*mat*Bit-Am-man-na-a-a); one mina of gold from the inhabitants of Moab (*Mat*Mu'-ba-a-a); ten minas of silver from the inhabitants of Judah (*mat*Ia-ú-da-a-a); [. . . mi]nas of silver from the inhabitants of Edom (*mat*[U-du-ma]-a-a). . . . (*ANET*³ 301; Pfeiffer, 1928: 185-86).

The reverse side refers to the city of Byblos (Gebal), or possibly to the northern area of Edom (modern Jibal), but no further information can be drawn from it. The reference to Edom on the first side is not absolutely certain, but is strongly suggested by the context and the word-ending; the amount paid in this case, however, is unfortunately lost. If the list has been arranged according to the size of the amount paid, beginning with the largest, then Edom's contribution was not more than Judah's, and probably less. Of all these countries, Edom was still probably the poorest.

Though the poorest, however, Edom was now (to judge from the archaeological evidence) entering upon the period of her greatest prosperity. To date four important sites have been excavated. The first was Tell el-Kheleifeh, excavated by Nelson Glueck 1938-1940. This site came under Edomite control in 733 BCE, and Glueck published in 1967 his examination of the pottery from this Edomite period of the tell's history. He concluded that

> The Edomite inscriptions and pottery in the completely Edomite Level IV of Tell el-Kheleifeh, which with its various sub-divisions can be dated no earlier than the latter part of the eighth century B.C., and no later than the sixth century B.C., testify to the existence there of a vigorous Edomite civilisation.' 'There was a striking renaissance of Edomite power in the seventh-sixth centuries BC, and beginning with the end of the eighth century B.C. (Glueck, 1967a: 8-38 [10,23]).

Glueck's work at Tell el-Kheleifeh has recently been re-examined by G. Pratico, who finds two main architectural phases at the site, a casemate fortress being succeeded by a fortified settlement with an offset/inset wall (Pratico, 1985: 1-32 [2-22]). The precise dates of the first phase are uncertain for lack of clear, stratified pottery evidence, but 'the pottery that can be associated with the levels of the offsets/insets settlement dates between the 8th and the early 6th century B.C.' (*ibid.*, 26). (Subsequent occupation is evidenced down to the fourth century BCE.) One might guess (though it is no more than a guess) that this second architectural phase represents the rebuilding and enlargement of Tell el-Kheleifeh by the Edomites after 733 BCE. The earlier, ruined casemate fortress, itself about 45 metres square, was partly incorporated into the north-west quadrant of the fortified settlement with its solid offsets/insets wall (measuring 56 metres [north] × 69 metres [east] × 59 metres [south] × 63 metres [west]. There was a four-chambered gateway in the southern wall, and outside the main wall a smaller external defensive wall (such as the Greeks called a *proteichisma*; A.W. Lawrence, 1979: 276-79). Within the main wall Glueck thought there were open courtyards, at least in the early phases of this period, but Pratico's reappraisal has suggested that interior architecture was there from the start. Associated pottery includes hand-made Negev ware, and a range of wheel-made forms: 'Edomite' cooking pots, bag-shaped jars, inverted-rim kraters (each of these three types were found bearing the inscription 'belonging to Qos'anal, servant of the king' stamped on the handle), 'Assyrian' bowls and cups in local limitation and pointed bottle fragments and censers, juglets, bowls, decanters, saucers. Pratico notes the absence of the typical late Judaean Iron Age wide-rimmed, holemouth jars and high-based lamps, and follows Glueck in emphasizing 'the regional character of the pottery with affinities close to assemblages of central and southern Transjordan and the Negev' (Pratico, 1985: [22-26]; see Glueck, 1967a: 8-38; 1967b: 124-27; 1969: 51-59; for the Qos'anal inscriptions, see below, p. 214). However, much work remains to be done on the material from Tell el-Kheleifeh; in particular, we lack a published inventory of the small finds, which would throw much light upon Tell el-Kheleifeh's local activities and trading relationships. However, Glueck noted evidence of contact with Arabia in a sixth-century BCE jar bearing an inscription of two letters in Minaean script, a variety of objects, including a faience amulet head of the god Bes and a cat amulet indicating contact with Egypt, and nails, pitch, fragments of palm-fibre rope perhaps suggesting boat-building, together with fish-hooks, weapons, copper dishes, fibulae, beads, cloth and baskets (Glueck, 1970: 126-34).

Exactly how 'Edomite' Tell el-Kheleifeh was is not clear. Though it was under Edomite control from 733 BCE onwards, and evidences Edomite pottery forms, its very position meant that it was open to other influences and that its population was probably not limited to Edomites. Fully Edomite, however, are three sites excavated in the central mountain range of Edom, Umm el-biyara, Tawilan, and Buseira. The one short period of occupation of Umm el-biyara, a settlement on the almost inaccessible top of a dramatically steepfaced mountain rising above Nabataean and Roman Petra, belongs only to the first half of the seventh century BCE (Bennett, 1966: 372-403). It seems to have been a small, domestic site, whose occupants practised weaving. Important small finds included a royal seal, an inscribed weight, a decorated palette, an ostracon and a stamped jar handle (Bennett, 1966: 395-401; 1967: 197-201). The site of Tawilan, east of Petra above the village of El-ji, is larger (Bennett, 1967-68: 53-55; 1971a: v-vii; 1984: 1-23). Occupation here seems to have begun with the use of the site as a clay-pit in the tenth-ninth centuries BCE, though the earliest buildings appear to be eighth century, and the major activity to date from the 8th-5th centuries BCE. Within this period there seem to have been two main building phases (2 and 3) visible in each of the three trenches dug; in Trench III the simple architecture of Stages 1 and 2 was 'superseded by a complicated arrangement involving split-levels and circulation spaces' (Bienkowski, 1984: 17), which apparently functioned as a unit rather than as a collection of separate area. In Trench II the 'Southern Complex' of Phase 2 and the 'Northern Complex' of Phase 3 were followed by a period of destruction and abandonment. A cuneiform tablet dating probably from the time of Darius I (522-486 BCE) was found just above the original surface of the Northern Complex in the fill-accumulation deposits (Petocz, 1984: 12-13; Dalley, 1984: 19-22), which suggests that the Northern Complex was abandoned a little earlier in the sixth century BCE. The major period of architectural activity at Tawilan, therefore, seems to fall, as at Tell el-Kheleifeh, between the eighth and sixth centuries BCE. Umm el-biyara's *floruit* falls within this period, and so also does that of Buseira. After the fourth season of excavation at Buseira, the excavator wrote,

> Nothing has been discovered in this latest season of excavations to alter the conclusion that the major *floruit* of ancient Buseirah was the 7th century B.C. and that the city was divided into upper and lower towns: the former was represented by the palatial and/or temple buildings on Area A and the latter by the ordinary domestic buildings on the terraces, Areas D and B, surrounding the 'Acropolis' Area A.

The excavator further concluded that

> Buseirah . . . only becomes of importance with the resurgence of the Assyrian empire and fairly late, at that, in her short lived supremacy (Bennett, 1977: 1-10 [9]).

One wonders when the major development of Buseira (Old Testament Bozrah) took place. The answer must surely be that the city was growing in population and importance through the eighth century BCE as the Edomite kingdom established itself, and that the major building operations revealed by excavation took place during Edom's vassaldom to Assyria. The function of the earlier building on the Acropolis site—Building B—is still in some doubt, but it seems to have been a palace or a temple. It was a large building or complex of buildings, some 77 metres by 38 metres, with stone foundations in places 3 metres deep, set into what may have been an artificially created mound. The building perhaps had two phases (Bennett, 1973: 1974a; 1975; 1977; 1983). The domestic buildings of area B to the west of the acropolis area had three main building periods, of which the second, belonging to the seventh century BCE, was the most important (Bennett, 1977: 1-10 [7]). To this period belongs the beautifully carved *tridacna squamosa* shell of Syro-Phoenician workmanship found in one of the houses, and also fragments of high quality pottery, probably imported, bearing the impressed stamp of a cow-and-calf motif (Bennett, 1977: 1-10 (7, Pl.I); 1975: 1-15 [14-15], fig. 8:10).

This is not the point at which to survey all the more interesting finds and epigraphic fragments from eighth-sixth century BCE Edom, but it may be noted here that it is from this period that we have a small number of seals and ostraca relevant to the reconstruction of Edom's history. Thus from Umm el-biyara we have a seventh-century seal reading *lqws g*** *mlk* '**, probably to be restored to read *lqws gbr mlk 'dm*, 'belonging to *qws gbr*, king of Edom', a king known to us from the records of Esarhaddon and Ashurbanipal in the first half of the seventh century BCE (Bennett, 1966: 399-401, Pl.XXIIb. See below, p. 213). At Tell el-Kheleifeh were found twelve jar-handles bearing the impression of a seal which read *lqws'nl/'bd hmlk*, 'belonging to *qws'nl*, the servant of the king'. Which king is not known; the seal is probably late seventh or early sixth century BCE (Glueck, 1938b: 3-19, fig. 6; see below, p. 214). From Buseira comes an enigmatic seal reading *lmlklb' 'bd hmlk*, 'belonging to *mlklb'*, the servant of the king', and another seal with the inscription *ltw*, 'belonging to *tw*'; the name is non-Semitic and the owner of the seal was perhaps a foreigner or a foreign official in Bozrah. These two seals belong to the late eighth or seventh century BCE (Bennett, 1974a: 18-19, Pl.VIB; Lemaire, 1975: 18-19; Puech, 1977: 11-20 [17-18, fig. 6]; see below, pp. 212-13, 215).

Tell el-Kheleifeh, Umm el-biyara, Buseira, and Tawilan thus all appear to belong to the eighth-sixth centuries BCE, the Assyrian period. This age seems to have been the most developed and prosperous period of Edom's history. Further evidence of this comes from survey work at the southern end of the Edomite plateau in the region of Ras en-Naqb. Here, in an area measuring about 24 kilometres from north to south and 12 kilometres from east to west, S. Hart identified 3 large fortresses (or walled villages), 7 small fortresses, 2 probable fortresses, 2 unwalled villages, 2 hamlets, 1 isolated building, with 23 other sites where sherds only were found, all dated by the pottery to the seventh–sixth centuries BCE (Hart, 1986c: 51-58). Hart emphasises that, though 'cultivation is not impossible, especially with hillside terracing', this is a 'water deficit region', unsuitable for growing citrus, olives, grapes, wheat or barley, and he concludes that

> Given these disadvantages there must be strong incentives for settlement to occur at all. In the seventh century BCE incentive for settlement must have come from Assyrians, anxious to protect a long border with the desert. Our small area represents the southern end of a long defensive line that stretched far to the north (*ibid.*, 54).

Hart raises further speculation

> whether Assyrian fortification of the region would be sufficient

stimulus [for the development of an extensive sedentary population from a nomadic one] or whether some forcible settlement was necessary or indeed, whether the Assyrians, with their policy of moving peoples around, imported population from elsewhere in the Empire (ibid., 57).

During a subsequent survey further north in Edom, Hart made soundings at six sites, noting 'a good corpus of seventh-sixth centuries BCE pottery' at Ghrareh, a fortress 10 kilometres west of Sadaqa, and late Iron Age remains at Khirbet el-Megeithah, Khirbet Ishra, and Khirbet Ain Jenin (possibly the necropolis for Buseira; Hart, 1986a: 77-78; 1987: 33-47). To all this one must add the evidence of B. MacDonald for the region between the Wadi el-Ḥasā and Tafila in northern Edom (see above, pp. 71-74); he attributes some 35 sites to Iron I-II or Iron II, over half of which appear to be occupied for the first time in this period. At most of these the evidence is limited to a scatter of sherds, but among the better evidenced sites west of the Wadi Laban are no. 24, Rujm Karaka, a signal or communication tower; no. 211, Kh. el Bureis (walls, rectangular structures of chert blocks); no. 187, Al Maqhaz; no. 71, Al Habes North (MacDonald, Banning, Pavlish, 1980: 169-83 [176-77]). In the Wadi Laban are sites 367, Ed-Dair (tower, major building) and no. 248, Rujm Muhawish (large fortress), and in Wadi Ja'īs no. 311, Rujm Ja'īs (fort-site with tower) (MacDonald, Rollefson, Roller, 1982: 117-32 [126-217]). There is also evidence of Iron II presence further east in the Wadi el-'Ali, though virtually nothing east of this (MacDonald, Rollefson, Banning, 1983: 311-23). It is true that the dating and classification of these sites remains imprecise, and that MacDonald appears to date his sites a little earlier than Hart dates his, but the overall impression remains that in Iron II, the period of Assyrian vassaldom, the central mountain plateau of Edom was defended by small forts and occupied by small settlements or hamlets, with the occasional larger village or town. Whether the Assyrians imported people or not, the development of Edom in the eighth-sixth centuries BCE probably has much to do with the political stability, and improved public security and economic circumstances established by Assyrian control.

The importance of Edom to the Assyrians in the seventh century BCE is revealed by references to Edom in the records of Esarhaddon and Ashurbanipal. Esarhaddon (680-669 BCE) records that

> I called up the kings of the country Hatti and (of the region) on the other side of the river (Euphrates) (to wit): Ba'lu, king of Tyre, Manasseh, king of Judah, Qaushgabri, king of Edom, Musuri, king of Moab, Sil-bel, king of Gaza, Metinti, king of Ashkelon, Ikausu, king of Ekron, Milkiashapa, king of Byblos, Matanba'al, king of Arvad, Abiba'al, king of Samsimuruna, Puduil, king of Beth-Ammon, Ahimilki, king of Ashdod—12 kings from the seacoast .... 10 kings from Cyprus amidst the sea, together 22 kings of Hatti, the seashore and the islands; all these I sent out and made them transport under terrible difficulties, to Nineveh, the town (where I exercise) my rulership, as building material for my palace: big logs, long beams (and) thin boards from cedar and pine trees, products of the Sirara and Lebanon mountains, which had grown for a long time into tall and strong timber, (also) from their quarries (lit.: places of creation) in the mountains, statues of protective deities (lit.: of Lamassu and Shedu) made of asnan-stone, statues of (female) *abzaztu*, thresholds, slabs of limestone, or asnan-stone, of large and small-grained breccia, of *alallu*-stone, (and) of *gi.rin.hi.li. ba*-stone (*ANET*³ 291).

The provision of labour, and perhaps of materials, was a new demand on Edom, but how it was organised and how great a burden it was we do not know. Manasseh of Judah is one of those mentioned as taking part in this exercise, but the Old Testament historians make no mention of it, unless it is concealed in the Chronicler's reference (2 Chron. 33.11) to 'the commanders of the army of the king of Assyria, who took Manasseh with hooks and bound him with fetters of bronze and brought him to Babylon', a statement which has not otherwise been satisfactorily explained. Presumably the various kings were expected to supply a labour force of a certain size. To judge from what we know of the comparative prosperity of Edom in this first half of the seventh century BCE, this Assyrian demand does not seem to have been particularly burdensome on the country, however unpopular it may have been among those involved.

Under Ashurbanipal (668-632 BCE) the Edomites were compelled to share in Assyria's military campaigns. In his first campaign, against Egypt, described on the Rassam Cylinder, Ashurbanipal says that he took twenty-two kings from the seashore, the island and the mainland with him (*ANET*³ 294), and if the list of twenty-two kings in Cylinder C belongs to this event (Streck, 1916: II.138-52; Luckenbill, 1927: II. §876), Qosgabri, king of Edom, was involved together with Manasseh, king of Judah, Musuri, king of

Moab, Amminabdi, king of Beth-Ammon, and other contemporaries. Such a campaign can hardly have been very welcome to the Edomites, who, along with the other south Palestinian states, probably tended to look to Egypt as a source of help against invaders from Syria and Mesopotamia. But as Assyrian vassals they had little choice; Ashurbanipal refers to the twenty-two kings as 'servants who belong to me', and he describes them as having 'brought heavy gifts (*tâmartu*) to me and kissed my feet' (*ANET*[3] 294). Edom seems to have remained loyal to Assyria throughout her vassalage. We do not hear that she rebelled, had her king removed, her people deported, and her kingdom turned into an Assyrian province, with an Assyrian administration, as happened elsewhere. But on the whole, Edom probably benefitted from Assyria, whose rule prevented Edom's major enemy, Judah, from hostile action of any kind. A similar benefit is revealed by the last appearance of Edom in the Assyrian records, also from the Rassam Cylinder. In his ninth campaign, Ashurbanipal marched against Uate', king of Arabia:

> Upon the oracle-command of Ashur, and Ishtar I called up my army and defeated him in bloody battles, inflicted countless routs upon him (to wit) in the *girû* of the towns of Asaril (and) Hirata (-)kassaia, in Edom, in the pass of Iabrudu, in Beth-Ammon in the district of Haurina, in Moab, in Sa'arri, in Harge, in the district of Zobah. In the (se) battles I smashed all the inhabitants of Arabia who had revolted with him, but he himself escaped before the powerful 'weapons' of Ashur to a distant region. They set fire to the tents in which they live and burnt (them) down. Uate' had misgivings and he fled, alone, to the country Nabate (*ANET*[3] 297-98).

Uate' was a member of the Qedarite tribe, which was to be found in the Syrian desert east and south-east of Damascus, and in certain circumstances ranging and raiding as far as the borders of Moab, Edom, or even the Teima region (Bartlett, 1979: 53-66 [59-62]). Edom could not escape involvement in this campaign, which appears to have been fought in part over her own territory. Edom probably found herself providing not only men but military bases, supplies and food, and the advantage of having Assyrian help against a local enemy may not have been without costly disadvantages.

From these Assyrian references to Edom we can reconstruct in outline the history of Edom from the beginning of her vassalage under Tiglath-pileser III in 732 BCE to Edom's part in the ninth campaign of Ashurbanipal, probably somewhere between 660 and 650 BCE. During this period, the Old Testament historians do not refer to Edom at all, probably because Judah had no military involvement with Edom. The Assyrian records mention three kings—Qosmalak in 732 BCE, Aiarammu in 701 BCE, and Qosgabri in the reigns of Esarhaddon and Ashurbanipal. Qosgabri's name is confirmed, as we have seen, by a seal found at Umm el-biyara. There may have been at least two other kings in this period; but there is room for one between Qosmalak and Aiarammu, and perhaps for one between Aiarammu and Qosgabri, and for one after Qosgabri. But we have no means of knowing how long any of these three kings ruled, except that Qosgabri seems to have had a fairly long reign. These kings probably followed one another in a dynastic succession, but it is noticeable that the Assyrian records do not name the kings' fathers—possibly because each name appears with many other kings in a list rather than in a narrative concerned with that particular king. The nature of the succession, then, remains in slight doubt. The place of rule was almost certainly Bozrah, modern Buseira, though it is not mentioned in the Assyrian texts.

One of the signs of Edom's self-confidence and expansion in this Assyrian period is perhaps to be found in the evidence, slight though it is, that Edomites were beginning to settle in southern Judah. We have already noted the Edomite seizure of Elath and attack on Judah, probably in 734 or 733 BCE, mentioned in 2 Kgs 16.6 and 2 Chron. 28.16-17, and the possible attack on Arad at that same period. The account in Num. 20.14-21 of Israel's request for passage through Edom after the exodus has the Israelites describe their presence 'in Kadesh, a city on the edge of your territory'. Kadesh is about 125 kilometres north-north-west of Elath and the Gulf of 'Aqaba, about 110 kilometres west of Bozrah, and about 120 kilometres south-south-east of Hebron. If Kadesh is on the edge of Edomite territory, the writer of this passage may be thinking of the mountainous region between Kadesh and the Wadi 'Araba as Edomite territory; but at what date is he writing? Recent analysis of Num. 20.14-21 has suggested that verses 15-16, in which this reference to Kadesh appears, are Deuteronomic or even post-Deuteronomic, and certainly no earlier than the seventh or sixth century BCE (Mittmann, 1973: 143-49). A similar picture appears in Num. 20.23; 21.4; 33.37, in which the people move from Kadesh to Mount Hor, on the border of the land of Edom: Aharoni, noting that Mt Hor always appears on the line of the journey from Kadesh-barnea to Arad (Num. 20.22-29; 21.4; 33.7-9; Deut. 32.50), locates Mt Hor some 13 km north of Kadesh-barnea (1979: 202; cf. earlier G.A. Smith, 1966: 368). The boundary descriptions of Judah given in Num. 34.3-5, Josh. 15.1-4, and Ezek. 47.19 also suggest that the territory of Edom began south of a line which ran from the southern end of the Dead Sea south of the ascent of Aqrabbim and Kadesh (Aharoni, 1979: 69-72). The same boundary could be inferred from the geographical extent of the list of Judah's southern cities in Josh. 15.21-32. Precise dating of these boundary descriptions is difficult, but in their present form they presumably describe the land claimed by Judah as its own in the monarchic or late monarchic period. Beyond Judah's southern border and the limits of Judah's urban or village settlement, the land could be seen and described as 'the border' or 'the side' of Edom. How much of this south-eastern Negev region Edom's king claimed or controlled as his rightful territory we have now way of knowing.

However, recent archaeological discoveries have suggested that in the seventh and early sixth centuries BCE there was growing Edomite influence and presence in the Negev of Judah (Bartlett, 1982: 13-24 [15-16]; for earlier discussion cf. Torrey, 1898: 16-20; Glueck 1935: 112-13; 1936a: 141-57; 1967c: 429-52 [436]; Bartlett, 1972: 26-37 [33-34]). Particularly important are the ostraca from Arad (which lies some 30-40 kilometres to the north of the line from the southern end of the Dead Sea past the ascent of Aqrabbim towards Kadesh), which show that Arad perhaps as early as 701 BCE and certainly a century later was an important military post responsible for monitoring military movements on the border with Edom (Aharoni, 1970: 16-28; 1981). We have already noted the correspondence relating, perhaps, to diplomatic messages passing through Arad from Edom to Judah in 701 BCE (see above, p. 131); among the ostraca dating from about a century later were three (Aharoni, 1981: nos 3, 21 and 24) that referred to Edom or Edomites, and two (nos 3, 26) with personal names incorporating the divine name *qws*, whose bearers might be of Edomite descent. Ostracon 24 (Aharoni, 1970: 16-28; 1981: 46) dated by Aharoni to 598/7 BCE, contains an order that troops be sent from Arad and Qinah to Ramath-negeb 'lest anything should happen to the city' and 'lest Edom should come there'. Qinah is perhaps Khirbet Ghazzeh at the head of Wadi el-Qeini south-south-east of Arad (Abel, 1933: I.272; 1938: II.88; Lemaire, 1977: 191), or Kh.eṭ-Ṭaiyib north-north east of Arad (Aharoni, 1970:21); Ramath-negeb is perhaps Khirbet Ghazzeh (if Qinah is not) (Aharoni, 1970:23; this site 'is the first point against which an Edomite attack would be expected') or Khirbet el-Gharrah (Tell 'Ira) a few miles further west (Lemaire, 1977: 191-92). Clearly, Edom's military presence was feared by the military command in Judah.

Edom's presence in the region, however, was apparently not purely military. Ostracon 12 (Aharoni, 1981:26) instructs a certain Eliashib to give a jar of oil and two measures of flour to a man probably called [Qo]s'anal, a name attested from the fortified settlement phase of Tell el-Kheleifeh and dated to the seventh-sixth century BCE (see below, p. 214). The name appears to be an Edomite name (cf. the fragmentary name . . . -qws on ostracon 26), but not the name of an enemy. Edomite names were perhaps not uncommon in this area at the time, for an Aramaic ostracon said to be list of names comparable with those known from Tell el-Kheleifeh was found at Tell el-Milḥ (Tell Mall.ata), twelve miles west of Arad (Kochavi, 1977: 771-775; for the various attempts to identify this site, see Bartlett, 1982: 13-24 [23, n. 2]). According to its excavator, 30 per cent of Malhata's late Iron age pottery is 'Edomite' ware, comparable with material from Tell el-Kheleifeh, Tawilan and Umm el-Biyara (Kochavi, 1967: 272-73; 1977: 771-775). Similar pottery has been discovered in the upper stratum of ruins outside the walls of the late pre-exilic city at Tell 'Aro'er, whence also comes a seal bearing what seems to be another name of Edomite origin, Qosa' (Biran, Cohen, 1976: 139-40; 1977: 273-74, Pl.IXd). Similar seventh-sixth century Edomite ware, including painted sherds and bowls with triangular knobs, has been excavated at what seems to be an Iron Age II cultic site at Ḥ.Qiṭmiṭ, 10 kilometres south of Arad (Beit-Arieh, 1984: 93; 1985: 201-202). At Tell Meshash (Tel Masos), a few kilometres west of Tell el-Milḥ, in a fill of seventh-century material was found a figurine head and a model of a bed, both decorated in Edomite style, and part of a jug of Edomite ware (Kempinski, 1977: 816-19). Again at Tell 'Ira the Late Iron Age pottery included painted sherds of the Edomite type (Beit-Arieh, 1981: 243-45). At Kh. Ghazzeh (Ḥorvat 'Uza), a seventh-century BCE fort south of Arad, among the ostraca found one is 'with distinctively Edomite script' (Beit-Arieh, Cresson, 1983: 271-72; 1985: 96-101; the ostracon appears to be an instruction from an Edomite official to an Edomite officer in Ḥorvat ʿUza [Ramath-negeb?] to supply food to the bearer). All these sites seem to have been occupied and active in the seventh-sixth centuries BCE, and though in Judah's territory to have clear links culturally with sites in Edom to the east.

What this suggests is that by the end of the Assyrian period a number of Edomites, or people with Edomite affinities, were settled among the population of the region roughly south of a line drawn from Arad to Beersheba. It has often been suggested that the Edomites migrated westwards under pressure from Arabs invading Edom from the east (cf. Bright, 1965: 332; Ephʿal, 1982: 178-79 (though note Ephʿal's caveat on p. 179); Dumbrell, 1971: 27-44 [41]), but this explanation is oversimple. The settlement of Edomites west of the Wadi ʿAraba was probably a process extending over several centuries, fluctuating with changed economic and social conditions. The Edomites probably had enough in common with the tribes of the border country of southern Judah—Kenites, Jerahmeelites, Kenizzites—to make movement and intermarriage relatively easy; certainly the editor of Gen. 36 could draw on names from this region when compiling his lists of 'Edomite' clans. In the post-exilic period, the author of Obad. 19 could speak of the Negev as the 'mount of Esau' and promise that on the Day of the Lord the people of Judah would re-possess it. In the eighth-seventh centuries however, individual Edomites, their horizons widened by the political and economic developments of the Assyrian period, perhaps found the prospect of settlement on the southern fringes of Judah more attractive than the future of farming in the higher, wilder mountains of Edom. Just how sharply the boundary line was drawn between land that was distinctively Judahite and land that was distinctively Edomite is not clear. There was probably no sharply defined border line, but rather a border zone in which the population might be somewhat mixed. By the end of the seventh century, the king of Edom might have had considerable political and military interests in the region. But there is no evidence that he ever controlled it.

Additional note: Jehoshaphat's campaign in 2 Chronicles 20

The account of the joint campaign against Moab in 2 Kings 3 has been replaced in 2 Chronicles 20 by a lengthy description of how Jehoshaphat of Judah, with much help from the Lord and with no help from Israel, defeated a coalition of enemies in the region of Tekoa and Engedi, in the valley of Beracah. Williamson (1982: 279) sees Jehoshaphat's success in 2 Chronicles 20 as being in deliberate contrast to the disaster of 2 Kgs 3.27, and as part of the Chronicler's concern to present Jehoshaphat in a wholly favourable light. Noth (1944-45: 45-71) and others following him have argued that the topographical details of 2 Chron. 20.1-30 are based on authentic local tradition; Noth believed that the account reflected a 3rd century BCE Nabataean invasion, though others have preferred to think of earlier events and have not ruled out the possibility of an event from Jehoshaphat's own reign (Petersen, 1975: 70-71; Williamson, 1982: 292-93). It is generally agreed that the Chronicler is far more concerned with the contribution of the Levitical prophets and singers to the campaign than with the historical details of the event, but for us the major problem concerns the identity of the enemies who attacked Judah. The MT lists them (2 Chron. 20.1) as the 'sons of Moab, the sons of Ammon, and with them some of the Ammonites'. This last grouping (*mehā'ammônîm*) reads strangely, and most scholars have read, by a simple change, *hammē'ûnîm*, 'the Meunim' or Meunites. Montgomery (1934: 182) suggested that the Arabian Minaeans were meant, or perhaps the people of Ma'ān in Edom (cf. Noth, 1944-45: 45-71). The third party to the unholy alliance against Jehoshaphat is also described later in the narrative as the men or inhabitants of Mount Seir (2 Chron. 20.10, 22-34), by which the Chronicler probably intended the reader to understand the Edomites. (This may also be indicated by verse 2, where the MT 'from Aram' may perhaps be an error for an original 'from Edom'; but in either case the phrase is perhaps an additional gloss; cf. Noth, 1944-45: 63, n. 2.) However, the only other biblical reference to the Meunim (2 Chron. 26.7) notes that God helped Uzziah against the Philistines, the Arabs that lived in Gur-baal, and the Meunim. Williamson (1982: 335) reads the name Gur-baal simply as Gur, emending *baal* to *wĕ'al*, which he takes with the following Meunim: i.e., 'and against the Meunim'. Williamson identifies Gur with the *Gari* of the el-Amarna letters somewhere between the Arabs of Gur and the Dead Sea; possibly they should therefore be connected with the place Maon about 10 kilometres south of Hebron in the Negev (cf. Josh.

15.55; 1 Sam. 23.24; 25.2; 1 Chron. 2.45; cf. Bartlett, 1969: 1-20 [6]; Williamson, 1982: 294). The Meunim would then be the people of the town and locality of Maon.

The results of this excursus can now be summarised. Somewhere at the heart of the narrative of 2 Chron. 20 lies the tradition of a battle in the region between Tekoa and Engedi, in the valley of Beracah, possible involving the Meunim from Maon, a little further south. The addition of the Ammonites and Moabites is unhistorical; the Chronicler, having identified the Meunim as people from Seir and so from Edom, involved the two obvious peoples to make up the alliance of three. The Chronicler composed the story for his own didactic purposes (cf. Petersen, 1975: 69-77; Williamson, 1982: 227-80, 291-301). If we could be sure that the campaign against the Meunim might properly be credited to Jehoshaphat (it is possible, in view of 2 Chron. 26.7, that the tradition really belongs to the reign of Uzziah), then we would at least have some further evidence of Jehoshaphat's interest in controlling the approaches to the Wadi 'Araba; but there is no evidence here of a campaign extending further into Edom, or of the involvement of Edomites from east of the Wadi 'Araba in a campaign against Jehoshaphat.

Chapter 8

THE END OF THE KINGDOM OF EDOM

Events to 587 BCE

The progressive decline in power of the Assyrian empire in the second half of the seventh century BCE inevitably meant that Assyria's hold on Edom weakened, and perhaps that Edom ceased to pay tribute as soon as she could safely do so. In Judah, Manasseh (696-642 BCE) probably remained faithful to Assyria, unless 2 Chron. 33.11 refers to some act of rebellion for which Manasseh was punished. His successor Amon (641-640 BCE) was murdered by conspirators, whose motive may have been the wish to remove a pro-Assyrian king. This was a period of unrest in the western Assyrian empire, and Ashurbanipal campaigned in the west for the last time in 640 BCE. It has been suggested that Samaria joined the revolt, the result being the settlement of foreign population there by Ashurbanipal (cf. Ezra 4.9ff.). But after this Assyria's power declined under pressure from Babylon, the Medes, and the Umman-manda from the north, and in Judah king Josiah set about re-establishing an independent Judah, acquiring for Judah in the course of his reign the Assyrian provinces of Gilead, Galilee, and Samaria. The process of release from Assyrian control must have been roughly contemporary in Edom, and there is evidence that the other two states in southern Jordan, Ammon and Moab, took advantage of the new situation. Zeph. 2.8 refers to the taunts of Moab and Ammon against Judah:

'I have heard the taunts of Moab
    and the revilings of the Ammonites,
how they have taunted my people
    and made boasts against their territory.'

Jer. 49.1 refers to the Ammonite invasion and dispossession of Israelites of the tribe of Gad settled at the north-eastern end of the

Dead Sea; pottery from Heshbon in this period 'confirms very definitely the ceramic tradition of the Amman tombs' while south of Heshbon the pottery tradition is essentially different (Lugenbeal, Sauer, 1972: 62-64). Towards the end of the seventh century BCE, the Transjordanian states were becoming free to be aggressive.

In 612 BCE the Assyrian empire gave way before the Babylonians, and from 605 BCE Judah and her neighbours had to come to terms with the new master of the Levant, Nebuchadnezzar king of Babylon (605-562 BCE). After the independence of Josiah's reign, Judah did not take kindly to renewed subservience, and after three years of vassaldom to Nebuchadnezzar rebelled (2 Kgs 24.1). The result of Jehoiakim's act of defiance, according to the Deuteronomistic historians, was that

> the LORD sent against him bands of the Chaldaeans, and bands of the
> Syrians, and bands of the Moabites, and bands of the Ammonites,
> and sent them against Judah to destroy it (2 Kgs 24.2).

These attacks are usually dated to 599 or 598 BCE and seen as a preliminary to Nebuchadnezzar's siege and capture of Jerusalem in January-March 597 BCE (Herrmann, 1975: 278; Gray, 1980, 756-57). Nothing is known of any Chaldaean (i.e., Babylonian) attack on Judah in 599 or 598 BCE from the Babylonian chronicles, which mention only an attack on the Arabs which may be the subject of the oracle in Jer. 49.28-33 (Wiseman, 1956: 70-71; Noth, 1958: 133-57 [=1971: III. 132]). Equally, nothing is known of any Moabite, Ammonite or Syrian attacks at this time, though Moabite and Ammonite activity would not be out of keeping with their threats against Judah perhaps a generation earlier, recorded in Zeph. 2.8, or with the Ammonite attack on Gadite towns mentioned in Jer. 49.1-6. That the Syrians might campaign against Judah with the Babylonians is clear from Jer. 35.11. Many scholars have followed the Peshitta and Arabic versions of 2 Kgs 24.2 and read 'Edomites' for 'Syrians', on the grounds that Edom rather than Aram (Syria) is to be expected in connection with Moabites and Ammonites (e.g., Burney, 1903: 365; Oded, 1977: 435-88 [470-71]; Eph'al, 1982: 172), and some scholars have speculatively connected this alleged Edomite act of hostility with the fear expressed in Arad ostracon number 24 that Edomite forces might come to attack Ramath-negeb (Aharoni, 1970: 16-42 [16-28]; Myers, 1971: 377-92 [390-92]; Lemaire, 1977: 235).

But there is no pressing need to emend the text of 2 Kgs 24.2, and no clear evidence of Edomite aggression in 599/8 BCE, though it might not be surprising to find Edom taking advantage of Judah's difficulties.

Much has been made of the possibility that Edom was active against Judah in the Negev in 597 BCE when Nebuchadnezzar attacked Jerusalem. Some scholars have dated to this occasion the oracle in Jer. 13.18f. (Alt, 1925: 100-16 [=1953: 276-88]; Noth, 1960: 283):

> Say to the king and the queen mother:
> 'Take a lowly seat,
> for your beautiful crown
>   has come down from your head.'
> The cities of the Negeb are shut up, ['besieged', NEB; cf. Josh. 6.1]
>   with none to open them;
> all Judah is taken into exile,
>   wholly into exile.

As it is clear that Nebuchadnezzar's short campaign of the winter of 598-7 BCE allowed him no time, after the capture of Jerusalem in March 597 BCE, to campaign in the Negev (Shea, 1979: 113-16), it has been suggested that the oracle refers to Edomite invasion of the Negev, and the evidence of ostracon 24 from Arad is again quoted. Lemaire argues that once Ramath-negeb had succumbed to Edomite attack, 'tout le Negeb passa sous le controle édomite', including Arad, whose destruction (Stratum VI) he dates to 597 BCE (Lemaire, 1977: 235, following Aharoni, 1970: 18). Unfortunately there is too much speculation here. Ostracon 24 does not tell us that Ramath-negeb was destroyed, nor that it was destroyed by Edomites. Excavation of H. 'Uza and T. 'Ira (the two sites proposed for Ramath-negeb) has shown that their seventh-century occupation was in each case brought to an end by fire, but at what date and by whose agency is unclear (cf. Beit-Arieh, Cresson, 1983: 271-72; Beit-Arieh, 1981: 243-45; 1982: 69-70). The dating of the destruction of Arad to 598/7 BCE rather than to 588/7 BCE depends upon the association of the events described in the ostracon with the alleged Edomite attack evidenced by 2 Kgs 24.2 (emended). (Aharoni himself notes [1970: 28] the possibility 'that the letter pertains to the second campaign of Nebuchadnezzar which marked the fall of the Judaean monarchy'.) The oracle of Jer. 13.18f., with its reference to siege and coming exile for the people of Judah, surely refers to Babylonian rather than Edomite activity; the disaster Jeremiah quite plausibly predicted for the Negev in 597 BCE did not in fact happen until ten years later. The evidence for Edomite military 'control' of the Negev, as distinct from population settlement, in this decade can be overstated, and the destruction of Arad probably belongs with the Babylonian destruction of the other major cities of Judah such as Lachish (Tell ed-Duweir), Azekah (Tell Zakariyah), Debir (Tell Beit Mirsim), Bethshemesh (Kh.er-Rumeileh), Bethzur (Kh.et-Tubeigheh), Beth-haccherem (Ramat Rahel), and Engedi (Oded, 1977: 475; Weinberg, 1969: 80). In 587 BCE, Judah still extended south past Bethzur and Engedi towards Arad in one dirction and towards Lachish and Debir in another. Aharoni has argued that the region between Arad and Lachish remained populated down to the time of Nehemiah in the mid-fifth century BCE by Judaeans who had escaped deportation in 587 BCE, for a number of cities of this region listed in Josh. 15.21-32 reappear in the list of Neh. 11.25-30: Dimonah (=Dibon?), Kabzeel (=Jekabzeel), Moladah, Bethpelet, Hazar-shual, Ziklag (Aharoni, 1979: 410). If this is so, and we may trust the Nehemiah list, then the evidence for an Edomite military takeover of southern Judah in the sixth century BCE remains uncertain. That there was continuing settlement of individual Edomites in this area, however, seems highly likely, but this took place over a long period of time until, by the late fourth century BCE, the region had become known (in Greek) as Idoumaia.

When Nebuchadnezzar seized the western states for his expanding Babylonian empire, it is likely that the king of Edom became his vassal at the same time as the kings of Judah and the other Syro-Palestinian states. At all events, we hear of the presence of the envoy or envoys of the king of Edom, along with envoys from the kings of Moab, the Ammonites, Tyre, and Sidon, at a meeting in Jerusalem under the chairmanship of Zedekiah, king of Judah. According to Jer. 27.9 the kings are being misled by the various advisers—prophets, diviners, dreamers, soothsayers and sorcerers—to rebel against the king of Babylon; following such advice would lead to exile and disaster, but acceptance of the Babylonian yoke would bring peace and security. In particular, Jeremiah attacks Zedekiah and the priests and prophets of Judah, and it was probably Zedekiah who summoned this meeting of representatives of the several vassal states. The king of Edom was doubtless willing enough to join in the council and have knowledge of what was planned, but it is unlikely that Edom was anxious to join any rebellion. The king of Edom probably took the view expressed by Jeremiah, that rebellion would lead to disaster, for when Judah openly rebelled in 589 BCE, only Egypt, Tyre, and perhaps the Ammonites associated themselves with her. Edom, as a long-standing enemy of Judah, was ready enough to leave Judah to her punishment.

Edom and the Fall of Jerusalem, 587 BCE

Hard evidence for Edom's behaviour when the Babylonians finally attacked and besieged Jerusalem in 589 BCE is less easy to find than is often supposed. Perhaps the most reliable piece of evidence comes from Jer. 40.11:

> When all the Jews who were in Moab and among the Ammonites and in Edom and in other lands heard that the king of Babylon had left a remnant in Judah and had appointed Gedaliah the son of Ahikam, son of Shaphan, as governor over them, then all the Jews returned from all the places to which they had been driven and came to the land of Judah, to Gedaliah at Mizpah; and they gathered wine and summer fruits in great abundance.

Transjordan, which was not attacked in 598-7 BCE, seems to have been the natural refuge for those of Judah who could escape. It is interesting, in view of previous history, that people from Judah could find refuge in Edom, but individual and national relationships are not always the same thing. If the Babylonians campaigned as far south as Arad in 589 BCE, the destruction they brought would have affected inhabitants of Edomite as well as of Judahite stock, and for all occupants of that area Edom would have been the obvious refuge.

The remaining evidence for Edom's behaviour in 589-7 BCE comes mainly from prophetic and liturgical sources. Most of the passages usually quoted in this regard picture Edom's attitude rather than her actions, and behind these complaints lies the communal memory of Edom's enmity as much as any precise knowledge of recent wickedness. Lam. 4.21f., for example, says nothing precise:

> Rejoice and be glad, O daughter of Edom,
>   dweller in the land of Uz;

> you to you also the cup shall pass;
>> you shall become drunk and strip yourself bare.
> The punishment of your iniquity, O daughter of Zion, is accomp-
>> lished,
>> he will keep you in exile no longer;
> but your iniquity, O daughter of Edom, he will punish,
>> he will uncover your sins.

Edom's iniquity is not specified; it does not appear to be necessarily recent. Zion's punishment is done; Edom's is still to come. Similarly, Isaiah 34 lyricizes over the sword which will descend in judgment upon Edom, but there is no mention of Edom's crimes, unless (vv. 5f.) it is a case of 'they that take the sword perish with the sword'; but Edom's reputation for coming out with the sword went back, as we have seen, for several centuries. Mal. 1.2-5 again reveals that the Lord hated Edom, and that Edom will be called the wicked country with whom the Lord is angry for ever, but no explanation for this is given. Joel 4.19 (EVV 3.19) at least brings a charge against Edom:

> Egypt shall become a desolation,
>> and Edom a desolate wilderness,
> for the violence done to the people of Judah,
>> because they have shed innocent blood in their land.

But this concluding addition to the book of Joel owes much to prophetic tradition. Both Edom and Egypt are long-standing arch-enemies—both feature, with the catchword 'desolation', in earlier prophecies about the Day of Yahweh (cf. Ezek. 29.10, 12 and 32.15 for Egypt, and Ezek. 35.3, 4, 7, 9, 14, 15 for Edom). The violence (*ḥămas*) perhaps echoes Obad. 10; the thought is present, if not the word, in Amos. 1.11. Wolff (1977: 84) rightly concludes that 'this piece of the addition is also determined much more strongly by received prophetic words than by present distress'.

We are on no firmer ground with Ezek. 25.12. Ezek. 25 is a collection of four undated oracles of doom against foreign nations. The first two oracles, against Ammon and Moab, show close similarity and parallelism, as do the second pair, against Edom and the Philistines. Edom's crime is that it has 'acted revengefully against the house of Judah and has grievously offended in taking vengeance upon them', and the Philistines are indicted in similar terms. Why

Edom took revenge, how, or when is not specified, any more than it is in the case of the Philistines. If 587 BCE is in mind (as Ezek. 25.23 suggests), then Edom appears, if anything, rather less guilty than other nations.

Ezekiel 35 attacks Edom, under the name of Mount Seir (used in contrast to 'the mountains of Israel' in ch. 36). There are four oracles, with a number of minor expansions (vv. 7f., 10b, 13, 15). The first oracle (vv. 3-4) brings no accusation. In the second (vv. 5-9) Mt. Seir is threatened 'Because you cherished perpetual enmity, and gave over the people of Israel to the power of the sword at the time of their final punishment', which repeats in different words the accusation of Amos 1.11, and 'Because you are guilty of blood' (Ezek. 35.6, RSV and NEB, following the Greek; cf. Zimmerli, 1969: 852), which is a very general accusation. The third oracle (vv. 10-12) brings a new charge, 'Because you said, "These two nations and these two countries shall be mine, and we will take possession of them"'. This charge is a conventional charge which might be made against others beside Edom and which appears elsewhere in Ezekiel, mainly in secondary material (cf. Ezek. 33.24; 36.2-5; see Wevers, 1969: 76, 254; Bartlett, 1982: 19-20). The accusation is based not so much on any material threat from Edom—the idea of Edom's taking possession of Israel and Judah would be somewhat unrealistic—as on the general understanding of how enemies of Israel might be expected to behave. An enemy of Israel is above all one who threatens to take possession of her land. The fourth oracle (vv. 14-15) appears to accuse Edom of gloating over Israel's fate (for text and meaning, see Wevers, 1969: 267; Bartlett, 1982: 20). Thus Ezek. 35 brings a number of charges against Edom couched in familiar and conventional terms. None of them necessarily reflects any specific action of Edom's in 589-7 BCE. In Ezekiel, Edom is but one enemy among several of whom similar charges are made.

Perhaps the most famous accusation against Edom is that of Ps. 137.7:

> Remember, O Lord, against the Edomites
>   the day of Jerusalem,
> how they said, 'Rase it, rase it!
>   Down to its foundations!'

Dahood has suggested that the Edomites' words might be translated 'Strip her, strip her to her buttocks' (Dahood, 1970: 273; Bartlett,

1982: 20), but whichever way we take the words, they do not amount
to a charge of Edom's physical involvement in any military act. They
are simply an imaginative, dramatic presentation of what was taken
to be Edom's attitude towards Jerusalem.

It is the oracle of Obadiah 1-14, 15b that appears to make the most
explicit charges against Edom. Particular complaints begin with
v. 11:

> On the day that you stood aloof,
>   on the day that strangers carried off his wealth,
> and foreigners entered his gates
>   and cast lots for Jerusalem,
>   you were like one of them.

This seems to make it clear that Edom was not among the strangers
and foreigners but that, on the principle that those who are not with
us are against us, was 'like one of them'. Verses 12-14 however,
especially in the RSV, appear to suggest that Edom's part was much
more active. These verses speak of Edom's gloating, rejoicing,
boasting, 'entering the gate of my people', looting his goods, cutting
off fugitives, and delivering up survivors. Gloating, rejoicing, and
boasting refer to attitudes rather than to any active participation in
Jerusalem's fall. The charges of cutting off fugitives and delivering up
survivors could have some foundation, in spite of the note in Jer.
40.11 that some refugees found safety in Edom; others, after all, may
not have been so lucky. The charges in v. 13, however, of entering
the gate of God's people and looting are more serious. They appear to
pick up the description of Babylonian activity in v. 11. Edom is
pictured as behaving just as Babylon behaved; 'you were like one of
them'. Edom, the arch-enemy, is being credited with Babylon's
behaviour.

There is, however, good reason for caution against assuming too
easily that these verses can be taken as an authentic chronicle of
Edom's activities in 587 BCE. The RSV translates these verses with
the repeated phrase 'you should not have. . . ', imparting to our ears
the suggestion that Edom *had* behaved in these particular ways. In
fact the author is projecting himself, in lively fashion, into the past,
looking back vividly to the day of Judah's misfortune, ruin, distress
and calamity. He addresses the Edomites directly with a series of
prohibitions, 'do not gloat', 'do not rejoice', and so on. There is a
dramatic sense of the contemporaneity of the occasion in which the

prophet, in some excitement, warns Judah's ancient enemy against typical hostile behaviour. 'You should not have gloated', as a translation, misses the immediacy of the original. The prophet is not simply criticising Edom for what she did; he is vividly imagining the fall of Jerusalem—the enemy rejoicing, boasting, entering the gates, looting and killing—and he imagines Edom taking part in all this. It is interesting and perhaps important to note that in vv. 1-10, Obadiah threatens Edom herself with all the usual miseries of conquest—the enemies' taunts (v. 2), the plundering (vv. 5f.), the failure of allies (v. 7), the slaughter (v. 8)—and then in vv. 11-14 he warns Edom against indulging in precisely these activities, in terms sometimes reminiscent of the Old Testament wisdom tradition:

> Do not rejoice when your enemy falls,
> and let not your heart be glad when he stumbles.
> (Prov. 24.17)

These verses in Obadiah should not be understood as an historian's description of Edom's behaviour in 587 BCE. The poet derives his picture largely from his imagination.

In all this prophetic accusation against Edom, the charges are general and conventional rather than specific and circumstantial. Most of these passages look back over a considerable span of time to condemn Edom's gloating attitude, vengefulness or violence, and interest in Judah's land; but none give details of any particular event. It is not until the third or second century BCE that we meet any specific accusation. 1 Esdras is a Greek version of the final chapters of 2 Chronicles, the book of Ezra, and part of the book of Nehemiah. Into it was incorporated the story of the three guardsmen, in which each of the three guardsmen argues his case before king Darius on the topic 'what one thing is strongest'. The winner is the third guard, identified by the Jewish editor with Zerubbabel the son of Shealtiel (1 Esd. 5.5; cf. Ezra 5.2). When the king asks Zerubbabel to choose his prize, Zerubbabel reminds the king that he once vowed to rebuild Jerusalem and restore the temple vessels which Cyrus removed, and that

> You also vowed to build the temple, which the Edomites (Gk. *'Idoumaioi*) burned when Judea was laid waste by the Chaldeans.

Whether the story of the three guardsmen was originally in Aramaic or Greek, it is quite clear that this text (which is part of the redactional work of 1 Esd. 4.42-46, linking the story of the three guardsmen with the main theme of 1 Esdras) comes from a time long enough after 588 BCE for the real part played by the Edomites at that time to have been irrelevant. The author indeed happily ignores the fact that the Chronicler himself unambiguously ascribes the burning of the temple to the Babylonians (2 Chron. 36.19; cf. 2 Kgs 25.9). For this author, rewriting Chronicles and Ezra, the Babylonians are past and gone; but the Idumaeans are a very present reality. In 312 BCE we hear of an eparchy of Idumaea (Diod.Sic. XIX.95.2; 98.1); in 259 BCE we read in the Zenon papyri of Idumaeans at Marisa (PZC 59006, 59015 verso, 59804; see Edgar, 1925: I.10, 34). From this and from various references in 1 and 2 Maccabees it is clear that by the end of the third century BCE the border of Judah and Idumaea ran between Bethzur and Hebron, and westwards north of Marisa (cf. 1 Macc. 4.15, 61; 5.68; 2 Macc. 12.38; Josephus notes that Adoreon and Marisa lay in Idumaea (*BJ* I.2.6 (63); *Ant.* XIII. 9.2 [257]; cf. Vermes, Millar, Black, 1979: II. 6; Hengel, 1974: II. 172). In pre-exilic times, Judah reached south to Hebron and Beersheba and beyond; by the third century BCE, the land south of Bethzur was totally alien, the home of Idumaeans living in hellenised cities like Adora, Marisa, Hebron and Beersheba. It is not surprising that 1 Esdras 4.50 makes Darius give orders that 'the Idumaeans should give up the villages of the Jews which they held' or that the Jewish historian, editing the Ezra narrative for his own contemporaries, should underline Idumaean wickedness, and improve upon already well-developed traditions of the villainy of the Idumaean ancestors in 587 BCE (see also 1 Esd. 8.69, which lists the Idumaeans (where Ezra 9.1 speaks of Amorites) among those with whom the Jews had contracted mixed marriages. (This indicates another grievance felt against the Idumaeans.) Obadiah in his imagination pictured Edom sharing in the looting and slaughter; 1 Esdras went a stage further in crediting the Idumaeans (and by implication their Edomite ancestors) with burning the temple, a crime in fact perpetrated by the Babylonians.

A review of the complaints made against Edom by the Jewish writers of the post-exilic period shows clearly their prejudice and lack of circumstantial evidence. The roots of this prejudice, and of Judah's hatred for Edom, go back to the monarchic period; the Davidic conquest of Edom and Edom's later successful fight for independence left a legacy of bitterness which turned Edom into the archetypal enemy of Judah. When Judah fell to the Babylonians, and Edom remained unscathed, it was inevitable that Edom should come in for harsh language; naturally such an enemy on Judah's borders coveted the land, would gloat over Judah's distress, would kill fugitives, join in the looting, and eventually be blamed, most unfairly, for the most painful catastrophe of all, the burning of the temple. In fact, Edom played no direct part in the events of 587 BCE. The only firm evidence suggests that some Judaean refugees found sanctuary in Edom. For the destruction of Jerusalem and Judah in 587 BCE Edom cannot be held responsible.

The End of Edom

The Transjordanian states of the Ammonites, Moabites and Edomites appear to have survived Nebuchadnezzar's expedition to Palestine unscathed (though Ezek. 21.18-23 suggests that the Ammonites at least were at some risk of invasion). The Edomite kingdom continued intact. According to Josephus, however, the Ammonites and Moabites were attacked and subjected to Babylonian rule in the fifth year after the destruction of Jerusalem (*Ant.* X. 9.7 [181]). If Josephus is right, the attack on the Ammonites, at least, may have been in retaliation for the Ammonites' continued resistance to Babylon, for according to Jer. 40.14 it was Baalis king of the Ammonites who instigated the murder of the Babylonian governor of Judah, Gedaliah. We know nothing further about this Babylonian campaign, though it has often been supposed that the Babylonians took the opportunity to overrun Edom as well. However, neither Josephus nor the Old Testament writers give any indication of this; indeed, the several prophetic oracles from exilic or post-exilic times threatening Edom with coming destruction (Amos 9.11f.; Isa. 11.14; 34; Jer. 9.25; 25.21; 49.7-22; Lam. 4.21; Ezek. 32.29) suggest that Edom has not yet suffered due retribution. Edom had given Nebuchadnezzar no cause for punitive action, and Edom therefore probably survived Nebuchadnezzar's campaigns in 582 BCE (cf. Lury, 1896: 65). It has been suggested it was not Nebuchadnezzar who brought about the end of the independent vassal kingdom of Edom, but one of the later Babylonian rulers, Nabonidus (555-539 BCE), in his campaigns of 552 BCE in southern Transjordan and northern Arabia (Lindsay, 1976: 23-29). In its description of Nabonidus' march through

Transjordan, the Nabonidus Chronicle says '[Against the town A] dummu they pitched (camp) . . .' (*ANET*³ 305). If [A] dummu refers to Edom, as seems most likely, it may have been preceded in the text by the name of a city, possibly Bozrah (Lindsay, 1976: 36,38). (The context required that -*dummu* be the name of a city, or of a land or country preceded by a city-name; cf. S. Smith, 1944: 37-38, 137, 139, who follows Musil in locating -*dummu* in Edom. Eph'al [1982: 188] suggests [U] dummu, Edom, as the most likely reconstruction of the name, and argues that Nabonidus' march to Teima lay 'not through the Syro-Arabian desert, but through the Fertile Crescent, a longer but more convenient campaign route'.) Bozrah (Buseira) seems to have suffered at least one major disaster, to which the signs of burning and destruction and the clearing of the acropolis bear witness, but the precise date of this is very far from clear on present evidence. The excavator connects it with the end of the earlier Acropolis building (Building B), before the later Persian Building A (Bennett, 1977: 1-10 [5]; 1983: 9-17). At Tell el-Kheleifeh, Glueck described his Period IV, the final Edomite period, as 'destroyed before the end of the sixth century BCE', but again, the dating is not precise (Glueck, 1970: 164). Re-examination has suggested that the pottery associated with the second major architectural phase, the fortified settlement with offset/inset wall, must be dated between the eighth and early sixth century BCE (though occupation of Tell el-Kheleifeh continued into the fifth and perhaps the fourth century BCE (Pratico, 1985: 1-32 [26]). The date of the end of Iron Age occupation at Tawilan is equally uncertain. The excavator notes that 'The site seems to have had a continuity of occupation at least down to the time of Nabonidus' (Bennett, 1984: 1-19 [19]), though once again the evidence seems imprecise. Apart from the pottery, the clearest indication of the date of the end of occupation, at least in Trench II in the south-eastern area of the site, was the discovery of a cuneiform tablet, probably from the time of Darius I (522-486 BCE) (though the possibility of Darius II (423-405 BCE) or even Darius III (335-331 BCE) is not totally excluded), from the fill-accumulation deposit of Phase IV overlying the destruction of the 'Northern Complex' buildings (Petocz, in Bennett, 1984: 1-19 [13-14]). Another pertinent find was the hoard of jewellery, probably from the late fifth or fourth century BCE (Petocz, *ibid.*; Maxwell-Hyslop, *ibid.* [Appendix B, 22-23]).

It is not easy to draw any firm conclusions from this evidence. Buseira, Tawilan, and Tell el-Kheleifeh seem to have been destroyed, perhaps in the sixth century BCE, but at each site there is evidence of further occupation (of limited nature at Tawilan) and activity. It is certainly possible that Nabonidus was responsible for the destruction of these places, but if so, it was probably in the interest of subjugation rather than annihilation. If Nabonidus was interested in controlling the trade of the region, as has often been suggested, the permanent destruction of places like Bozrah and Elath was hardly to his advantage. Both cities seem to have recovered and become centres of population and administration or trade in the early Persian period, and the presence of a cuneiform tablet from Harran at Tawilan suggests that Tawilan, though apparently somewhat run-down, was still a centre of activity.

The biblical evidence for events and conditions in Edom in the sixth century BCE is even more difficult to evaluate. Obadiah 1-10, already mentioned, threatens Edom with humiliation (vv. 1-4), pillage (5-6), betrayal (7), loss of political and military leadership (8-9) and final extinction (10). This may be genuinely prophetic, or it may be *vaticinium ex eventu*. In either case, those responsible for Edom's downfall are described in v. 7:

> All your allies have deceived you,
> they have driven you to the border;
> your confederates have prevailed against you;
> your trusted friends have set a trap under you.

Obadiah 11 shows that the prophet saw Edom as being on the Babylonian side in 587 BCE ('you were like one of them'), and for Obadiah the allies and confederates of v. 7 can hardly be any other than the Babylonians (for my earlier view, that Edom's allies and confederates were her Arabian trading partners, see Bartlett, 1972: 26-37 [36]). Obadiah notes with satisfaction that Edom's abstention from rebellion in 587 BCE (which he construes as support for Babylon against Judah) has not saved her in the end; Edomites have been deported just as the people of Judah were. This too may possibly be connected with the campaign of Nabonidus in 552 BCE. Obad. 1-6 reappears in slightly different form in Jer. 49.7-9, 14-16, together with other material including the prose oracles against Edom in vv. 12-13, 17-22. In these the prophet proclaims that Edom will be punished:

> For I have sworn by myself, says the LORD, that Bozrah shall become a horror, a taunt, a waste, and a curse; and all her cities shall be perpetual wastes (vv. 12-13).

> Edom shall become a horror; everyone who passes by it will be horrified and will hiss because of all its disasters. As when Sodom and Gomorrah and their neighbour cities were overthrown, says the LORD, no man shall dwell there, no man shall sojourn in her... (vv. 17-18).

> Therefore hear the plan which the LORD has made against Edom and the purposes which he has formed against the inhabitants of Teman: Even the little ones of the flock shall be dragged away; surely their fold shall be appalled at their fate. At the sound of their fall the earth shall tremble; the sound of their cry shall be heard at the Red Sea. Behold, one shall mount up and fly swiftly like an eagle, and spread his wings against Bozrah, and the heart of the warriors of Edom shall be in that day like the heart of a woman in her pangs (vv. 20-22).

The prophet threatens Edom with depopulation; the inhabitants of Teman, including the children, will be dragged away, and the warriors of Bozrah will be terrified at the approach of 'one... like an eagle', which, if human reference is intended, may indicate the Babylonian army. Ezek. 25.12-14 makes a similar threat:

> ... therefore thus says the LORD God, I will stretch out my hand against Edom, and cut off from it man and beast; and I will make it desolate; from Teman even to Dedan they shall fall by the sword.

Again, there is no explicit reference to the agent of destruction, but the geographical reference of 'from Teman even to Dedan' is highly appropriate to the activities of Nabonidus, who campaigned precisely in this region south of Edom. The most interesting description of the devastation of Edom appears in Mal. 1.2-5:

> 'I have loved you', says the LORD. But you say, 'How hast thou loved us?' 'Is not Esau Jacob's brother?' says the LORD. 'Yet I have loved Jacob, but I have hated Esau; I have laid waste his hill country and left his heritage to jackals of the desert.' If Edom says, 'We are shattered but we will rebuild the ruins,' the LORD of hosts says, 'They may build, but I will tear down, till they are called the wicked country, the people with whom the LORD is angry for ever.' Your own eyes shall see this, and you shall say, 'Great is the LORD, beyond the border of Israel!'

Malachi appears to describe Edom as a land of ruins, and he allows for the possibility that the Edomites might wish to rebuild them. He does not say who was responsible for the destruction, but if Malachi belongs to the end of the sixth century BCE or the first half of the fifth, Nabonidus is a possible and perhaps even a probable candidate. It should be noted that these passages in Obadiah, Jeremiah, Ezekiel and Malachi nowhere suggest that Edom was invaded, overrun or occupied by Arab tribes from the east (though the Ammonites and Moabites are threatened with occupation by 'the people of the East', Ezek. 25.4,10); the references to deportation (Obad. 7), military attack on Bozrah (Jer. 49.22), the location 'from Teman to Dedan' (Ezek. 25.13), and the shattered ruins which need rebuilding (Mal. 1.4) all seem more appropriate to a Babylonian campaign than to a speculative and unevidenced invasion of nomadic Arabs.

There seems little doubt that sometime in the sixth century BCE the kingdom of Edom suffered a disaster. It was most probably inflicted by Nabonidus, king of Babylon. Why he considered it necessary we do not know; he may well have thought it important to have Edom secure in his rear as he marched south to Teima in north-west Arabia. We hear no more of the monarchy in Edom; Nabonidus perhaps replaced the Edomite king with a Babylonian governor, as Nebuchadnezzar had done in Jerusalem. It was at this stage that Edom ceased to exist as an independent state.

Chapter 9

THE LAND OF EDOM IN THE PERSIAN PERIOD

Edom from Babylonian to Persian Rule

If Nabonidus placed Edom under Babylonian administration, we hear nothing of it. It would in any case have been short-lived, for whether Cyrus II of Persia (559-530 BCE) conquered Arabia before or after capturing Babylon, Babylon fell to him in 539 BCE, and any Babylonian administration in Edom would not have survived long. Unfortunately, evidence for Persian administration of Edom and Arabia to its south is almost equally sparse. It will help to mention briefly the relationship of the Arabs to the Persian empire. The fifth-century BCE Greek historian Herodotus, describing the empire of Darius I (522-486 BCE), includes the Arabs in his list of peoples who 'paid no settled tribute, but brought gifts to the king', 'every year a thousand talents of incense' (Hdt. III.97). Herodotus is here probably thinking mainly of the inhabitants of southern Arabia, famous for their frankincense, myrrh, cassia, cinnamon and ladanum (III.107), but he knows of other Arabs in the north, on the southern borders of Palestine, whose help Cambyses II (530-522 BCE) solicited when he crossed the desert region from Palestine to attack Egypt in 525 BCE (III.4-5). These Arabs probably belonged to that Arabian district which Herodotus describes as excluded from the bounds of the fifth satrapy (i.e., Abar Nahar, or Trans-Euphrates) and locates in the coastal region between Gaza and Ienysus (III. 91; III. 5). This district thus appears to have provided the Arabs with trade access to the Mediterranean. Herodotus carefully notes that this district was untaxed, which is consistent with his earlier statement that 'the Arabians were never subject as slaves to the Persians, but had a league of friendship with them from the time when they brought Cambyses on his way as he went into Egypt'. Eph'al, however, noting that 1000 talents of incense (i.e., about 30 tons) is 'an extraordinarily onerous levy', argues that what Herodotus call 'gifts' was in fact revenue from the incense trade for the Persians via the Arabian king to whom they had delegated the collection (Eph'al 1982: 206-10). Presumably the Arabs, beyond the boundaries of the fifth satrapy, preserved a much greater degree of freedom from direct Persian control than those peoples within the satrapy. One might expect this to be true of the difficult Hejaz region to the south of Edom, but an inscription found near the oasis of El-'ula (Old Testament Dedan) (JS 349 Lih.; cf. Jaussen, Savignac, 1914: II. 524-25; Atlas, Pl. CXXXIX; Winnett, 1937: 50-51, pl.VIII; Winnett, Reed, 1970: 115-117; Eph'al 1982: 204) notes that

> Nīrān b.Ḥāḍiru inscribed his name in the time of Gashm b.Shahr
> and 'Abd the governor of Dedan, in the reig[n of . . .].

Winnett argues that the phrase 'governor of Dedan' (not 'governor of Lihyan') suggests the Persian period for this inscription, before the Lihyanite kingdom existed, and that 'the very use of *fḥt* governor implies that the Persians once had a governor in some part of Arabia; otherwise, it is doubtful if the author would have been acquainted with the word' (Winnett, Reed, 1970: 116; cf. Albright, 1953: 1-12). It is easy to go further and assume that the *fḥt ddn*, the governor of Dedan, was a Persian official. However, though the title *fḥt* may have an Aramaic or Akkadian ancestry rather than an Arabic one (Winnett, Reed, *ibid.*), there seems no reason why it would necessarily denote a Persian official. As the Teima inscription and several ostraca from Tell el-Kheleifeh show, Aramaic was known and used in this region in the fifth century BCE. The extent of Persian involvement and administration in northern Arabia remains very uncertain, but it seems unlikely that this region was subject to close control.

The Edomites, however, probably fell within the boundaries of the fifth satrapy, and were subject to Persian rule and administration, at least until the beginning of the fourth century BCE when Persia lost control of Egypt (Eph'al, 1982: 205-206). Unfortunately the Old Testament evidence is minimal, and not very helpful. While we hear of Persian governors in Judah, and a Persian official in Ammonite territory east of the Jordan (if Tobiah, 'the servant, the Ammonite' [Neh. 2.10] may be so described), we have no reference to any such officials in Edom. Mal. 1.2-5 has already been mentioned as suggesting that—perhaps sometime early in the Persian period—the

Edomites were anxious to make good the damage they had suffered. If the book of Joel belongs to the fifth or fourth century BCE, the threat in Joel 3.19 (MT 4.19) that Edom shall become a desolate wilderness 'for the violence done to the people of Judah' shows that Edom was still thought of as being in existence, and that the name Edom was still in use. The absence of the name from the books of Ezra and Nehemiah has been commented upon by many scholars, and it has been suggested that in Ezra 9.1 the MT's reading 'Amorites' in the list of 'peoples of the land' conceals an original 'Edomites', since this name appears in place of 'Amorites' in the parallel list at 1 Esd. 8.69. Whatever the original reading, however, not much weight can be put on this artificial list. At best it would tell us only that in Ezra's time there were still Edomites with whom the people of Judah might intermarry, and in view of the evidence for the settlement of Edomites in southern Judah from late pre-exilic times onwards, such intermarriage was perhaps a matter of real concern to Ezra and his colleagues. But this tells us little or nothing of the state of the population of Edom itself, or of its political situation, in the Persian period.

The archaeological evidence is more promising.

In 1935 Nelson Glueck expressed the view, based upon the results of his surface exploration of Edom, that

> From about the end of EI II in general, but in many sites from about the end of the eighth century on, there is another gap in the history of settled communities in Edom. It lasted till the appearance of the Nabataeans. By the fourth century B.C. they had definitely swung themselves into power by gaining control of the trade routes leading northward from Arabia (Glueck, 1935: 139).

This view of a gap in sedentary occupation of the land between the eighth and the fourth centuries BCE was generally accepted until the evidence from excavations at Umm el-Biyara, Tawilan and Buseira in the 1960s and 1970s revealed that settled communities flourished in Edom from the eighth century through the seventh century and into the sixth century BCE and probably beyond. At Buseira, the later phase of a large building complex in area C contained associated Persian period pottery, and the similarity of this building to the later 'winged' building A on the acropolis suggested to the excavator that this building also might be dated to the Persian period (Bennett, 1977: 1-10 [8-9]). It appears to have been built above the destruction

level of the preceding Iron II building B. Buseira-Bozrah was clearly
an important centre, and after the departure of the Babylonians it
probably remained the centre for whatever Persian administration
was imposed upon the land. This administration might have been
responsible for a stamped jar-handle which has been tentatively
assigned to the fifth century BCE (Bennett, 1975: 1-15 [15]). The
evidence for the dating of the later phases at Tawilan is not easy to
assess; the excavator notes a continuity of occupation from the
eighth century 'at least down to the time of Nabonidus' (Bennett
1984: 1-19 [19]). However, in Trench II a cuneiform tablet dated to
the 'accession year of Darius king of the lands' (whether Darius I, II
or III is not clear) was found in the fill-accumulation deposit (Phase
IV) above the destruction level of the Northern Buildings, and a
hoard of jewellery whose use has been dated to the late sixth-fifth
centuries BCE was found close to (though probably not associated
with) a burial interred in Phase IV of the same Trench (*ibid.*:
Appendix A [Dalley], 19-22; Appendix B [Maxwell-Hyslop], 22-23).
These finds indicate at least some human activity at the site in the
Persian period, though this area of Tawilan seems to have been at
least partly ruined. What is particularly interesting is that the
cuneiform tablet witnesses to trade contacts between Edom and
Harran in northern Syria in the Persian period, and that the gold
jewellery witnesses to 'the possible connections between Tawilan
goldsmiths . . . and jewellers and goldsmiths working within the
neighbouring Persian province of Idumaea or at the sites with a
tradition of jewellery production open to influence from other parts
of the Achaemenid empire' (Maxwell-Hyslop, 1984: 22). Whatever
the state of Tawilan in the late sixth-fifth century BCE, the tablet and
the jewellery are important pieces of evidence for the continuance of
human activity and society in Edom into the Persian period. The
tablet also indicates that the Akkadian language and cuneiform script
might be understood by at least some officials and traders in Edom;
Horsfield and Conway noted in 1930 that 'five stone pencils,
seemingly for writing cuneiform, were dug up at Petra (Pl:10), but no
cuneiform tablets have yet been found' (1930: 369-90 [379]).

There is no evidence that the settlement on the top of Umm el-
Biyara lasted beyond the seventh century BCE, but its very existence
suggests that there was Edomite occupation in some sense of the
valley beneath, endowed as it is with running water. What the level

of occupation was through the sixth and fifth centuries we do not know. Greek pottery from the late fourth century BCE attests trade (cf. Horsfield, Conway, 1930: 369-90 [379], who note also the presence of Rhodian jar-handles and 'a terra-cotta head of a horse, 1½ inches long, in style and perhaps in date of a type that approximates closely to those from the pediments of the Parthenon [Pl.11]'). A.H.M. Jones commented that '[Petra's] wealth in the Persian period is attested by the persistent attempts made by Antigonus, only twenty years after the Macedonian conquest, to destroy it' (Jones, 1971: 232). The Semitic name of the place, preserved by Josephus (*Ant.* IV.4.7 [82], 7.1 [161]) and attested by an inscription discovered in the Siq (Starcky, 1965: 95-97), was Reqem, a name connected by Num. 31.8 with the Midianites. The date of this reference is not certain, but if we see Num. 31 with most scholars as among the later strands of the Pentateuch (Noth, 1968: 229-30) it may indicate that the name Reqem was known and associated with the Midianite area early in the post-exilic era. Another pointer to the earlier importance of Reqem/Petra may be the Nabataean sanctuary of the Great High Place of Zibb Atuf, which, Glueck argued, has much in common with the sanctuary at Khirbet Tannur (Glueck, 1966: 63, 78, 85, 86). Both sanctuaries are likely to have had a long cultic history behind them before the Nabataeans developed them.

Tell el-Kheleifeh was certainly occupied and active in the Persian period. Glueck noted that his Period IV, which he saw as the final Edomite period, was 'destroyed before the end of the sixth century BCE', and that 'a new industrial city [Period V] was built over it which lasted from near the end of the sixth or from early in the fifth century B.C., mainly under Persian administration' (Glueck, 1967c: 429-52 [442]; 1970:134). Aramaic ostraca were found witnessing to trade with Arabia (see ch. 12 below, ostraca nos. 4, 6, 8 [Glueck's nos. 2069, 2071, and 7094]; for the probable use of the Aramaic language and script in Edom for official purposes during the Persian period, see Bartlett, 1979: 53-66 [55-56]); fifth-fourth centuries BCE black-glazed Greek pottery indicated trade or contact with Greece. 'Tell el-Kheleifeh was abandoned thereafter, and the subsequent Nabataean settlement was located further to the east, at Aila, close to present day Aqabah' (Glueck, 1967c.: 443; 1970: 135-57).

There can be little doubt, therefore, that occupation of the land of Edom continued from the Babylonian period into the Persian period.

The Edomite monarchy might have been removed by Nebuchadnezzar or Nabonidus, and some devastation inflicted upon the towns and villages, but we have no evidence of any wholesale deportation of people, and we must assume that for most people, especially in the country, life went on much as usual. If the Babylonians sacked Bozrah, the Edomite capital, destroying its royal, administrative and cultic buildings, it is hard to believe that the peasant farmers, shepherds and goatherds in the surrounding hills would not have continued to exist, living as far above or below subsistence level as their skill and the climate allowed. It is most unlikely that the towns and villages of Edom were erased permanently by Babylonian activity; settlements depend on the presence of a local water supply and that presence would inevitably attract the occupation and rebuilding of that site as soon as the destroying army had passed. Thus Malachi portrays the Edomites as saying, 'We are shattered but we will rebuild the ruins' (Mal. 1.4). Malachi went on to prophesy that their attempts were doomed to failure, and the evidence from Tawilan does not indicate any great or lasting success. There is sufficient evidence to show that life went on, though Eph'al's suggestion that Persian administration did not last beyond the death of Darius II (1982: 205-206) may well be right.

Edom and the Qedarites

It has often been argued that after the Babylonians came the Arabs, with final devastating effect upon Edom. Thus, for example, John Bright noted that 'By approximately the end of the sixth century Edom had been entirely taken over by Arab tribes, and sedentary occupation there had ended' (Bright, 1965:332). The picture here drawn of a nomadic Arab occupation of the land of Edom is the correlative of an over-simplified view of the absence of sedentary occupation there between the Edomites and the Natabaeans. We have already seen that this thesis can no longer be supported from the archaeological evidence. The question of Arab invasion, however, needs further examination. In particular, we need to consider which Arabs might have been involved, and what evidence there is for Arab occupation of Edom.

The Arab groups most likely (on geographical and other grounds) to have attacked, invaded or occupied Edom are the Nebaioth and the Qedarites, named in Gen. 25.13 and 1 Chron. 1.29 as the first and secondborn sons of Ishmael. They were famous for their animal husbandry; the flocks of Kedar and the rams of Nebaioth are among the gifts that will be brought to Israel from the wealth of the nations (Isa. 60.7), and similarly Ezek. 27.21 describes the princes of Kedar as 'favoured dealers in lambs, rams, and goats'. The Qedarites lived in tents (Ps. 120.5; Cant. 1.5) or in villages (*ḥăṣērîm*, Isa. 42.11). Jer. 49.28-33 describes the Qedarites as 'a nation at ease, that dwells securely, that has no gates or bars, that dwells alone' (v. 31), and prophesies the pillage of their tents, flocks, curtains, goods, camels, and herds of cattle. Isa. 21.16f. prophesies the end of 'the glory of Kedar': 'the remainder of the archers of the mighty men of the sons of Kedar will be few; for the Lord, the God of Israel, has spoken'.

These Old Testament references give little clue to the precise geographical location of the Qedarites or to their history (except for Jer. 49.28-33, which pictures Nebuchadrezzar's campaign against them). The Assyrian records, however, are more helpful. Sennacherib campaigned c. 690 BCE against the Arabs, who were led by Te-'-el-ḫu-nu, queen of the Arabs, and Hazael, king of the Qedarites. The campaign ended at *uruAdummatu* (Dumat al-Jandal, perhaps the biblical Dumah, at the south-eastern end of the Wadi Sirhan [see Eph'al, 1982: 118-23]), to which the Arab leaders had fled. Under Esarhaddon (681-669 BCE), Hazael was succeeded by his son Yauṭa' (in some texts spelt *Ia-u-ta'*, and in others *U-a-a-te-'*, apparently by confusion with another Arab king, his uncle *U-a-a-te'* son of Birdāda, king of *Su-mu-AN* [see Eph'al 1982:146]). Yauta' rebelled and was defeated (Eph'al, 1982: 128-29). Under Ashurbanipal (668-627 BCE), Yauta' again rebelled, and was active in the regions of Syria and Transjordan. We hear that Ashurbanipal defeated him in various places, including

> the *girû* of the towns of Azaril (and) Hirata (-) kasaia, in Edom, in the pass of Iabrudu, in Beth-Ammon, in the district of Haurina, in Moab, in Sa'arri, in Harge in the district of Zobah (*ANET*³ 298; Eph'al, 1982: 147-55, especially 147-50).

This list perhaps indicates that there was a chain of Assyrian garrisons stretching along the western edge of the Syro-Arabian desert from the district of Zobah in the north to Edom in the south, along the route of the 'King's Highway' (Oded, 1970: 177-86 [184-

86]). Ashurbanipal could apparently count on the help of his vassal kings against the Qedarites, for when another Qedarite king, Ammuladi, apparently a contemporary of Yauta's successor Abiyaṭe', rebelled,

> Kamashaltu, king of Moab, a servant belonging to me inflicted a defeat in open battle upon Ammuladi, king of Qedar who, like him (Abiate'), had revolted and had continuously made razzias against the kings of the Westland (*ANET*[3] 298: Eph'al, 1982: 151-52).

When Abiyaṭe' himself rebelled, joining Uaiṭe' son of Birdāda, king of *Su-mu-An* and Natnu king of Nebaioth, Ashurbanipal defeated them in a three-month campaign which began in the Tadmor (Palmyra) region and moved via Damascus to the el-Leja region (Eph'al, 1982: 157-64). Nebuchadrezzar's campaign against the Qedarites, mentioned in Jer. 49.28-33 and probably in the Babylonian Chronicle (see Wiseman, 1956: 31-32, 70-71), also belongs to the Syrian desert east of Damascus rather than to the Transjordan further south. (If Nebuchadrezzar was based in Syria, the Arabs whom he plundered are more likely to have been from the regions of south-eastern Syria and northern Jordan than from further south; see Bartlett, 1982: 13-24 [16], and Eph'al, 1982: 172-73. This makes it surprising that Eph'al should wish to emend 2 Kgs 24.2 to read 'Edomites', for the MT 'Syrians' here makes perfectly good geographical and historical sense [Bartlett, 1982: 16].) All these references suggest that the Qedarites might be found ranging the Syrian desert almost anywhere between Palmyra and Damascus in the north and the borders of Moab and Edom in the south or the oasis of Dumah in the Jauf region of Wadi Sirhan to the east. And while they suggest that in the declining years of the Assyrian empire, the Qedarites might raid the Assyrian vassal kingdoms of Syria and Transjordan, they do not suggest anything like Qedarite occupation and settlement in them.

It has been argued, however, that with the decline and fall of the Assyrian and Babylonian empires, Qedarite power and control expanded, developing into a 'kingdom', whose 'confederate or allied peoples were distributed from the Syrian desert to North Arabia and were found in the Persian period to the south of Palestine and in the Delta region' (cf. Dumbrell, 1971: 33-44 [44]: Lemaire, 1974: 63-72 [70]). (Lemaire's support is based on his reading and interpretation of an inscription on an incense altar from Lachish as referring to a king of Qedar, Iyas the son of Mahlai; but for other readings of this inscription, see Dupont-Sommer in O. Tufnell, *Lachish* III [1953]: 358-59; Milik, 1958/59: 334, no. 4; Cross, 1969: 19-24; Aharoni, 1968: 163-64. Lemaire's identification of Iyas as a king of Qedar remains a guess.) In the fifth century BCE, Judah's major enemies were Sanballat, the governor of Samaria, Tobiah, a ruler in the former Ammonite territory, and Geshem the Arab (Neh. 2.19; 6.1f., cf. 4.7). The growing importance of the Arabs to the south of Judah is revealed by various references in the work of the Chronicler (2 Chron. 17.11; 21.16; 22.1; 26.7) (for the 'Arabs that dwelt in Gurbaal' (2 Chron. 26.7) see Williamson 1982: 335). Geshem has been seen as the *de facto* ruler in Edom in the mid-fifth century BCE. Thus J.M. Myers states; 'By the time of Nehemiah, Geshem was in control of both Edom proper and the Edomite territory seized from Judah, since Edom is nowhere mentioned in either Nehemiah or Ezra' (Myers, 1971: 377-92 [386]). This Geshem has been identified by many with Gašmu, who is named on an inscription on a silver bowl found at Tell el-Maskhūṭa near Ismailia in the eastern delta region of Egypt. The typology of the bowl and the palaeography of the inscription suggest a date c. 400 BCE. The inscription reads:

> That which Qaynu, son of Gašmu, king of Qedar, offered to Han-'ilat (Dumbrell, 1971: 33-44, and references there given).

The identification of Gašmu, king in the mid-fifth century BCE, with Nehemiah's opponent Geshem is clearly possible, if not absolutely certain. The further identification of Gašmu and/or Geshem with a certain Gashm son of Shahr who appears on a Lihyanite inscription from near El-'ula (Dedan) is much less certain and indeed unlikely, for Gashm is not called 'king of Qedar', and the name *gšm* was not uncommon in that region (JS 349 Lih.: Winnett [1937:51] identified Geshem the Arab and Gashm son of Shahr, but later [1970:116] said that the identification of these names and the Gašmu of the bowl was 'a moot question', the name *gšm* being not uncommon, and particularly common in Safaitic).

The presence of Arabs in the fifth century BCE to the south of Palestine, excluded from the boundaries of the satrapy of Trans-Euphrates, is clear from the evidence of Herodotus, and this fits well with the reference to Geshem the Arab as an opponent of Nehemiah and with the presence of the dedicatory bowl at Tell el-Maskhūṭa bearing the name of Qaynu son of Gašmu, king of Qedar. But these references do not allow us to infer that the Qedarites had occupied and taken political control of Edom, which, like Judah, fell within the Persian satrapy and under Persian administration at least until 400 BCE. In the absence of further evidence, the extent of Qedarite influence in Edom in the fifth century must remain very uncertain. What Qedarite influence there may have been, by way of raiding or settlement, does not seem to have left any mark on later understanding or memory of the subsequent history of Edom. From the late fourth century onwards the inhabitants of what had been Edom called themselves Nabaṭu and were known to Greek writers as Nabataioi and to modern historians as Nabataeans. The Qedarite name, if it was ever important in Edom, did not survive.

Edom and the Nebaioth

In the Old Testament the people of Qedar are closely associated with a people called the Nebaioth (Isa. 60.7; Gen. 25.13; 1 Chron. 1.29), and a similar association is found in the Rassam Cylinder accounts of Ashurbanipal's campaigns against the Arabs, in which Abiyaṭe' the king of Qedar allies himself with Natnu, king of the Nabaiati (*ANET*³ 299; Eph'al, 1982: 157). There is little doubt that the Assyrian *Na-ba-a-a-ti* and the Old Testament Nebaioth are the same people. But whereas the people of Qedar are not connected in any way with Edom in the biblical tradition, the Nebaioth are. According to Gen. 28.9 and 36.3, Esau, whom the Israelite tradition came to identify as the ancestor of the Edomites, married Mahalath and Basemath; both were daughters of Abraham's son Ishmael and sisters of Nebaioth. Because the Edomites were later succeeded in the region south-east of the Dead Sea by the Nabataeans, it has always been tempting to identify the Nebaioth with the later Nabataeans. The identification is attractive on several grounds. The names are reasonably similar (though not quite identical). Both Nebaioth and Nabataeans are identified in the historical sources as Arabs. The Nebaioth lived in the North Arabian desert east of Edom in the seventh century BCE, while the Nabataeans appear to be people with desert traditions occupying Edom from the fourth century BCE onwards. The Old Testament links the Nebaioth and the Qedarites, and similarly the first century CE. Roman historian Pliny (*Nat. Hist.* V.12) links the Nabataei and the Cedrei. The identification, however of the Old Testament Nebaioth and the Nabataeans has been firmly opposed by many scholars on the linguistic grounds that, first, the *t* of the Assyrian *Na-ba-a-a-ti*, the O.T. Nebaioth, and the *nbyt* mentioned in the Jebel Ghunaym inscriptions as enemies of the people of Teima is unlikely to have become the emphatic ṭ of the Nabaṭu of the Nabataean sources, and, secondly, the final elements - *a-ti* (Assyrian records), -ôṭ(O.T.), or -*t* (Jebel Ghunaym) are inflectional endings, the root of the name being *nby* rather than *nbt* or *nbṭ* (cf. Montgomery, 1934: 31, n. 16; Starcky, 1966: cols 886-1017 [902-903]; Eph'al, 1982: 221-23). On this view, the Nabataeans are not to be identified with the Old Testament Nebaioth and the Assyrian *Na-ba-a-a-ti*, and their origin remains a mystery. A recent attempt to explain how the change from *Na-ba-a-a-ti*, Nebaioth or *nbyt* to *nabaṭu* might have come about (Broome, 1973: 1-16) has met the serious criticism that it is relying on 'the spelling *mar Na-bat-ta-a-a* in ABL 305, which does not necessarily refer to the *Nabayati*', and 'systematically ignores the phonetic value *ca-a-a* = *aya* in *Na-ba-a-a-ti/te*, *Na-ba-a-a-ta/ta-a-a*, which is customary in Assyrian sources' (Eph'al, 1982: 223, n. 33), and the philological objections to the identification therefore remain.

However, there can be no doubt that the Old Testament tradition thought of the Nebaioth as the most important of the Arab tribes (cf. the genealogy of Gen. 25.13 and 1 Chron. 1.29) and as being linked by marriage with the Edomites (Gen. 28.9; 36.3). This last point suggests that the Nebaioth were also thought of as belonging, at least originally, to much the same part of the world as the Edomites. The available evidence is limited, but the location of the Nebaioth can be plotted with reasonable certainty from the evidence of the Assyrian inscriptions and by inference from the position of other Arab tribes. After being defeated in Syria and Transjordan, Yauta' king of Qedar fled to Natnu, king of the *Na-ba-a-a-ti*, whose country, Ashurbanipal noted, lay at a great distance (Rassam Cylinder viii.24ff.: *ANET*[3] 298; Eph'al, 1982: 250) and had not submitted to Assyria (Ishtar Temple inscription, 123f.: *ANET*[3], 300). Clearly the Nebaioth lived in the desert beyond normal Assyrian rule and administration, and the texts from Jebel Ghunaym referring to the wars (of Teima?) against the *nbyt* suggest that the *nbyt*, the Nebaioth and the *Na-ba-a-a-ti* belong to the region south of that controlled by the Qedarites. The obvious area for them to occupy is that bounded by the mountains of Edom to the west, the Ḥismā plateau to the south-west, Teima to the south, the Nafūd to the east, and the Wadi Sirhan to the north-east (see Bartlett, 1979: 53-66 [60, fig. 1]). Clearly the Nebaioth were in the best position of all the Arab groups to invade or infiltrate and occupy the land of Edom immediately to their west. There is no documentary evidence to suggest that they attacked or occupied Edom, but it would hardly be surprising to find that individual members of this group had settled and inter-married with Edomites. While it is true that there remain obstacles to the equation of the names Nebaioth and *Nabaṭu*, it is nevertheless interesting and perhaps significant that while the Nebaioth are famous for their rams (Isa. 60.7) the Nabataeans are said by Diodorus Siculus to be breeders of cattle, camels and sheep and to practise the life-style of the desert: they eat meat and milk and foods that grow wild; they do not plant grain or fruit trees or cultivate vines, and they do not build houses—indeed, these activities are forbidden. When threatened, they retreat to the desert, which they use as their refuge, having perfected the art of conserving water in concealed cisterns (Diod. Sic. XIX:94). All this suggests that the Nabataeans, who according to Diodorus and his source Hieronymus of Cardia were already in occupation of Edom by 312 BCE when Antigonus' general Athenaeus attacked them, were a people with recent experience of a desert existence. Their life-style as described by Diodorus was hardly very different from that of Nebaioth, and their place of origin must have been in much the same general area as the home of the Nebaioth.

The Edomite monarchy came to an end in the mid-sixth century BCE and lapsed into the administration of first the Babylonian and then the Persian empire. Human occupation and activity did not cease, but social and economic conditions must have changed as urban life suffered disaster or decayed, and peasant farmers cultivated their crops as their fathers had done, but increasingly alongside newcomers who pastured their flocks over the hills and competed for the use of the springs. On the wider political field, Edom had ceased to count for anything, as is shown by the absence of any reference to her in the books of Ezra and Nehemiah. There is no certain evidence that the Persians took much thought for this mountainous region on the desert fringes of the Trans-Euphrates satrapy. It was not until the arrival of the Hellenistic world that the land which had once been called Edom began to revive socially, economically and politically; and just over a century later the new Nabataean dynasty began its rule.

Chapter 10

EDOM AND JUDAH

Edom and Esau

As has already been noted, much of our evidence for the history of ancient Edom comes from the literature of the kingdom of Judah, Edom's principal enemy. All the Old Testament writers who mention Edom owed allegiance to Jerusalem—the Yahwistic and Priestly editors of Genesis—Numbers, the Deuteronomist, the Deuteronomistic historian, the Chronicler, the author of Lamentations, the prophets Isaiah, Jeremiah, Ezekiel, Joel, Amos (though his words were spoken in the kingdom of Israel), Obadiah, Malachi and their editors, and the author of 1 Esdras. We are therefore in a strong position to observe Judah's attitude towards Edom, and perhaps to relate it to their political history. It is clear that Judah consistently regarded Edom as a fierce enemy, and later as a particularly treacherous enemy who would receive her deserts from Yahweh. At no time in history does Edom seem to have had a friendly relationship with Judah. Relationships between Edom and Judah seem to have been worse, on the whole, than relationships between the other Transjordanian states and Judah and Israel. Yet Edom is called in several places 'brother' to Israel or Judah, a position and title not given to Moab or the Ammonites. This peculiar relationship, illustrated in Genesis by the stories of Jacob and Esau, demands explanation.

According to Gen. 25.21-25:

> Isaac prayed to the LORD for his wife, because she was barren; and the LORD granted his prayer, and Rebekah his wife conceived. The children struggled together within her; and she said, 'If it is thus, why do I live?' So she went to inquire of the LORD. And the LORD said to her,

'Two nations are in your womb,
and two peoples, born of you, shall be divided;
the one shall be stronger than the other,
the elder shall serve the younger.'

When her days to be delivered were fulfilled, behold, there were
twins in her womb. The first came forth red, and all his body like a
hairy mantle; so they called his name Esau.

This story identifies Rebekah's children, Jacob and Esau, as the
ancestors of two nations, and the description of Esau as 'red'
(Hebrew *'admônî*) appears to pun on the name Edom, thus
connecting Esau with Edom. The connection is made explicit in the
famous story of the selling of Esau's birthright for pottage (Gen.
25.29f.)

Once when Jacob was boiling pottage, Esau came in from the field,
and he was famished. And Esau said to Jacob, 'Let me eat some of
that red pottage, for I am famished!' (Therefore was his name
called Edom.)

The theme of the identification of Jacob and Esau as ancestors of
nations appears to be continued in the blessings given to each by
their father Isaac. To Jacob Isaac says:

'See, the smell of my son
is as the smell of a field which the LORD has blessed!
May God give you the dew of heaven,
and of the fatness of the earth,
and plenty of grain and wine.
Let peoples serve you,
and nations bow down to you.
Be lord over your brothers,
and may your mother's sons bow down to you.
Cursed be everyone who curses you,
and blessed be everyone who blesses you!'

(Gen. 27.27-29)

By contrast, to Esau Isaac says:

'Behold, away from the fatness of the earth shall your dwelling be,
and away from the dew of heaven on high.
By your sword you shall live,
and you shall serve your brother;
but when you break loose
you shall break his yoke from your neck.'

(Gen. 27.39-40)

As this material stands in Genesis, there can be little doubt that the reader is meant to see it as referring to the historical and political relationships known to exist between Edom and Judah. Esau is linked with Edom by being described as 'red' at birth and as eating 'red pottage', the pun on Edom being made explicit in the latter case (Gen. 25.30). In this context, the references of Gen. 25.23 ('the elder shall serve the younger'), Gen. 27.29 ('Let peoples serve you . . . be lord over your brothers'), and Gen. 27.49 ('you shall serve your brother') are probably intended to bring to mind the period of Edom's subjection to Judah from the time of David to the revolt from Judah in Jehoram's reign in the mid-ninth century BCE. The words of Gen. 27.40b ('but when you break loose you shall break his yoke from your neck') recall the Edomite revolt and may, as some scholars think, have been added to the original oracle in the light of it; if, however, they are an original, integral part of the oracle, as they might well be, the author or editor is probably writing after the mid-ninth century BCE, which is likely on other grounds (for fuller discussion of these passages, see Bartlett, 1977: 2-27 [18-20]; Blank, 1936: 159-92 [177]).

However, it is also clear that the identification of the two brothers with the two nations is unlikely to have been an original element in the Jacob-Esau stories. The old stories of the rivalry of Jacob and Esau have been used to illustrate the rivalry of Judah and Edom, but it is unlikely that this was their original function. There are signs that the stories have been made to fit a new situation. For example, there is no immediately obvious reason why Esau should be the eponymous ancestor of the Edomites. The name Esau is quite unlike the name Edom, and in order to make the connection, Esau has to be described as born red or as eating red pottage. In each case, the redness has been deliberately introduced into the story. In Gen. 25.25, the adjective 'red' comes awkwardly into the verse, for it does not explain the name Esau and is not necessarily appropriate to a hairy mantle; and as we know from Gen. 27.11, Esau is properly described solely as 'a hairy man' in contrast to his brother Jacob, who is 'a smooth man'. In Gen. 25.30, instead of asking for pottage (Heb. *nāzīd*), as one would expect, Esau asks for 'the red, that red (stuff)', which is either a deliberate change from 'pottage' to make the point of Esau's connection with Edom, or perhaps, as Gunkel suggested, an earthy joke at Esau's expense, Esau being portrayed as not knowing what else to call the pottage. The story-teller adds his gloss: 'Therefore was his name called Edom' (see further Bartlett, 1969: 1-20 [11-12]).

It seems, then, that Esau's connection with Edom is, as has long been recognised, secondary and not original. Von Rad, following M. Noth, held that:

> The Esau of [Gen.] ch. 27 and ch. 33 belongs in East Jordan in the history of tradition. He is not the ancestor of a nation at all, but just that type of hunter which the people of Jacob, who were colonising East Jordan, met and whom they as shepherds recognised ... as having a different way of life from their own. Only after a subsequent transfer of this narrative complex into the Judaean south did that connection with Edom occur according to which the Judaeans identified the figure of Esau with those neighbours who were their greatest rivals (von Rad, 1972: 275-76).

Esau became identified in the Israelite tradition as the eponymous ancestor of Edom because as a 'hairy man' and a hunter he seemed an appropriate figure, and because no other eponymous figure was known to tradition. This choice of eponymous ancestor for Edom also expressed the knowledge that there was some fairly close if historically indefinable relationship between the people of Israel and the people of Edom; through the figure of Esau the relationship became one of brotherhood.

We can see to some extent the process by which this tradition developed. If the Esau tradition originally was at home (as von Rad suggested) in the central Transjordan, it became newly connected with the regions of Beersheba and southern Palestine when the Jacob-Esau traditions became attached to the traditions about Abraham and Isaac. Thus Esau became a figure whom Judaeans could connect with the wilderness regions on the southern borders of Judah, and it was probably at this stage that Esau became connected with the region of Seir. The connection between Edom and Seir is strong in the tradition, and is probably earlier than the connection between Esau and Edom. When Esau is described as 'a hairy man' (Gen. 27.11), the Hebrew phrase (*'îš śā'îr*) clearly puns on the place-name Seir (*śē'îr*), and the same pun appears in Gen. 25.25 with the description of Esau as 'like a hairy mantle' (*kĕadderet śē'ār*). An examination of the material in Gen. 36 shows clearly that there too Esau belongs primarily to Seir, and that the connection with Edom has been made secondarily. If we ignore the king-list (Gen. 36.31-39), which has no reference to Esau or Seir, and the two lists of 'chiefs' (vv. 15-19, based on vv. 9-14, and vv. 40-43, based on several place-names), the remaining material deals primarily with Esau and Seir, the only references to Edom appearing in the editorial explanatory phrases 'that is, Edom', 'Esau is Edom', 'the father of the Edomites', and 'in the land of Edom' in vv. 1, 8, 9, 21. These phrases belong to the same tradition as the references in Gen. 25.25, 30 discussed above. The connection of Esau with Seir appears again in the story of the meeting of Jacob and Esau in Gen. 32.3–33.17; the story begins when Jacob sends messengers to Esau 'in the land of Seir' (to which has been added the explanatory phrase 'the country of Edom') and ends with Esau returning to Seir (Gen. 33.14, 16). Deut. 2.4, 5, 8 locate the sons of Esau in Seir, as does the Deuteronomic passage Josh. 24.4 (see Bartlett, 1969: 9-11).

It was this previous connection of Esau with the region of Seir (which lay to the south-east of Judah, between Judah and Edom) (see above, pp. 41-44) that facilitated the identification of the figure of Esau with the country of Edom. According to the tradition, Esau, the brother of Jacob, was a fierce and hostile figure, whose clans belonged to the wilderness regions on the southern borders of Judah (see above, pp. 86-90). It was an easy step to make such a figure, from the borders of Judah and Edom, the ancestor of the Edomites, notoriously fierce and hostile towards Judah; and in this way, Edom became 'brother' to the people of Judah. Esau was the older brother, and so the oracle of Gen. 25.23 has it that 'the elder shall serve the younger' (cf. Gen. 27.40), probably with references to the conquest of Edom by David and the ensuing status of Edom as 'David's servants' (2 Sam. 8.14). The fact that Esau was the elder brother may also have something to do with the attribution to Edom in Gen. 36.31 of a monarchy earlier than Israel's.

It is hard to date Judah's identification of Edom with Esau and his clans, but it is unlikely to have happened before hostilities arose between the two peoples. As we have seen, it is impossible to reconstruct with any confidence any hostile meeting between Israelite and Edomite clans at the time of the Exodus or in the time of the Judges. It is not until the time of Saul and David that we see evidence of real conflict. The references in Genesis to Judah and Edom under the guise of Jacob and Esau suggest that Edom's vassaldom to Judah and her subsequent rebellion are known. It was probably in the early monarchic period that the identification of Edom with Esau arose and became established in Israelite tradition. At all events, the picture of Edom as a fierce brother, sword in hand (Gen. 27.40), appears again in the oracle against Edom in Amos 1.11f., which, if authentic, dates from the mid-eighth century BCE (cf. Bartlett, 1977: 10-16):

> Thus says the LORD:
> 'For three transgressions of Edom,
> and for four, I will not revoke the punishment;
> because he pursued his brother with the sword,
>   and cast off all pity,
> and his anger tore perpetually
>   and he kept his wrath for ever.
> So I will send a fire upon Teman,
>   and it shall devour the strongholds of Bozrah.'

Much of the case against the authenticity of this oracle depends on an assumption that the reference of these lines is to Edom's behaviour in 587 BCE, but as we have seen, the other evidence does not suggest that Edom behaved in this way in 587 BCE, and the more likely reference of these lines is to the rebellion of Edom from Judah in Jehoram's reign (2 Kgs 8.20-22), some eighty years before Amos' day. Amos' language suggests an act of violence some time in the past and a subsequent period of continued Edomite hatred, both of which are appropriate if the reference is to the Edomite rebellion. But there is also direct criticism here of Edom's unbrotherly behaviour. Edom is no longer simply identified with Esau, from whom one might expect uncouth behaviour—Esau in fact is not mentioned. Here Edom is blamed for assault unworthy of a brother—a relationship which Edom doubtless would have disclaimed—and the historical reasons for Edom's behaviour are ignored. Edom is blamed for her perpetual enmity, and the idea of brotherhood is brought in to underline the enormity of the offence.

Edom's Brotherhood with Israel: The Deuteronomic View

A further reference to Edom's brotherhood with Israel appears in the story of Israel's encounter with Edom in the wilderness period (Num. 20.14-21). Mittmann argues that this story is basically a copy of the similar story about Israel's encounter with Sihon in Num. 21.21-23, with the inclusion of Deuteronomic material from Deut. 26.5-9, and that the whole is the late result of a redactor's compilation (Mittmann, 1973: 143-49). Van Seters argues that Num. 20.14-21 is a late, post-Deuteronomic piece, the messenger speech in vv. 17-19 being dependent on Deut. 2.27-28, and he dates it to the sixth century BCE (van Seters, 1972; 182-97; see further Bartlett, 1978: 347-51; van Seters, 1980: 117-24). As has already been argued (above, pp. 90-93), a number of points suggest that the story as it stands is hardly earlier than the Assyrian period. There is one obvious difference between it and the Sihon story of Num. 21.21-23: Sihon is not stated to be related to Israel, while the king of Edom is addressed with the words, 'Thus says your brother Israel' (Num. 20.14). The author or editor thus knows the tradition of brotherhood (though he describes Israel, not Edom, as the brother). He knows also the tradition of the sword: 'Edom said to him, "You shall not pass through, lest I come out with the sword against you" . . . . . . And Edom came out against them with many men, and with a strong force.' (The Sihon story merely says that 'Sihon would not allow Israel to pass through his territory'.) The author of Num. 20.14-21 was perhaps familiar with the tradition of the Edomite revolt known to Amos and Gen. 27.40.

Another version of the encounter with Edom in the wilderness period appears in Deut. 2.1-8. Interestingly, this version plays down hostility towards Edom. The author speaks of 'your/our brethren the sons of Esau who live in Seir' (accepting the identification of Esau with Edom, clearly well known by his time), and refers to them without bitterness. Indeed, he makes the Lord warn Israel not to contend with the sons of Seir (v. 5), which suggests that he knows the tradition of enmity but disapproves of it. Whether he derives this tradition from Num. 20.14-21, or from Amos 1.11, or Gen. 25–27, or from a generally accepted Israelite attitude, is not clear. Deuteronomy ch. 2 in fact says nothing of an actual encounter, but only that Israel will buy food and water from the sons of Esau (v. 6).

There are some similarities between this passage and the other passage in Deuteronomy which mentions Edom. Deut. 23.7 (MT 23.8) knows of the Edomite as Israel's brother, and makes this the reason for not 'abhorring' an Edomite. Compared with the Ammonites and Moabites, the Edomites are to be given preferential treatment, for the children of the third generation that are born to the Edomites may enter the assembly of the Lord, whereas 'No Ammonite or Moabite shall enter the assembly of the LORD; even to the tenth generation none belonging to them shall enter the assembly of the LORD for ever; because they did not meet you with bread and water on the way, when you came forth out of Egypt. . . ' Deuteronomy ch. 23 and ch. 2 have in common the idea that food (or bread) and water were or were not supplied by the Edomites, Moabites and Ammonites to Israel when Israel came out of Egypt. Israel would be able to buy food and water from Edom (2.6), but was not met with bread and water by the Ammonites and Moabites (23.4). The two passages taken together give a consistent picture, and clearly the Deuteronomist had a higher regard for the Edomites than for the Ammonites and Moabites. The Edomite is different: he is Israel's brother.

The Deuteronomist doubtless derived this idea from the material we have examined above, or perhaps from the tradition represented in that material, but in order to understand what the Deuteronomist meant by describing the Edomite as the Israelite's brother we should examine how the Deuteronomist uses the word elsewhere. In a few passages (13.6; 25.5-10; 28.54; 32.50) he uses it of normal physical brotherhood in the context of a human family. But usually in Deuteronomy the word is used to refer to an Israelite as opposed to an alien (cf. 1.16; 15.2f.; 7; 9; 11f.; 17.15; 23.19f.; Deut. 19.18f. and 22.1-4 probably have fellow Israelites alone in mind). This suggests that in 23.7 the Deuteronomist is saying that the Edomite is not to be treated as a pagan alien, but as a fellow Israelite—at least one whose standing is higher than that of a bastard (cf. Deut. 23.2). Deut. 23.1ff. lists those who are not allowed to enter the assembly of the Lord. Men whose genital organs are damaged are prohibited absolutely; bastards, Ammonites and Moabites are prohibited down to the tenth generation; but Edomites and Egyptians, for reasons given, are not to be abhorred, and 'the children of the third generation that are born to them may enter the assembly of the LORD' (see Bartlett, 1977: 5-8).

This attitude towards the Edomites, and this understanding of the Edomites' brotherhood, is so unlike what we find elsewhere in the Old Testament that it looks very much as if the Deuteronomist is consciously and deliberately opposing the usual abhorrence of Edom. He is clearly well aware of his contemporaries' or his predecessors' dislike of Edom ('you shall not abhor an Edomite'), and meets it by underlining, and subtly reinterpreting, the now established idea that Edom is brother to Israel to mean that the Edomites are to be thought of as related to the Israelite religious community rather than to the pagan world. The Deuteronomist defers to the contemporary view of Edom to the extent that he limits the entry to the assembly to 'the children of the third generation', but at least the Edomites' situation in this respect is much better than that of bastards, Ammonites and Moabites. But why the Deuteronomist took this view is not clear. It is certainly not easy to find a period in the history of Edom's relations with Judah when the Jerusalem community might show any warmth in their feelings towards Edom. It has been suggested that Deuteronomy's friendly tone towards Edom is a surviving echo of the anti-Assyrian league of Ashdod, Judah, Edom and Moab in Hezekiah's time (Cannon, 1927: 129-40; 191-200); but there is little evidence that Edom was a convinced member of any such league, and the Deuteronomist's stress on the point seems more than an echo of a past event or situation. Carmichael argued that the Deuteronomist based his attitude towards Edom on his interpretation of Genesis 33: Deuteronomy's 'positive attitude towards Edom is based on the fact that Esau (Edom) received Jacob (Israel) with brotherly affection after Jacob's flight from Laban' (Carmichael), 1974: 176). One wonders, however, whether this one not very convincing reference to brotherly affection between Jacob and Esau (Gen. 33.4) is enough to make the Deuteronomist oppose the prevailing view of Edom so strongly. Noth related the attitude of Deut. 23.7 to the Deuteronomist's account in Deut. 2.1-8, the difference of which from Num. 20.14-21 derives, according to Noth, from the Deuteronomist's theological view of the conquest: Yahweh had ordained separate settlement areas for Edom and Israel, with the result that for the Deuteronomist Edom had no need to oppose Israel on her journey to the promised land, and Israel had no need to use force against Edom (Noth, 1957: 33-35). Noth is surely right to suppose that the Deuteronomist had theological reasons for his attitude, over and above the received tradition that the Edomite was a 'brother'. The Deuteronomist was above all a theologian; and in particular, a theologian with strong views about Israel's need to reject the admission of non-Yahwistic beliefs and practices into the cult.

The Deuteronomist would have needed a very strong reason for distinguishing Judah's notorious enemies, the Edomites, from such peoples as the Moabites and Ammonites, whose gods were abominations, and for accepting the Edomites, even to a limited degree, into the Israelite worshipping community. Even Noth's suggestion does not adequately explain the Deuteronomist's attitude, for on this view the Deuteronomist's attitude would have to apply to other countries besides Edom. The possibility remains that the Deuteronomist's readiness to accept the Edomites into the religious community of Israel (after a purging period of three generations) may have been based on some knowledge and understanding of the early connection and essential similarity between the Edomite and the Israelite religion. This will be explored in a later chapter, but for the present it must be noted that the Israelite tradition is singularly lacking in condemnation of Edomite religious practices (with which we may contrast its condemnation of those of the Moabites and Ammonites), and indeed speaks of its own deity Yahweh as marching to Israel's aid from the region of Edom and Seir (Judg. 5.4). The Deuteronomist's attitude, in fact, reveals the fundamental reason why the Edomites could be thought of as brothers; they were believed to have a common religious background. This in turn shows why the Edomites became so hated; actively hostile behaviour was only to be expected from peoples like the Ammonites and Moabites, who worshipped abominations and whose origins might be portrayed in the scandalous story of Lot and his daughters (Gen. 19.30-38), but could not be condoned from people who might be seen as co-religionists. From the Edomites, hostility meant treachery.

Post-exilic Views of Edom

We have already examined the part played by Edom in the events surrounding the second capture of Jerusalem by the Babylonians in 587 BCE, and seen something of how Edom's role could be presented and misrepresented in the subsequent Jewish literature. A number of other passages from the later Old Testament writers make it clear that Edom was regarded with little favour in the exilic and post-exilic periods. Thus Jer. 49.12-13, material belonging perhaps to the Deuteronomic prose editors of Jeremiah (cf. Jer. 25.28f.), argues that Edom must, with other nations, drink the cup of punishment. The surrounding verses (Jer. 49.7-11, 14-22), composed from material found also in Obad. 5-6, 14-16 and in Jer. 50.40, 44-46, describe the disasters come or coming upon Edom. Lam. 4.21-22 ironically calls upon Edom to rejoice, threatening her with having to drink the cup that symbolizes punishment. Ezek. 32.29 pictures Edom, her kings and all her princes, along with Egypt, Assyria, Elam, the princes of the north and the Sidonians, lying in Sheol 'with the uncircumcised, with those who go down to the pit'. In Ezek. 36.5 a specific reference to Edom has been added to a general oracle against those who possessed and plundered Israel's land. Mal. 1.2-5 presents Edom as Esau, hated by the Lord (in contrast to Jacob/Israel, who is loved), and proclaims that Edom will be called 'the wicked country, the people with whom the LORD is angry for ever'. A further lesson is to be drawn from this: 'Your own eyes shall see this, and you shall say "Great is the LORD, beyond the border of Israel."' Isa. 11.14 promises that Judah and Ephraim will attack the Philistines, plunder the people of the east, attack Edom and Moab and subdue the Ammonites. (This list of nations to be conquered in Isa. 11.14 has probably influenced the list of enemies in the opening lines of the scroll of *The War of the Sons of Light against the Sons of Darkness.*) A similar hope of reconquest appears in the appendix to the book of Amos:

> 'In that day I will raise up
>> the booth of David that is fallen
>> and repair its breaches,
>> and raise up its ruins,
>> and rebuild it as in the days of old;
> that they may possess the remnant of Edom
>> and all the nations who are called by my name,'
>> says the LORD who does this (Amos. 9.11-12).

The author of Obad. 15-21 vividly expresses his hopes that Jews will again possess Edomite territory:

> The house of Jacob shall be a fire,
>> and the house of Joseph a flame,
>> and the house of Esau stubble;
> they shall burn them and consume them,
>> and there shall be no survivor to the house of Esau;
>> for the LORD has spoken.
> Those of the Negeb shall posses Mount Esau...

> and the exiles of Jerusalem who are in Sepharad
>   shall possess the cities of the Negeb.
> Saviours shall go up to Mount Zion to rule Mount Esau;
>   and the kingdom shall be the LORD's (Obad. 18-21).

A particularly vivid picture of the coming destruction of Edom appears in Isaiah 34. The poem is in fact basically concerned with God's judgment on the nations as a whole (cf. 34.1-4), who are to be slaughtered. The slaughter of Edom, described in terms of a sacrifice (verses 5-7), and the consignment of her land to the fate of Sodom and Gomorrah (verses 8-10) and its future destiny as a wilderness for wild animals (verses 11-17) appear to offer a symbolic example of the wider process of universal destruction. In Isa. 63.1-6 God is pictured as coming from Edom and Bozrah in garments stained from the blood of the peoples he has trodden down in his anger. B. Cresson noted 'a developing tendency to use "Edom" as a designation of the enemies of the Jews' (Cresson, 1972: 125-48 [137]). Edom certainly became the classic example of the enemy of God's people. In later times, Edom was used to refer to Rome and the kings of Edom identified with Roman emperors; thus, for example in Midrash Rabbah Genesis 83-4 Magdiel, as the penultimate chief in the list of Gen. 36.43, is identified with Diocletian (whose successor the rabbinic commentators believed would be the last emperor before the destruction of Rome), and in Leviticus Rabbah 13.5 Rome, under the name of Edom is compared with a boar, as is Esau in 1 Enoch 89.12 (see Freedman, Simon 1939: II. 768; IV. 174; for later Jewish views of Rome, see Vermes, 1975: 215-24).

This very mixed bag of post-exilic references to Edom demonstrates how Edom acquired a symbolic status in post-exilic Israel. Edom was a nation that deserved punishment and would be punished, a people deserving of the Lord's eternal anger. The idea of the reconquest of Edom was used as an expression of the hope of a restored Davidic kingdom. The destruction of Edom was a parable of the destruction of the nations as a whole; indeed, the destruction of the peoples might be pictured as taking place in Edom itself. Edom could be named to symbolise a world empire, seen in opposition to God. It is remarkable that such a small, remote and unsuccessful nation should have had such a deep psychological effect upon its former masters.

Chapter 11

RELIGION IN EDOM

Archaeological Evidence

It is always difficult to describe the place and importance of religion in a society, particularly when that society belongs to the distant past. It is never easy to present accurately the religious practices and beliefs of a society, even with the help of extant historical records, for the written record does not always manage to convey the depths of inner commitment and devotion shared by the faithful. It is practically impossible to give an adequate account of the religion of a people who have left no literature and for whom the architectural and artefactual evidence is hitherto so limited. It is almost inevitable that any attempt to portray Edom's religion will draw on assumed ancient near eastern common religious heritage; on present evidence, for example, it is hard to say how Edom's religion differed from that of her neighbours in north-west Arabia, Transjordan, or even in Israel and Judah. In fact, Edom's religion may not have differed very much from that of Israel and Judah, for various Old Testament texts present Edom and Seir as the homeland of Israel's god Yahweh, and Doeg the Edomite as worshipping at a Yahwist shrine. The point is perhaps strengthened by the fact that the biblical writers neither condemn the Edomite god or gods nor identify him or them by any proper name, though they name and strongly condemn Milcom and Chemosh, the gods of the Ammonites and Moabites respectively.

We shall return to discuss the biblical evidence for Edomite religion, and the name of the Edomite god, in due course. We shall begin by listing the architectural and artefactual evidence currently available to us. The most obvious evidence for Edomite religion might be the presence of sanctuaries or temple buildings. In 1930 George Horsfield and Agnes Conway (1930: 375-76, fig. 2, Pl.V) published their discovery of a megalithic circle 72 feet in diameter outside the north wall of Petra on a rock whose highest point it encloses. The exterior of the wall was plastered with lime and the joints between the stones filled in and wedged with small ones. It has the appearance of typical Mediterranean bronze age masonry, not uncommon in other parts of Trans-jordan, in watch towers and foundations of strong places. This was a retaining wall, a single stone thick, showing no sign of tooling, the inside filled to the peak of the rock with red sand. Beyond this again on the face of the fall of rock is cut a flight of steps. . . . This may have been a primitive sanctuary of the period before the revelation of Moses, when Edomites and Israelites followed the same religious tradition; a natural rock altar, enclosed by a wall because it was sacred.

This sanctuary appears to be located above the city of Petra, overlooking it from the north, on Jebel Me'esara. Without further evidence its dating must remain uncertain, but as described it seems not unlike other 'high places' at Petra. Mountain sanctuaries tend to be revered as holy places for many generations, sometimes being adopted by a succession of cults and religions, and this may have been the case at another site in ancient Edom, Jebel et-Tannūr, a white conical mountain lying immediately south of the Wadi el-Ḥasā, just west of the main north-south road, the 'King's Highway'. The Nabataeans erected a temple there in the first century BCE, and Glueck guesses, reasonably enough, that the Edomites had worshippped there before them (1966:85); he found there a small crude animal figurine 'which might possibly have been handed down somehow or other from an earlier period. It seems too crude to be Nabataean, and has affinities in general workmanship with the early Iron Age figurines found near Buseirah; it is, however, impossible to date' (Glueck, 1938: 8-9). A Nabataean inscription found here dedicates a stele to Qos or Qosallah (Glueck, 1966: 514f., Pl. 196), but this need not suggest that Qos was worshipped here in pre-Nabataean times, though certainly Qos may have been.

Excavation on the acropolis at Buseira revealed a building which has been interpreted as either a temple or a palace (Bennett, 1977: 1-10 [9]). This was 'Building B', covering an area of some 2,400 square metres, and apparently founded on a deep fill of some 2-4 metres thick; the excavator suggests this was 'to give the Acropolis an overall dominance over the surrounding countryside' (Bennett, 1983: 9-17 [13]), but it seems more likely that it was to provide a large level area for building, for the natural shape of the hill already gave a fair dominance to the building. However, the building appears to face north-east, and to have been fronted by a rectangular plastered courtyard of about 25 by 20 metres. In the south corner of this, against the main building, was a small room from which a drain led across the yard to a central cistern. Another drain led out of the courtyard, apparently from the cistern and through the entrance by the northern corner. These drains, as described, are a little puzzling. It is not clear that the first drain actually empties into the cistern; it may skirt it and become the second drain which exists through the north corner. Certainly, if the small room in the south corner was used for washing purposes, the users would not wish the contaminated water to be fed back into the cistern. Where the cistern water came from is not clear; possibly it was fed partly from rainwater run off in the courtyard, but it may have been necessary to carry water from some other source. All this becomes very relevant if the building was, as the excavator suggested, a temple (Bennett, 1976: 63-67 [66]; 1978: 165-71 [169]). Further indications which might point to this interpretation are the steps leading from the courtyard on its south-west side into the main building; the steps are flanked by two podia or column bases. The excavator notes that the plinths form the bases of two columns, 'the marking of their circumferences plainly visible on the surface of the plinths' (Bennett, 1977: 5-6), though elsewhere she suggested the possibility that the plinths carried statues (Bennett, 1978: 169: see also Bennett, 1975: 1-15, Pl.IVb).

The interpretation of this large building must remain in some doubt. The groundplan is uncertain, for the excavation is incomplete, and there are no associated artefacts by way of confirmatory evidence. It is tempting to see the building as a temple, but it might equally have been a palace or other important public building. After the destruction of Building B, and an intervening period of uncertain, but probably fairly short, duration, Building A was superimposed. It measures 48 × 36 metres, and its north-east wall is located a few paces inside (i.e., west-south-west of) that of Building B. Again, there is no evidence to show for certain what the function of Building A was, but it does not seem to have the same ground plan as the building beneath it, and its entrances were in different places; in particular, it does not seem to have its major entrance in the middle of the north-east side, as did Building B, but on the south-west wall at the other end of the building. This might suggest that it was not a temple building. Mrs Bennett originally dated this building to the Assyrian period, but later to the Persian period (Bennett, 1977: 3).

On general grounds, it is highly likely that Bozrah had a temple, and that the temple would be located near the royal palace on the acropolis. It is worth noting that Mesha of Moab, Edom's next-door neighbour, recorded on his stele as the first item the building of a sanctuary for the god Chemosh (lines 3-4). Unfortunately, there is no trace of Mesha's temple in the excavated remains of Dibon (Tushingham, 1972: 24), so comparisons with the Buseira building cannot be made. The Old Testament mentions Bozrah on several occasions; what is probably the earliest reference (Amos 1.12) threatens the palaces (*'armĕnôt*) of Bozrah with fire (Isa. 34.13 also uses the word with reference to Edom). However, the word *'armĕnôt* is used of eight different places apart from Edom in Amos 1 and 2, and thus does not suggest special knowledge of Bozrah. But there is no Old Testament reference to any temple at Bozrah, unless Isa. 34.6 and 63.1 gained some of their point from knowledge of the existence of a temple at Bozrah. The Old Testament thus does not help us much with the identification of major buildings at Bozrah; it supports the presence of palaces, but has no certain knowledge of any temple.

Excavations at Ḥorvat Qiṭmiṭ 10 kilometres south of Arad have revealed two complexes. The one complex so far excavated

> comprises a single structure divided into three long rooms, a platform . . . surrounded by an enclosure wall, and nearby another enclosure with a stone-built basin and an altar cut from a flint boulder. Within the platform enclosure were excavated about ten pottery stands together with many pottery figurines and reliefs . . . The reliefs included human figures with well proportioned limbs. Also found were the head of a three-horned goddess, a seal, some small bronze objects and everyday pottery vessels (Beit-Arieh, 1985: 201-2).

Beit-Arieh identifies the site as a temple from the seventh-sixth centuries BCE. Ḥorvat Qiṭmiṭ is not in Edom proper, but lies in an area which became at least partly settled by Edomites in the eighth and following centuries, and Beit-Arieh notes that:

> the ceramic finds include . . . Edomite ware such as painted sherds and bowls with triangular knobs. The layout and interior elements of the temple, as well as its iconography, are entirely alien to the eastern Negev. Moreover, the temple and its finds are unparalleled in Palestine or neighbouring countries, though there is a similarity to some figurines discovered at Buseirah in Edom (*ibid.*).

The excavation of Tawilan has revealed no major building which might be identified as either a temple or a palace, though the excavator does refer to the discovery of fragments of stone altars (Bennett, 1971a: v-vii [vii]; 1980a: 371-74 [373, Pl. XIc]). Incense altars of various kinds were found by Glueck at Tell el-Kheleifeh from Level V, which he dated to the fifth century BCE. Glueck describes a group of four-legged pottery altars, variously decorated (one portrayed a camel and possibly a cameleer, perhaps indicating the transport used by the incense trade from south Arabia), together with a similar small altar made of semi-porous stone and another of chalk (Glueck, 1970: 325-29). With these may be compared three similar incense altars (or 'incense burners') found at Petra (Parr, 1962: 747, fig. 7; Bennett, 1962: 233-43 [239]), and two found at Kh. Tannūr (Glueck, 1966: 511, Pl. 193b, c), and a fine example from Tell es-Sa'idiyeh in northern Transjordan (Pritchard, 1972: 1-17). Glueck notes that similar objects have been found at Gerar, Tell Jemmeh, Tell Far'ah (S), Ashdod, Lachish, Gezer, Samaria, as well as at Timna, Hureidha, Thaj and Aden in Arabia, and Uruk, Babylon and Assur in Mesopotamia and with Albright dates them from the sixth (or late seventh) century BCE to the fourth century BCE, the tradition in fact carrying on into the Nabataean period (Glueck, 1970: 325-29 [327-28]). Pritchard notes that the crudely executed designs of the Transjordanian examples compare badly with the Palestinian and Arabian examples (Pritchard, 1972: 14). If these altars were common from the Neo-Babylonian period onwards, earlier incense burners are perhaps represented by a cauldron shaped pot from Buseira of rough ware, 12 cm. diameter and 12.5 cm. high. The base is tripodic, and below the rim are two rows of holes (Bennett, 1975: 1-19 [12, fig. 7.18]). This may belong to the seventh century, together with a fragment, bearing two incised letters, *lk*, from what may have been a round, stone incense altar (Puech, 1977: 11-20 [11, fig. 1; Pl.IVA]). Glueck finds Assyrian influence in seventh-sixth centuries BCE censers from Tell el-Kheleifeh with flaring rims (Glueck, 1967a: 8-38 [30-33, fig. 3]; 1969: 51-59 [53, pl. 7]), similar to the 'Assyrian' type cups but with three stump legs, two horizontal rows of perforations, a double body carination, and a rounded or flattened loop handle (Pratico, 1985: 1-32 [25, and fig. 15.8], cf. Beit-Arieh, 1984: 193). From the same context comes a mug-shaped censer with a ring base, five rectangular windows (instead of round perforations) in the body of the pot below which is a denticulated fringe, and a lid on top

(Glueck, 1967a: 33-34, fig. 2.1; 5.1; Pratico, 1985: 25, fig. 15.9). Incense may have been comparatively expensive, a luxury item, but it seems to have been fairly commonly used, and its use was not necessarily restricted to temples or sanctuaries.

Another artefact which needs mention here is the figurine. These seem to be equally common either side of the Jordan in the Iron Age. Not all figurines discovered in Edom have been published. In 1939 Glueck published three female figurines found near Buseira, each bearing a saucer lamp on its head, which he compared with a similar 'lamp goddess' figure from Ain Shems. One of these figurines was holding before it a round object (as was perhaps originally the case with one of the other two figurines); the object has been identified as a loaf of bread, or, with greater probability, a tambourine (Glueck, 1937/39: 32-37, fig. 19; 1970: 185-88; Dornemann, 1983: 136). In 1935 Glueck noted several Astarte figurine fragments, together with fragments of a hand clutching a cone-shaped object; also an animal, and what he identified as a phallus but was probably a fragment of a pillar figurine (Glueck, 1935: 136: Pl. 30A). From Tell el-Kheleifeh Glueck published a crude pottery plaque representing a pregnant woman or goddess; 'a figurine of equal ugliness representing the same type of fertility goddess was found in another room. With it was found a tiny cup in which incense may have been burned' (Glueck, 1940b: 2-18 [16]). Thus from Glueck's work alone comes evidence for the presence in Edom of the main types of female figurine known west of the Jordan. In his study of Palestinian Iron Age baked clay figurines (Holland, 1977: 121-55 [156-57]), Holland divided the human figurines typologically into three main groups (each with a number of sub-groups): A, human pillar figurines with solid, hand-modelled bodies; B, human pillar figurines with hollow bodies; and C, female plaque figurines. For Buseira and Tawilan (the only Edomite sites on his chart) he registered as follows (*ibid.*, 126-27):

Site	A	B	C
Buseira	6	1	13
Tawilan	-	-	-

It should be noted, however, that a mould for plaques was found at Tawilan (Holland, 1977: 127), so presumably they were manufactured there.

Animal figurines are also known in Edom. Dornemann comments that only a few animal figurines from Transjordan do not represent horses (1983: 140), and a fragmentary horse figurines, with indications of riders, were found by Glueck at Medeiyineh (1970: figs 97, 98) in Moab: complete horse and rider figurines were found in the Meqabelein tomb (Harding, 1950: 44-48), while riderless horse figurines were found in tomb F at Amman (Dornemann, 1983: 141; figs. 86.9 and 89.5) and from tomb 84 at Mt Nebo (Saller, 1966; 261, 263, fig. 28.3). Holland lists the presence of his type D, solid hand-modelled horses and riders, also at Amman (1), Deir 'Allā (9), Nebo (1), Saliyeh (1), with one horse fragment at Buseira. From his type H, 'hollow hand-modelled animal figurines not spouted', Holland lists from Edom three horses from Buseira and two from Tawilan (none with riders). (From the comparatively high number of examples of this type recorded from Tawilan, Deir 'Allā and Buseira, Holland speculates on the east bank as the home of origin of these hand-modelled vessels [1977: 127].) Of other types of figurines charted by Holland as present at Buseirah and Tawilan, the most significant are those of his type J, 'zoomorphic spouted vessels', of which 10 are credited to Buseira and 3 to Tawilan. Of these vessels, Holland comments.

> Their wide-spread distribution indicates they were extremely popular. Many of these vessels could also be associated with cult use which would explain their presence in such large numbers on the sites of major importance where one would expect to find formal centres of worship (1977: 127).

The question remains, however, as to the religious significance of these various figurines. The presence of similar human and animal figurines together with cult vessels in the caves from squares AXXVI and AXXI-XXII of Kenyon's excavations at Jerusalem suggest strongly that these figurines had cultic significance and purpose and were not just toys. Kenyon interpreted the Jerusalem evidence as relating to cults associated with fertility worship and sun worship, some of the horse figurines bearing a clay disc or wedge between the ears which has been identified as a 'sun disc', i.e., a symbol of the sun (Holland, 1977: 149-41, and references there given). Such cults may have been more popular than official (especially in Jerusalem), and their presence in Edom and elsewhere in the Transjordan hardly surprising. Whether such practices in Edom were official or unofficial, however, it seems likely that the women presented female figurines as votive offerings, perhaps particularly in connection with child-birth and its attendant risks, while the men presented horse, or horse-and-rider figurines, perhaps particularly in time of war or economic adversity.

It is not easy to identify the god or gods, goddess or goddesses to whom the Edomites dedicated their votive plaques and figurines. Some of the female figurines and plaques may represent the goddess Astarte, who was probably known to the Edomites along with such deities as Hadad, El and Baal (see below). It has been suggested that some indication of Edomite religion may be given by a scarab found at Tawilan. The scarab shows at the top centre a star set inside a crescent. The crescent is supported by a pole, at the top of which are two fillets each pointing obliquely downwards towards the ground. The pole is mounted on a cross-hatched podium of some kind (an altar?), with short legs at the front corners. On either side stand two stylised trees, of slightly differing design. The central motif of the crescent on the pole is known from a number of examples as the symbol of the moon-god Sin, the centre of whose cult was at Harran (Spycket, 1973: 383-395). The discovery of a scarab at Tawilan symbolising the moon-god Sin of Harran has been made less surprising (if it was surprising) by the more recent discovery at Tawilan of a cuneiform tablet, a contract concerning the sale of livestock, drawn up at Harran perhaps in the reign of Darius I (Dalley, 1984: 19-22). Clearly business and communications were possible between Tawilan and Harran, and the discovery of such a scarab at Tawilan is not necessarily evidence for the native Edomite religion or an Edomite god (as Bennett suggested (1971: vi); the presence of this scarab indicates only that the name and cult of Sin might have been known in Tawilan, as elsewhere in the Levant. Unfortunately we do not know whether the scarab was owned by an Edomite or by a visitor from the north.

Biblical Evidence

It is a surprising fact that the biblical writers, most of whom thought of Edom as a major enemy to Judah and Israel, say little or nothing about the religion of Edom, and do not identify the god or gods worshipped in Edom by any name. This is all the more surprising in that they refer without hesitation to the god of the Ammonites as Milcom and the god of the Moabites as Chemosh, and to both of them as an abomination (1 Kgs 11.5, 7; 2 Kgs 23.13). The Edomites are not described as the sons or daughters of any deity, as the

Moabites are of Chemosh (Num. 21.29; Jer. 48.46). We have no mention of any sacrifice or other ritual performed by the Edomites, as we have of the Moabites (Num. 23.1, 14, 29: 2 Kgs 3.27; Isa. 15.2; 16.12), apart from the behaviour of Doeg, 'detained before the Lord' at Nob (1 Sam. 21.7). There is only one clear reference in the literature of ancient Israel to the religion of the people of Edom, and that is in the Chronicler's version of the story of Amaziah's victory in the Valley of Salt over the Edomites (2 Chron. 25.5-24). Here it is recorded (verse 14) that

> After Amaziah came from the slaughter of the Edomites, he brought the gods of the men of Seir, and set them up as his gods, and worshipped them, making offerings to them. Therefore the LORD was angry with Amaziah and sent to him a prophet, who said to him, 'Why have you resorted to the gods of a people, which did not deliver their own people from your hand?'

Amaziah's success with Edom prompted him to attack Israel. The king of Israel warned him against it (2 Chron. 25.18-19),

> But Amaziah would not listen; for it was of God, in order that he might give them into the hand of their enemies, because they had sought the gods of Edom (verse 20).

The Chronicler's purpose is clear; and it is is also clear that he has no genuine knowledge of the religion of Edom. By his day the kingdom of Edom had been extinct for nearly two centuries.

This absence of explicit reference to Edomite religion in the biblical writings demands explanation. It seems unlikely that the Old Testament writers deliberately suppressed all reference to Edomite religion as the ultimate abomination without leaving hints of their intention. It is perhaps more likely that they knew very little about it, just as they knew little about Edom's geography or history; yet even so, it would be surprising if they did not know the name of Edom's god or gods, for they knew those of the Ammonites and Moabites. F. Buhl suggested (1893: 50) that the absence of prophetic attack upon Edomite religion indicated that religion perhaps did not play such a dominant role among the Edomites as among Israel's other neighbours, and Charles Doughty remarked that natives of this part of the world were not particularly religious (1888: I. 38). But the biblical writers nowhere suggest that Edom was known for irreligiosity, though it is true that Edom's ancestor Esau is portrayed as one who would sell his birthright for a mess of pottage. The real solution to this problem probably lies, as we shall see, in the close relationship that originally existed between the Edomite and Israelite religion.

Several attempts have been made to identify the gods worshipped by the early Edomites and to explore the nature of their religion. W. Robertson Smith saw a religious significance in the animal names given to many Semitic tribes, and drew attention to the number of animal names among the tribes listed in Gen. 36.20-30 (*šôbāl*, young lion; *zib'ôn*, hyaena; *'ǎnâ*, wild ass; *dîsôn*, *dîsān*, antelope; *'ayyâ*, kite; *'ǎrān*, ibex); he suggested that the tribal members were known as the 'sons' of these animal totems, which they treated as their ancestors and deities. He detected two other Arabian gods in Jalam (ibex, Gen. 36.14) and Jeush (the Arabic lion-god Yaghûth, 'the protector', Gen. 36.14), and in Akan (Gen. 36.27; cf. Jaakan, Deut. 10.6 and 1 Chron. 1.42) he identified the Arabian Ya'ûq (Robertson Smith, 1912: 455-83). Both the general theory and certain etymological details have met serious criticism (E. Meyer, 1906: 309; F. Buhl, 1893: 49), but even if these tribes are to be accounted Edomite, there is no suggestion in the biblical literature that the historical Edomites practised such animal worship. The references to 'Obed-edom the Gittite' in 2 Sam. 6.11, and another Obed-edom in 2 Chron. 25.24, have suggested the existence of a deity called Edom (see Engnell, 1943: 164; Kraeling, 1928: 156n), but there is no evidence that this supposed deity was in any way connected with or worshipped in Edom. If the name Baal-hanan, which has become attached to the Edomite king-list (see above, p. 99), is genuinely Edomite, the Canaanite deity Baal was known in Edom, and if so, it is also likely that the deity Hadad was also known there, whether Hadad the son of Bedad (Gen. 36.35) was Edomite or Moabite. The deity El was almost certainly known in Edom (cf. the name Magdiel, Gen. 36.43). El is evidenced in the seal from Tawilan (?) bearing the name *sm'l* (see below, pp. 214-215), and Baal on a seal from Petra (see below, p. 211) and on ostracon 2070 from Tell el-Kheleifeh, though here the names may be Phoenician (see below, p. 218).

It must be admitted that the evidence considered so far is decidedly scrappy. It suggests that, like the Israelites and their other neighbours in the Levant, the Edomites worshipped in temples and sanctuaries, made plaques and figurines, used incense altars and burners of various kinds, and knew and probably used the names of the gods El, Baal and Hadad (to which we can probably add Astarte). We can add to this, that like the Israelites, Egyptians, Ammonites and Moabites, the Edomites were circumcised (cf. Jer. 9.25f.). All this suggests that Edomite religion would not have seemed very strange to their neighbours in Moab, Ammon and Israel, and conversely that an Edomite abroad would have found little difficulty in adjusting to religious practice and belief in Israel, Ammon or Moab. Thus the author of 1 Sam. 21.7 notes without surprise the presence of Doeg the Edomite, 'detained before the Lord' at the sanctuary of Nob. An Edomite, it seems, might be found worshipping Yahweh and paying vows to him.

Not surprisingly, therefore, several scholars have suggested that the Israelite Yahweh was known also in Edom, or that the Edomite god had features in common with Yahweh (cf. Waterman, 1938: 25-43; Gray, 1953: 278-83 [280-81]; 1954: 148-54 [153]; Rose, 1977: 28-34; Bartlett, 1978: 29-38; see also Vriezen, 1965: 330-53 [353, n. 1]). Certainly, the biblical writers and the traditions they inherited connected Yahweh directly with Edom, together with such other places to the south as Sinai, Horeb, Seir, Mount Paran, Kadesh, and Teman. Thus in the 'Blessing of Moses' (Deut. 33.2) the poet begins by describing the arrival of Yahweh:

> The LORD came from Sinai,
>> and dawned from Seir upon us;
>> he shone forth from mount Paran,
> he came from the ten thousands of holy ones [see above, p. 43]
>> with flaming fire at his right hand.

The 'Song of Deborah' (Judg. 5.4) similarly pictures the theophany of Yahweh, and explicitly links him with Edom,

> LORD, when thou didst go forth from Seir,
>> when thou didst march from the region of Edom,
> the earth trembled,
>> and the heavens dropped,
>> yea, the clouds dropped water.
> The mountains quaked before the LORD,
>> yon Sinai before the LORD, the God of Israel.

A similar description appears in Hab. 3.3:

> God came from Teman,
>> and the Holy One from Mount Paran.
> His glory covered the heavens,
>> and the earth was full of his praise.

The prophet of Isa. 63.1-6 pictures God returning, bloodstained, from taking vengeance on the peoples:

> Who is this that comes from Edom
>   in crimsoned garments from Bozrah,
> he that is glorious in his apparel,
>   marching in the greatness of his strength?

(F. Buhl [1893: 76], following a conjecture of Lagarde and Duhm, would remove reference to Edom and Bozrah from Isa. 63.1 by reading 'Who is this that comes reddened (*me'āddām*), in crimsoned garments from the grape-gathering (*mibbōsēr*)?', thus making the verse a description of the physical appearance of the Judge of the world.) The theophanies of Yahweh on Mount Sinai (Exod. 19.16-25) and on Mount Horeb (1 Kgs 19.8-18) are well known. The Israelite tradition thought of Yahweh as being at home in the mountains to the south, and could include among these equally Sinai/Horeb, Seir, Edom, Paran and the region of Teman; it could even specifically connect Yahweh with Bozrah (by way of poetic parallelism with Edom). That the Israelites could link Yahweh with the land of Edom (together with other places in the south) does not necessarily suggest that the people of Edom worshipped Yahweh as their god, and the Israelite tradition does not say that they did. In the Israelite tradition, it was Jethro, the priest of Midian, Moses' father-in-law, who blessed Yahweh and offered burnt-offering and sacrifices to him (Exod. 18.12), and there is no suggestion that the Edomites were also early worshippers of Yahweh, though, indeed, many scholars have identified the Kenites as early Yahwists and as related to the Edomites (see de Vaux, 1971: I.313-21). As is well known, the Old Testament speaks of Israel's 'brotherhood' with Edom; this is traced back to the brotherhood of the respective ancestors of Israel and Edom, Jacob and Esau (see above, Chapter 10). It is certainly possible that behind this relationship lies an early recognition in Israel that in matters of religion the people of Israel and the people of Edom had something in common, and that the cult of Yahweh was known in Edom as well as in Israel. Israel, however, absolutized Yahweh, and demanded allegiance to him alone: 'You shall have no other gods before me' (Exod. 20.3; Deut. 5.7). Israel claimed Yahweh for her own exclusive possession, and Israel's relationship with Yahweh was summed up in the statement, 'I will be their God, and they shall be my people' (Jer. 31.33). There is no evidence that the

Edomites took this line; though they may have recognised Yahweh, they seem to have recognised other gods as well, and in particular a deity called Qos. It is not impossible that the worship of Yahweh fell out of favour in Edom and disappeared there precisely because the Edomites knew that Yahweh was the god of their rulers and oppressors from the kingdom of David. And if the cult of Yahweh was practised in early times among the Edomites, and this was known in Israel, it is also possible that Israel's writers were silent on the matter because they did not like to admit too readily that the hated Edomites also worshipped Yahweh. The notion of brotherhood, however, remained, and was exploited by frequent reference to unbrotherly behaviour (see above, Chapter 10). A late acknowledgement of Edom's religious affinities with Israel, however, perhaps appears in Deut. 23.8:

> You shall not abhor an Edomite, for he is your brother; you shall not abhor an Egyptian, because you were a sojourner in his land. The children of the third generation that are born to them may enter the assembly of the LORD.

This passage follows a series of prohibitions in Deut. 23.1-7 which forbid entrance to the assembly of the Lord to three groups of people: males with damaged genitalia; bastards; Ammonites and Moabites. None of these or their descendants shall enter the assembly of the Lord 'until the tenth generation'. With the Edomites and Egyptians, however, it is different. The Edomites are not to be abhorred—clearly the Deuteronomist knew that they were—and their descendants may be allowed entrance in the third generation. Compared with Ammonites and Moabites, the Edomites are favoured. The reason given is that the Edomite is the Israelite's brother (see the discussion above, pp. 181-83). In Deut. 23.7 the Deuteronomist is saying that the Edomite is not to be treated as a pagan alien, but as a fellow Israelite, and, moreover, as one whose standing is much higher than that of a deformed male or bastard. The Deuteronomist clearly rates the Edomites higher than do his contemporaries, but he has to make some concession (delayed entry to the assembly until the third generation) to his contemporaries' dislike of the Edomites. It is particularly clear that the Deuteronomist rates the Edomites much higher than the Ammonites or Moabites. The Edomite can eventually be accepted into the Israelite worshipping community; the Ammonites and Moabites, to all intents and purposes, cannot.

Edom and the Edomites

It cannot be denied that the relationship of the Edomites to Yahwism remains very uncertain. The Israelite sources clearly hint that in religious matters the Edomites were not totally beyond the pale; perhaps the Israelites of the monarchic period regarded the Edomites, at least in religious matters, much as the later Jews regarded the Samaritans. But the problem is complicated further by the fact that there is some evidence that the Edomites worshipped a deity called Qos.

Qos

Evidence for the actual worship of Qos is late. A Nabataean stele from Jebel et-Tannur (Savignac, 1937: 401-16 [408-9], Pl. IX.3, X; Milik, 1958: 227-51 [237-38]; Glueck, 1966: 514-15, Pl. 196, 197), dating from the first century BCE or the first century CE, bears an inscription which reads

> '[stele] which Qosmalak made for Qos, god of *HWRW*'.

A bilingual Nabataean and Greek inscription of the second-third century CE from Bosra (Syria) (Milik, 1958: 235-36) records that

> Muaino son of Zabdai has made the eagle in honour of Qos;
> Moainos Hulaipi son/of Taima, sculptor.

Earlier evidence for the worship of Qos is derived from a number of personal names which include the element Qos or -qos (*qws*). Known examples begin with Qosmalak, a king of Edom in the reign of Tiglath-pileser III of Assyria in the eighth century BCE, Qosgabri, king of Edom under the Assyrian kings Asarhaddon and Ashurbanipal in the seventh century BCE, and Qosa', whose eighth-seventh century BCE seal was found at Tell Aro'er in the Negev. From the seventh-sixth centuries BCE five different *qws* names are attested on a seal impression and an ostracon from Tell-el-Kheleifeh, and two more are attested from a cuneiform tablet found at Tawilan, dating probably from the end of the sixth century BCE. Two *qws* names are known from commercial documents from Nippur, from the reign of Artaxerxes I in the fifth century BCE (465-423 BCE); from the fourth century comes the Liḥyanite inscription referring to Galti-qos, governor of Dedan, and also a collection of 14 *qws* names from ostraca found at Tel Beersheba. One of these names may be restored as *b*[*r*]*qws*, which appears also in Ezra 2.53 and Neh 7.55. Possibly

Kushaiah of 1 Chron. 15.17 conceals a *qws* name; if it does, it links in one name the deity *qws* with the Israelite Yahweh. Perhaps five *qws* names are known in all from Liḥyanite inscriptions, and one from a Minaean inscription. From the third century BCE onwards a number of Idumaean names of this type are known from Greek inscriptions at Marisa, Alexandria, Old Memphis [Mitrahineh] and Hermopolis Magna and elsewhere, and Josephus mentions an Idumaean Kostobaros who belonged to the family of priests of the Idumaean god *Koze* (*Ant.* XV.8.9 [253]). Qosmalak appears on a Nabataean stele at Jebel et-Tannūr (see above), and Uriqos (*'rqs*) on a Nabataean altar found Buseira. (For a full list of these names, with references, see the end of this chapter.)

These names are typically Semitic theophoric names, and there is no reason to doubt that the element *qws* represents the name of a deity. To judge from the geographical distribution of these names, his worshippers could be found on both sides of the Wadi 'Araba, both in Edom and the Hedjaz and in Beersheba and the Negev, and among the emigrés both in Mesopotamia and in Egypt, as far away as Nippur and Cyrene. Although the earliest known example is the name of an Edomite king (and a *qws* name is also borne by one of his successors), it is not certain that the name is of pure Edomite origin. Some scholars have argued that the Edomites derived knowledge of this deity from their early Arab neighbours to the east and south of Edom (e.g., Buhl, 1983: 47-48; Rose, 1977: 28-34).

The Semitic name *qws* (*qop, waw, samek*), which we anglicise as Qos, is generally agreed to be related to the Arabic word for a bow, *qaus* (see Vriezen, 1965: 330-53; du Buit, 1979: 674-78). The bow, *qaus*, was the cult symbol of the pre-Islamic weather-god Quzaḥ, and the phrase *qaus Quzaḥ*, 'bow of the god Quzaḥ', became an Arabic term meaning 'rainbow' (Fahd, 1978: 803-804). The god Quzaḥ is probably the deity Josephus transliterates as *Koze*, the final *ḥet* disappearing in Greek transliteration (du Buit, 1979: 674-78 [678]). Wellhausen argued that the deity *qws* was a personification of the bow of the god Quzaḥ (Wellhausen, 1887: 77). This view was opposed by Th. Nöldeke, who distinguished between Qos and the deity Quzaḥ, seeing the latter as a storm god (1908: 660-61). Nöldeke also denied the derivation of Qos from Arabic *qaus*, 'bow' (review of Wellhausen, 1887: 707-27 [714, n.i]; but see Vriezen, 1965: 335-42). More recently Vriezen has dissociated *qws* from the phrase *qaus Quzaḥ* and the deity Quzaḥ altogether, and has argued cogently that *qws* was the god of the bow, the bow in the Semitic world being primarily the symbol of the war god. The deity *qws* was thus a personified and deified bow; the worship of *qws* was appropriate in Edom, whose ancestor Israelite tradition found in Esau, the hunter, the man of the field. The war-like *qws* became one of Edom's leading deities. However, Vriezen admits (1965: 330-52) that the bow was also associated with storm-gods, and recognizes that in later times *qws* became identified with the Arab deity Quzaḥ (perhaps this identification is implicit in Josephus' reference to the Idumaean deity Koze).

The cognate relationship of *qws* and the (later) Arabic *qaus* does not establish that the deity worshipped by the Edomites under the name *qws* necessarily had an origin and background in the neighbouring pre-Islamic Arab tribes, though of course this is possible. Martin Rose, noting the Liḥyanite and Nabataean distribution of *qws* names, has argued that *qws* was an Arab deity which penetrated Edom 'in the wake of the westward movement of Arab tribes beginning in the 8th and 7th centuries' (1977: 30). The matter is not as simple as this, however. While it is true that Arab tribes were active to the east of Edom, Moab and Ammon in the seventh century BCE, as the Assyrian records of Esarhaddon and Ashurbanipal show, the thesis of a 'westward movement of Arab tribes' into Edom and Moab in the eighth-seventh centuries BCE lacks support from either the archaeological or biblical evidence, and finds no confirmation in recent studies concerning the inter-relationships of settled farmers, semi-nomadic pastoralists, and true nomads in the near east. In this Assyrian period, Edom seems to have been at the height of her urbanization, well established and administered. When Arab tribes appeared threatening, Assyria reacted and campaigned against them. This is not a time when we might most naturally expect the Edomites to adopt and give pride of place to a god belonging to Arab tribes to the east, though it is a period when we might expect to find (as we do in Judah) a certain amount of religious syncretism, whether from Syria to the north or Arabia to the south, by way of the trade routes. Possibly we should be looking to the south for the homeland of *qws*, and perhaps to an earlier period than the eighth century BCE.

As we have seen, the Edomites established their independence from Judah and set up their kingdom in the mid-ninth century BCE, somewhere between 850 and 841 BCE. Between then and the time of the Assyrian Tiglath-pileser III we know nothing of the names of the Edomite kings. The first name known to us is that of Qosmalak (*qa-uš-ma-la-ka*). Sennacherib refers to an Edomite king named *a-a-ram-mu/me*, and Esarhaddon and Ashurbanipal mention an Edomite king *qa-uš-gab-ri*, who appears also on the royal seal from Umm el-Biyara. Unfortunately, from the whole of the independent Edomite kingdom, from the mid-ninth to the mid-sixth century BCE, these are the only royal names known to us. Two out of the three bear names incorporating the element *qws*, but the sample is a small one, and we do not know whether Qosmalak was the first Edomite king to include the divine name *qws* in his name. Even if he was, the fact that this divine name appears in a royal name suggests that *qws* was not a name that had only just arrived in Edom. Unless Qosmalak was the first of a new dynasty, or a religious reformer incorporating the name of a newly adopted deity into his throne-name, we must suppose that *qws* appears in his name precisely because *qws* was a generally accepted major god—perhaps the principal god—in Edom. The god *qws* may thus have been known in Edom (whatever his origin) for some time. Given Edom's geographical position and cultural and ethnic contacts with the Arabian world this is far from unlikely. If *qws* is of Arabian origin, we do not need to postulate westward movements of Arab tribes to explain the presence of *qws* in Edom.

The position of *qws* in Edom remains a little uncertain. In view of the incorporation of *qws* into royal names, it does seem likely that this was the deity adopted by the Edomite kings as their patron and officially supported by them. If there was a temple in Buseira, it may have been dedicated to Qos. Possibly Jebel et-Tannur was in monarchic times a holy place of Qos. The nature of the god may be seen from the theophoric names, at least to some extent. They compare closely with similar theophoric names from Israel and elsewhere. Thus we find such names as *qwsmlk* ('Qos is king', cf. Heb. *mlkyh*), *qwsgbr* ('Qos is powerful', cf. Heb. *gbry'l*), *'bdqws* ('servant of Qos', cf. Heb. *'bdyh*). Vriezen argued that the names *qwsmlk* and *qwsgbr*, together with such names as *pg'qws* and *qwsny* (which he translated 'Qos attacks/strikes down' and 'Qos restrain/ repel the attack') support the view that Qos was a god of hunting and war (1965: 331f., 345). However, the last two translations are doubtful, and many other names must be taken into account to give the full picture—for example, *qwsyd'* ('Qos has known', cf. Heb. *'lyd'*), *qwsb[n]* ('Qos has made'), *qwsyhb* ('Qos has given'), or *qwsnhr*

('Qos is light', cf. Heb. *nryh*). It has been suggested that Qos was a storm god (Lury, 1896: 37) or that storm-god traits were later attributed to him (Vriezen, 1965: 345). Teixidor (1977: 90) notes that at the Nabataean shrine of Khirbet et-Tannūr, Qos is represented as 'seated on a throne flanked by bulls and holding in his left hand a multi-branched thunderbolt, the symbol of the lord of rain. At Bostra, an inscription in Greek and Nabataean commemorates the offering of an eagle to him. The bulls, the thunderbolt, and the eagle seem to support the conclusion that Qos was a weather god.' However, the personal names considered above (and more fully listed below) do not suggest that Qos was understood exclusively as a war god or a storm god, but rather that his devotees (like the worshippers of Yahweh and of other gods) might hope for his help and support in various situations, personal and domestic as well as national.

List of Names Incorporating the Divine Name Qos

I. *Assyrian texts*

1. [1]*qa-uš-ma-la-ka* ('Qaus has become king'): Tiglath-pileser III, Nimrud (*ANET*[3] 282; Weippert, 1971: 82, 466)

2. [1]*qa-uš-gab-ri* ('Qaus is powerful'): Asarhaddon, Nineveh (Prism B, V. 56, *ANET*[3] 291; Weippert, 1971: 127, 466; also Ashurbanipal, Prism C, II.28, *ANET*[3] 294; Weippert, 1971: 141, 466)

II. *Achaemenid cuneiform texts*

3. [i.d.]*qu-ú-su-šá-ma-a'* ('Qos has heard'): Darius I (?), Harran/Tawilan (Dalley, 1984: 21)

4. [i.d.]*qu-ú-su-ia-da-a'* ('Qos has known'): Darius I (?), Harran/Tawilan (Dalley, 1984: 21)

5. [i.d.]*qu-ú-su-ya-da-'* ('Qos has known'); Artaxerxes I, Nippur (E. Schrader, 1903: 472f.; J.N. Strassmaier, 1897: 301, 16)

6. [i.d.]*qu-su-ya-a-ḫa-bi* ('Qos has given'): Artaxerxes I, Nippur (Schrader, 1903: 472f.: *BE* IX.1, 1.23.25 (Babylonian Expedition of the University of Pennsylvania, Series A, Cuneiform Texts). See P. Jensen *apud* W. Baudissin, 1899: 135, and the comment by Weippert, 1971: 711, note 1754.)

7. [1]*qu-us-da-na-'* ('Qos is judge'): BE IX.32.4. Coogan (1976: 65, note 83) argues that the name is Persian, not Edomite, and does not contain the element 'Qos'.

III. *Seals and ostraca from Edom and Judah*

8. *qwsg*[br] ('Qos is powerful'): Umm el-Biyara (Bennett, 1966: 399-401, Pl. XXIIB.

9. *qws'nl* ('Qos has answered [me]', or 'Qos has achieved'): Tell el-Kheleifeh (Glueck, 1938b: 16-18, fig. 6; 1938c: 12f., fig. 3; Albright, 1938: 13, n. 45; Milik, 1958: 239).

10. *bdqws* ('by the hand of Qos'): Tell el-Kheleifeh (Glueck, 1971: 228-9; Pl. 3).

11. *pq'qws* ('[son] asked of Qos', or, 'Qos attacks/ strikes down'): Tell el-Kheleifeh (Glueck, 1941: 3-6; figs 1, 2; Albright, 1941: 11-15; Vriezen, 1965: 339-353.

12. *qwsb*[nh] ('Qos has created'): Tell el-Kheleifeh (Albright, 1941: 11-15).

13. *qwsny* (possibly hypocoristic in -y for *qwsntn*, 'Qos has given'): Tell el-Kheleifeh (Glueck, 1941: 6, 13; Milik, 1958: 240.

14. *qws'* (a hypocoristic form): 'Aro'er (Biran & Cohen, 1976: 139, Pl. 28b).

15. *qwsnhr* ('Qos is light'); Tel Beersheba, Ostracon 28.2 (Naveh, 1979: 183).

16. *qwsynqm* ('Qos will avenge'): Tel Beersheba; Ostracon 33.3 (*ibid.*, 185).

17. *qwsbrk* ('Qos has blessed'): Tel Beersheba, Ostracon 33.4 (*ibid.*, 185).

18. *qwsml*[k] ('Qos is king): Tel Beersheba, Ostracon 33.4 (*ibid.*, 185). Father of preceding person.

19. *qws'wt* ('Qos has helped'): Tel Beersheba, Ostracon 34.1 (*ibid.*, 186).

20. *qwsy* (a hypocoristic form; cf. no. 7, *qws'* above): Tel Beersheba, Ostracon 34.3 (*ibid.*, 186).

21. *qws'dr* ('Qos has helped'): Tel Beersheba, Ostracon 34.6 (*ibid.*, 186).

22. *qwswhb* ('Qos has given'): Tel Beersheba, Ostracon 36.1 (*ibid.*, 187).

23. *qws . . .* ('Qos . . . . . .'): Tel Beersheba, Ostracon 36.6 (*ibid.*, 187).

24. *b.qws* (=? *bdqws* v.sup. no. 10; or *brqws*, cf. Ezra 2.53; Neh. 7.55. See below on *brqws*, no. 36: Tel Beersheba, Ostracon 37.1 (*ibid.*, 188).

25. *qwsgbr* ('Qos is powerful'): Tel Beersheba, Ostracon 37.4 (*ibid.*, 188).

26. *qws. . .* ('Qos . . . . . .'): Tel Beersheba, Ostracon 41.4 (*ibid.*, 189).

27. *qwshbn* (unexplained): Tel Beersheba, Ostracon 41.6 (*ibid.*, 189). Knauf (1981: 191) gives *qwshnn*.

28. *qwsm*[lk] ('Qos is king'): Tel Beersheba, Ostracon 42.3 (*ibid.*, 190).

IV. *Lihyanite inscriptions*

29. *gltqs* ('Terror of Qos' or, 'majesty of Qos'): JSLih 83.7 (cf. Albright, 1953: 6; Milik, 1960; Winnett & Reed, 1970: 125-7; Caskel, 1954: 146f.; MacDonald, personal communication).

30. *'dbqs* (probably metathesis for *'bdqs*, 'Servant of Qos'): JSLih 143. (See M.C.A. Macdonald, 1986: note 100).

31. *'kmqs* (unexplained): JSLih 265.

32. *qwsmlk* ('Qos is king'): JSLih 331

33. *qwsmlk* ('Qos is king'): JAL 61.1 (*qwsmlk bn lft*: A. Jamme, 1974: 56f., Pl.14. I owe this reference to M.C.A. Macdonald.)

34. *qwsbr* ('Qos is pure'): JSLiḥ 334, graffito; perhaps *qws*[g]br?

35. *slmtqs* ('peace of Qos'): JSMin. 117. (Milik, 1960: 96, notes 'en alphabet minéen (ou lithyanite ancien?), mais désignant sans doute un Lihyanite').

V. *Tabuki Thamudic/South Safaitic*

36. *brqs* (graffito, *l h:b bn brqs*: 'son of Qos'?): near Teima, Hu. 491/1 (C. Huber, 1891). Such an etymology, however, is unlikely if the name belongs to a language which uses *bn* rather than *br* for son. G.L. Harding and E. Littmann (1952; no. 110) list a Thamudic *brqš*, cf. Arabic *birqiš*, a small bird with bright plumage (cf. Milik, 1958: 241, n. 1).

37. *qs* (graffito, *l qs bn w'lt....*): west of Tabuk: JSTham. 607.

VI. *Safaitic*

38. *qs* CIS Pars V 1513.

39. *qs* CIS Pars V 3578.

40. *qs* CIS Pars V 2851 (graffito, *l qs bn 'zz*).

41. *qs* * WH 1001 (graffito, *l qs bn tm w t'mr šḥh f h lt ġnmt*).

42. *qsl* CIS Pars V 1740 (graffito, *l qn bn qsl*).

43. *qsl* CIS Pars V 3163 (graffito, *l qsl bn n.4.4.4*). * 'N.B. Divine names do occur as names of men in North Arabian (e.g., *'lh*, , *šms*), so there is no objection to a name Qos on that ground. It should, however, be borne in mind that *qs* could equally well come from Arabic qass ('a good herdsman') and that Qas, Qais, and Quss are known Arabic names.' (M.C.A. Macdonald, personal communication)

VII. *Nabataean*

44. *'rqs* ('Qos is light'): Buseira (Starcky, 1975: 16).

45. *qws'dr* ('Qos has helped') graffito, W. Mukatteb; CIS II. 923.2

46. *qsntn* ('Qos has given'): Hegra (tomb inscription, *hlp br qsntn*. CE 31; CIS II. 209 (Milik, 1958: 241).

47. *qsmlk* ('Qos is king'); Kh. Tannūr; R. Savignac, 1937: 408f., Pl.X (photograph), Pl.IX.3 (facsimile); N. Glueck, 1966: 514f., Plates 196, 197; Milik, 1958: 237f. Milik rejects Savignac's suggestion that *lqs 'lh* be read as one name, Qosallah, 'Qos is god'.

VIII. *Greek*

48. ἀβδοκως ('Servant of Qos'): Hermopolis Magna, Egypt; 80-69 BCE; J.G. Milne 1905: no. 9296.

49. κοσάδαρος (cf. *qws'dr*, nos 21, 45): Temple dedication from Old Memphis (Mitrahineh), Egypt, including Idumaeans; see J.G. Milne, 1905; 9283 I.27; κοσαδάρου (gen.), col.I. 4,21,22,31; II.27

50. κοσάδου (gen., form of *qws'd*', 'Qos has adorned', or hypocoristic form

of *qws'dr*, 'Qos has helped'): Marissa; J.P. Peters & H. Thiersch, 1905: 47, no. 13; see Milik, 1958: 240, n. 4.

51. κωσανέλου (gen., form of *qws'nl*, no. 9): Alexandria; 134 BCE; CIG III. 4582.8; Milik, 1958: 240.

52. κοσβάνου (gen., form of *qwsbnh*, no. 12): Old Memphis (Mitrahineh); Milne, 1905: 9283, col. I.35; Marissa; Peters & Thiersch, 1905: 46, no. 12.2

53. κοσβάρακος (form of *qwsbrk*, cf. no. 17): graffito from Cyrenaica: SEG IX 743; L. Robert (19.9): 179.

54. κοσγήρου (gen., 'Qos is host'): Old Memphis; Milne, 1905: 9283, col. III.33

55. κοσμάλαχος (form of *qwsmlk, qsmlk*; cf. 1,18,28,32,44: Old Memphis; Milne, 1905: 9283, col.I.17, III.39; gen. κοσμαλάχου, *ibid.*, I. 39, II. 17, III. 29. Milne, III. 34, reads κοσμάτανος; Lidzbarski, *Ephemeris* 341.2 suggests κοσνάτανος; E. Miller, 1870: 109-25, 170-183, reads κοσμάλαχος. (Weippert, 1971: 711, n. 1755)

56. κοσνάτανος (form of *qwsntn*, no. 4): Marissa; Peters & Thiersch, 1905: 44 no. 9.1; gen. κοσνατάνου, *ibid.*, 45.10.1, 11.1, 28.3; Old Memphis; Milne, 1905: 9283, col. I. 5.34.

57. κόσραμος ('Qos is elevated'): Old Memphis; Milne, 1905: 9283, col. I. 5, II. 5 (gen.)

58. κοστόβαρος (cf. Josephus, *Ant.* XV. 8.9. (253): of Idumaean priestly family; Herod made him governor of Idumaea and Gaza, and gave him his sister Salome in marriage): it has been suggested that the name arose by error from κοσγάβαρος or κοσγόβορος (S.A. Cook, 1930: 203f., n.5; Milik, 1958: 240, n. 7), but the error (a Greek *tau* for a *gamma*) can have occurred only in a Greek-speaking community unfamiliar with Semitic names.

59. κουσνάτανος (cf. no. 55): papyrus from Zenon archive, 259 BCE; see Tcherikover & Fuchs, *CPJ* I (1957), 3.10.

60. Πακειδοκώσῳ (Dat) (cf. *paqid* [governor]+*qws*): Delos; dedication of Magnes, son of Philodotos, to Pakeidosos, in virtue of a vow; Milik, 1960: 95f., with references.

Chapter 12

INSCRIPTIONS FROM EDOM

Introduction

Exploration and excavation in Edom have so far brought to light a number of seals, seal-impressions, fragments of pottery with inscriptions incised after firing, ostraca bearing inscriptions in ink, and one cuneiform tablet. Unfortunately no major monumental Edomite inscription has been found. The existence of the Moabite stone recording the achievements of king Mesha and the citadel inscription from Amman show that inscribed public monuments were known in Transjordan in the first half of the first millennium BCE, and it was a disappointment to the excavators of Buseirah that no fragments of anything that might have been a public inscription were found there. Probably any such public monuments were destroyed in antiquity.

The more humble epigraphic fragments that have survived from Edom show that in the period of the Edomite monarchy the Edomites used a regional variant of the north-west Semitic script and language. More precisely, L.G. Herr (1980: 21-34) has classified the scripts in use in the southern Levant from the ninth century BCE as Phoenician (the Phoenician city states and colonies), Aramaic (the Aramaic kingdoms and the Ammonites), and South Palestinian (subdivided between Israelite and Judaean scripts in Cisjordan, and Moabite and Edomite scripts in Southern Transjordan). Naveh argued that the use of open forms of the *bet*, *dalet*, *'ayin*, and *reš* in the *qws'nl* seal inscriptions, the graffito on a jar, and ostracon 6043 from Tell el-Kheleifeh, and the bulla from Umm el-Biyarah, show Aramaic influence from the seventh century BCE onwards on the Edomite script (Naveh, 1966: 27-30; 1982: 102: Naveh (*ibid.*) rejects Herr's thesis on the Transjordanian scripts, though without discussion); Herr (1980: 33) suggested that the Transjordanian scribes were influenced by the forms used by the Aramaic scribes of the Assyrian administration. The 'South Palestinian' script may first have been used in Edom—though this is but a guess—by the occupying Davidic adminstration in the tenth century BCE. Our earliest firm evidence for its use, however, does not go back beyond the eighth century BCE (the *lytm* seal from Tell el-Kheleifeh and the *lmlk l/b'bd/hmlk* seal from Buseira). (The *sm'l* seal purchased in Tafila has been dated as early as the ninth century BCE, but the date and provenance are far from certain.) The bulk of the inscriptional material so far discovered belongs to the seventh-sixth centuries BCE, with later material from Tell el-Kheleifeh and Tawilan, and this fact underlines the picture we have drawn of an Edom which flourished politically particularly in the Assyrian period.

With a few exceptions, these seals, impressions and ostraca bear personal names, not all of them necessarily Edomite. There is one royal seal, one seal belonging to a royal official, and one set of seal-impressions referring to another royal official. One seal from Tell el-Kheleifeh may bear the name of a king of Judah (though this is far from certain, for the inscription does not identify *ytm* as a royal figure), and another, from Buseira, the name of a foreign resident in Edom. The names of the king and the two royal officials mentioned are theophoric names including the element *qws*, and the same element appears incised on a pot fragment from Buseira and in no less than four names (if not five) on one ostracon from Tell el-Kheleifeh. Single names may have been written or incised upon pots to indicate ownership, but ostraca nos 2070, 2071 and 6043 from Tell el-Kheleifeh, with their lists of names, are less easily explained.

The remaining Edomite epigraphic material relates to weights, measures, and the contents of jars. A roughly cuboid piece of stone from Buseirah, weighing 9.5 gr., is marked *n* and *ns*, probably to indicate a *nsp* weight. A jar handle from Buseirah is incised *'b*, perhaps 'a tenth of a *bath*' (this might represent a liquid measure of 4-5 litres). Another ostracon from Buseirah perhaps gives a weight of grain in *kors* and *se'ahs*. A dome-shaped weight from Umm el-Biyara is incised '4 shekels'. Edom seems to have been well acquainted with the terms for weights and measures which were also known in Judah. One ostracon from Umm el-Biyara appears to refer to a delivery of olive oil, and two ostraca from Tell el-Kheleifeh to jars of wine.

There are some important examples of inscriptional material from abroad. From Tell el-Kheleifeh there are two jars incised with letters in the Minaean script, indicating, with other artefactual and literary evidence that the head of the Gulf of 'Aqaba was an important staging post in the trade route between southern Arabia and the kingdoms of Syria, Transjordan and Palestine. From Tawilan there is the recently discovered cuneiform tablet, written in Harran in the accession year of Darius king of the lands, witnessing to the purchase of oxen and sheep from an Aramaean by an Edomite. This document has interesting implications for the history of Edom in the Persian period, and is an indication of what might yet be discovered in further excavation in Edom.

Seals

1. *lb'zr'l/'bdyb'l*
Purchased at Petra, 1940

The seal is circular, of reddish stone, with a dome back. G.R. Driver read the inscription as giving two names: (1) *Be-'ezer-'el*, 'by the help of *'l*', and (2) *'Abdi-ba'al*, 'slave of Baal' (cf. Heb. *'Abdi-'el*, 'slave of El'). However, the second line might also be read *'bd yb'l*, 'slave of *yb'l*'. Driver's reading, if correct, attests knowledge of the gods El and Baal in Edom. Herr dates the seal to the second half of the seventh century BCE on the evidence of the open *'ayins* 'since in the other Trans-Jordanian scripts the *'ayins* do not seem to open before that period' (Herr, 1978: 166f.)

> G.R. Driver, 1945: 82; Pl. 18
> G.R. Driver, 1976: 113; fig. 63B
> L.G. Herr, 1978: 166-67
> L.G. Herr, 1980: 29-31

2. *lytm*
Tell el-Kheleifeh, Reg. no 7022

The seal, measuring 15 × 12 mm, is mounted on a copper ring. Beneath the name the seal bears the picture of a ram walking; in front of the ram appears an object which has been variously identified as a man, bellows, an ox-hide shaped metal ingot, and a scarab. The interpretation of this object as bellows or an ingot was probably suggested by the earlier (now abandoned) interpretation of Tell el-Kheleifeh as a copper-refining plant. The ram (*'yl*) has been interpreted as an allusion to the name of the city Elath (*'ylt*), though the name of the city may rather be connected with the word *'lh* (tree). The name *ytm* has frequently been identified with that of Jotham king of Judah in the mid eighth century BCE, Tell el-Kheleifeh probably being under Judah's control under the reign of Ahaz (2 Kgs 16.6), but the name *ytm* was not uncommon (cf. Judg. 9.5), and Herr dates the seal to the first half or the middle of the seventh century BCE on epigraphic grounds. The identification of *ytm* with king Jotham of Judah thus is unlikely.

N. Avigad, 1969: 18-22
D. Diringer, 1958: 224-25; Pl. 13
K. Galling, 1967: 131-34
N. Glueck, 1940b: 13-15
N. Glueck, 1970: 125; fig. 61a, b
N. Glueck, 1971: 225; Pl. 1
L.G. Herr, 1978: 163; fig. 78.2
L.G. Herr, 1980: 29-31
S. Moscati, 1961: 54, no. 9
F. Vattioni, 1969: 337-88 (373, no. 131)

3. *lmlkl/bʿbd/hmlk*
Buseira, Reg. no. 368

This seal is made of grey clay, and measures 11 × 6 mm. The upper register of the seal contains three designs which may represent towers or gateways (if so, presumably of Bozrah itself). A similar design appears on another seal found at Buseira (see *Levant* 9 [1977], plate IV D). The three lower registers give the name of a royal official, *mlklbʿ*. The name is otherwise unknown, but the second half of the name has been compared with a feminine Thamudic name *lbʿt*. The *dalet* (in *ʿbd*) has an upper extension to its shaft (compare the *qwsʿnl* seal impressions); this has prompted Puech (1977; 13, note 9) to suggest that the seals of Edom's royal officials derived from one scribal school. But the two *dalets* do not appear to be the same, and the two inscriptions are not of the same date or place. A. Lemaire argued that an illiterate engraver adjusted the lettering for the sake of symmetry, and that the name should be read *lmlkbʿl*, but that such a deliberate adjustment should be allowed on such an important thing as an official's seal seems unlikely. Herr dates the seal to the seventh century, possibly the first half.

A. Lemaire, 1975: 18-19
C.-M. Bennett, 1974a: 18-19; Pl. VIb

L.G. Herr, 1978: 163-64: fig. 78.3
L.G. Herr, 1980: 29-31

4. *'r 'r/lqws*
'Aro'er (in the Negev)

This jasper seal is divided by a single line into an upper and a lower register. The upper register appears to name the owner's home city, 'Aro'er, south-east of Beersheba. The seal was found in a stratified context which included painted pottery of the type known from Buseira and Tell el-Kheleifeh, and a stamped jar-handle of the *lmlk* (Ziph) type. In spite of the origin and archaeological context, and the use of the theophoric element *qws* on the seal, it is not completely certain that this was a specifically Edomite seal; the details of the lettering are unclear and slightly ambiguous. The seal came from an eighth-seventh century BCE building, and Herr dates it to the seventh century BCE.

A. Biran and R. Cohen, 1976: 139; Pl. 28
A. Biran and R. Cohen, 1977: 273-75; Pl. IXd
L.G. Herr, 1978: 165-66; fig. 78.6
L.G. Herr, 1980: 29-31

5. *qws g* [br] /mlk '[dm]
Umm el-Biyara

This seal is made of grey clay, and measures 19 × 16 mm. It shows a winged sphinx moving to the right, between the two lines of text, upper and lower. The sphinx has royal associations, and this seal is the only royal seal so far known in both Cis- and Trans-jordan. The thread marks on the back show that a leather document (the marks are not those of papyrus fibres) was once attached. The fire that destroyed the document baked and preserved the seal. The king named on it is probably the Qausgabri mentioned by Esarhaddon and Ashurbanipal (*ANET*[3] 29, 294) in the first half of the seventh century BCE, and if so, this dates the seal fairly closely. Herr notes the Aramaic style of the *waw* and the local, more Hebraic, style of the other letters.

C.-M. Bennett, 1966: 399-401; Pl. XXIIb
L.G. Herr, 1978: 162-63; fig. 78.1
J. Naveh, 1982: 102; Pl. 12[C]
F. Vattioni, 1969: 383, no. 227

6. *lqws'nl/'bd hmlk*
Tell el-Kheleifeh

This seal impression (the original seal has not been found) appears on a variety of pottery forms found in a storehouse of Glueck's Period IV at Tell el-Kheleifeh. 'All of the impressions were apparently stamped with the same small seal. Most of them belong to a type of large jug with one thin, broad loop-handle; others to bowls and cooking pots with rounded loop handles' (Glueck, 1938: 11; 1971b: 239). For the large jugs with thin, broad loop-handle, and the bowls ('inverted rim-craters') see Pratico, 1985: fig. 14.4; 15.1. The seal (cf. no. 3 above) was that of a royal official; his name includes the theophoric element *qws* and a verbal form which may mean 'has answered' or 'has answered me' or 'has achieved' (cf. Milik, 1958: 239 note 3; Malamat, 1966: 213). The script, styled 'lapidary' by Glueck, shows signs of Aramaic influence (e.g., the *waw* and open *'ayin*), and is generally agreed to date from the late seventh century—early sixth century BCE.

> W.F. Albright, 1938: 13, note 45
> N. Glueck, 1938b: 16-18; fig. 6
> N. Glueck, 1938c: 12-13; fig. 3
> N. Glueck, 1967a: 8-10
> N. Glueck, 1971b: 237-40; Pl. 11
> L.G. Herr, 1978: 164-65; fig. 78.4
> L.G. Herr, 1980: 29-31
> A. Malamat, 1966: 213
> J.T. Milik, 1958: 239
> J. Naveh, 1982: 102; fig. 92
> G. Pratico, 1985: figs. 14, 15, 17
> F. Vattioni, 1969: 372; no. 119

7. *šm''l*
Tafila (?)

The seal is made of chalcedony, and measures 20 × 18 mm. The face is divided into three registers. The upper and lower bear decorative motifs; the name (which lacks the usual *lamed* prefix) is in the middle. The name in this form does not seem to be recorded elsewhere, but compare the Old Testament Shemaiah (*šm'yh* or *šm'yhw*) and Ishmael (*yšm''l*). Harding originally dated this seal on general stylistic grounds to the ninth century BCE, but Herr finds the *m* typical of other Edomite seals, and the *'aleph* comparable to that on a Moabite and several Hebrew seals c. 700 BCE, and suggests a date in the first half of the seventh century BCE.

G.R. Driver, 1943: 34
G.R. Driver, 1976: 113; fig. 63A (wrongly attributed to Ammon)
K. Galling, 1941: 150, 171, 198; no. 183
G.L. Harding 1937: 255; Pl. X.10; fig. 12
L.G. Herr, 1978: 165; fig. 78.5
L.G. Herr, 1980: 29-31

8. *ltw*
Buseira, Reg. no. 856

This scaraboid seal measures 12 × 8 mm and is pierced lengthways. The name *tw* appears not to be Semitic, and possibly the seal's owner was an alien resident in Edom for political, commercial or military reasons. Another possibility is that *ltw* simply means 'for a mark'. The design is unusual, the inscription occupying the lower left face of the seal, surrounded by a crudely designed border on the upper and right-hand sides only. The design hardly suggests an owner of great wealth or style. Herr notes that the script, especially the *taw* and the *waw* would fit the Ammonite tradition, the *waw* being of Aramaising type, and he suggests a date of c. 700 BCE.

L.G. Herr, 1978: 167; fig. 78.8
L.G. Herr, 1980: 29-31
E. Puech, 1977: 17-18; fig. 6; Pl. VIB

Ostraca

1. Umm el-Biyara

line 1: *šmn r* [	oil p[ure, × measures]
line 2: *m'dr m*[	from 'Adr M[
line 3: *bd . . . . . bn.*[	(delivered) by . . . . . son of [

The ostracon is dated from its archaeological context to the seventh century BCE. The second line may refer to a place; the second word (*m*[. . .]) may be the second element of the place-name (e.g. M[oab]). The ostracon appears to be a docket recording the delivery of olive oil.

J.T. Milik, in C.-M. Bennett, 1966: 398-99; Pl. XXIIA

2. Buseira (reg. no. 816)

?]*hkrkb*[?

The first letter is not quite complete, the ostracon being broken at this point, but a *he* seems almost certain. It is not clear whether the *he* was preceded by other letters. The *reš* could be a *dalet*, and the final letter (if it is the final letter; but if there were any subsequent letters, they probably did not belong to the same word) could be a *reš*. Puech notes the biblical parallels at Exod. 27.5 and 38.4, where *krb hmzbḥ* appears to refer to a feature of the altar of the tabernacle— RSV, 'ledge'. This seems a very unlikely thing to write on a pot, even if the pot was destined for cultic use. A. Malamat suggested to me in conversation that the word should be read *hkdkd*, which is found in Ezek. 27.16 as one of the products of Edom (if Edom, not Syria, should be read here), and also at Isa. 54.12. However, in these two passages the word appears to refer to a hard, red stone (cf. Cooke, 1936: 303; Noth, 1964: 253). If the reference is to precious stones, the appearance of the word on a pot can be explained with reasonable ease. The interpretation of this ostracon, however, remains obscure. Puech dates it c. 700 BCE.

E. Puech, 1977: Pl. VB

3. Buseira (reg. no. 1191)

line 1: only an indistinct trace remains
line 2: *n k d* (or *r*) 1 (symbol) 2

The original number and length of the lines of this fragment are unknown. Only the end of the second line of the existing inscription can be made out. Puech suggests the reading *ḥṭn kr* 1 (symbol for *se'ah*) 2, i.e., 'wheat, 1 *kor*, 2 *seahs*'. (For *ḥṭn* Puech compares the Aramaising form *ḥiṭṭin* in Ezek. 4.9.) There were probably 30 *seahs* to the *kor* of grain, the *kor* being about 360 litres (cf. Gehman, 1951: 131) or about 240 litres (cf. de Vaux 1961, 202). Puech, however, calculates the amount of grain noted here as about 480 litres. Puech dates the ostracon to the seventh century BCE, noting that the *kap* resembles that in Buseirah ostracon no. 816 (see no. 2 above); the long, straight tails to the *kap* and the *nun*, however, are reminiscent of an earlier Hebrew style.

E. Puech, 1977: 19-20; fig. 8; Pl. VID.

4. Tell el-Kheleifeh (reg. no. 2069)

Glueck	Torrey
line 1: *qrplgs ṭpy'n* (?)	*ḥmr blgn ṭb y'n 5* (??)
line 2: *ḥmr ṭpy'n* 11	*ḥmr ṭb y'n 2*
line 3: *ḥmr* (?)	*ḥmr b* [*lgn*]...

In the first six letters of the first line Glueck sees the transliteration of the Greek *karpologos*, 'tax-gatherer' (following Albright, 1940: 9, note 12). It would be interesting (and perhaps not totally unexpected) to find evidence of an official with a Greek title in the Gulf of 'Aqaba in the fifth-fourth centuries BCE, but Torrey's reading, which supposes that the first letter of the first line is now lost but can be restored by comparison with lines 2 and 3, has merit. The two suggested translations are:

Glueck	Torrey
tax collector, jars, (?)	bottled wine, good quality, choice!
wine, jars, 2	5 (?) wine, good quality, choice! 2
wine (?)	wine b(ottled) ...

For *blgn*, 'in bottles', Torrey compares the use of *lgn* in Pap. 81 of Cowley, 1923. The difficulty with this reading is that the form of the *bet* (as Torrey himself remarks) is unusual, and at first sight Glueck's reading of a *pe* seems more probable. But an almost identical form occurs in two other places on this ostracon, and in each case Torrey and Glueck agree on the reading *bet*. The final *nun* of *blgn* seems more likely than Glueck's *samek*. In lines 1 and 2, Glueck reads *ṭpy'n*, which he interprets as one word meaning 'jars', (following H.C. Youtie's identification of *ṭpy'n* with Jewish-Aramaic *ṭpy'* and Mishnaic *ṭāfî*, 'jug with a narrow neck'. Torrey, however, reads these first letters as two adjectives, *ṭb, y'n*, 'fine, beautiful', which has the merit of simplicity. Albright proposed that the word *ṭpy'n* is derived from the Aramaic stem *ṭp'*, 'to close', 'to seal tight', and thus might mean 'sealed', 'closed'; but it seems unnecessary to state on a delivery docket that the wine will come in *sealed* bottles; how else would it come? In the second and third lines, the reference to the container is ellipsed (I owe this suggestion to W.G.E. Watson).

The script is Aramaic of the fifth-fourth centuries BCE.

W.F. Albright, 1941: 11
N. Glueck, 1940c: 6-10
N. Glueck, 1971: 232-33
C.C. Torrey, 1941: 15-16

5. Tell el-Kheleifeh (reg. no. 2070)

obverse

Glueck (1941)	Naveh (1966)	Glueck (1971)
1. *'(bd)plṭp.(š)*	---	*'(bd)--m*
2. *'bd's(ṭ)b(')l*	*'bd's-*	*'bd'š(m)n*
3. *'p(b)šlm*	*'bšlm*	*'bšlm*
4. *šlmlpsḥ(y)*	*šlmlḥy*	*šlmlḥy*
5. *š'db'l*	*š--b'l*	*š'db'l* (*sic.*: read *š'db'l*)

There are no names in this list containing the theophoric element *qws*, and the elements *b'l*, *'šmn* (Baal, Eshmun), together with the components *'b*, *'bd*, and *šlm* have suggested that this is a list of Phoenician names (Naveh, 1966: 27f.) The presence of Phoenicians in a coastal trading centre like Tell el-Kheleifeh is not surprising (cf. in earlier times 1 Kgs 9.26f.; 10.22). Similar names appear on ostracon 2071 (see below, no. 6). Naveh argues that the script is not, as Glueck and Albright originally thought, Aramaic, but a Phoenician cursive script from the Persian period.

reverse

Glueck (1941)	Torrey (1941)	Naveh (1966)	Glueck (1971)
1. *plg'*	*byt*	*p-'*	*plg'*
2. *knšh*	*knšh*	*knšy*	*knšy*
3. *wprš(ṭ)h*	*yršlm*	---	*(bdrmn)*

Much here is obscure. There appears to be agreement only on the first letter of line 1 and the first three letters of line 2. Torrey's suggestion that the ostracon refers to a synagogue 'Jerusalem' at Tell el-Kheleifeh begs too many questions. Naveh (1966: 28) again thinks of a Phoenician background, the form *knšy* (line 2) being a common name in the Punic onomasticon in the forms *knš*, *knš' knšy*, *knšm'*. The script of the reverse is also, according to Naveh, a Phoenician cursive script, though by a different hand from that on the obverse.

G.R. Driver, 1943: 34
N. Glueck, 1941: 7-11; figs 3-6
N. Glueck, 1971: 229; 31; Pl. 5.6
J. Naveh, 1966: 27-28
C.C. Torrey, 1941: 4-5

6. Tell el-Kheleifeh (reg. no. 2071)

line 1: *šlmn 'bd* (or, *šlmn 'br*)
line 2: *lḥy 'bd* (or, *lḥy 'br*)
line 3: *b'lyt(n)*
line 4: *'sb'(l)*

Glueck describes the script as cursive Aramaic of the fifth-fourth centuries BCE, though he ascribes line 4 to a different hand, 'related less to the Aramaic cursive script of the lines above it than to the Phoenician script of reg. no. 2070' (Glueck, 1971: 232, note 45). Torrey suggests that in the first two lines the strangely appended *'bd* should be read as *'br*, 'grain', and the text understood as a receipt, a companion to ostracon no 2069 (no. 4 above), which was a receipt for wine. A break in the ostracon has left us with an incomplete text. The break cuts through the last letter of line 1, allowing us to read a *dalet* or a *reš* (probably, with Torrey, the latter) and allowing us to restore the same letter to the end of line 2. If line 3 had the same word, it is now lost. Some indication of quantity may have been lost from all three lines. In the additional fourth line, the name itself appears to be incomplete. Glueck notes that beneath the visible lines may be seen traces of an earlier, erased text. The names on this ostracon contain elements (*b'l*, *lḥy*) which feature also on ostracon 2070; the distinctively Edomite element *qws* is also missing, though this is of little significance in such a short list. However. there is no certainty that these names can be counted as Edomite.

N. Glueck, 1940c: 3-10
N. Glueck, 1971: 232-33; Pl. 7
C.C. Torrey, 1941: 15

7. Tell el-Kheleifeh (reg. no. 6043)
The following readings of this ostracon have been proposed:

Glueck (1941)	Torrey (1941)	Albright (1941)	Naveh (1966)	Glueck (1971)
1. *lš'l*	*'š'l*	*n''l (r''l)*	*r''l*	*r''l*
2. *'d(y)'*	*'d'*	*bd'[l]*	*bd–*	*bdqw(s)*
3. *šlm*	*šlm*	*šlm*	*šlm*	*šlm*
4. *'bs b[r]*	*'wsb[r]*	*qwsb[nh]*	*qwsb–*	*qwsb[nh]*
5. *pgšqw[s]*	*tšqy*	*pg'qws*	*pg'qw[s]*	*pg'qws*
6. *y'kn (n'kn)*	*n'm (?)*	*nṭbn (?)*	*-db-*	*n'm(n)*
7. *škm*	*škm*	*škk*	*škk*	*škk*
8. *'ph ('py)*	*'py*	*rph (nph) (?)*	*rp'*	*rp'*
9. *pl(g)šq[ws]*	*tsqy (?)*	*pg'qws*	*pg'qws*	*pg'q(w)s*
10. *qwsny*	*qwsny*	*qwsny*	*qswn–*	*qwsny*

It is clear that Albright's readings mark an important stage in the decipherment of this ostracon. Rosenthal's opinion that the script of this ostracon shows 'an assimilation of the Canaanite cursive ductus to the then ruling uniform Official-Aramaic script' (Rosenthal 1942: 8f.) has received support from Naveh, who suggests that ostracon 6043 is in Edomite cursive script of the seventh-sixth centuries BCE, influenced by Aramaic forms, e.g., in the *bet*, *gimel*, *dalet*, *waw*, *kap*, *nun*, *samek*, *reš*; the *mem*, however, he compares with the forms found on the *qws'nl* seal impressions, the *l'myrn* (or *l'myrw*) graffito, and Moabite material, and he suggests that 'this *mem* may perhaps be a special form which was developed independently by the Moabites and Edomites' (Naveh, 1966: 30, note 24).

On Glueck's 1971 reading, half the names of this list contain the theophoric element *qws*. Four different *qws* names are attested.

1. *bdqws*: 'by the hand of *qws*'; cf. Phoen. *byd'l*, 'by the hand of El', and the eighth century BCE Ammonite king Buduili of Beth-Ammon (*ANET*[3] 287).

2. *qwsb[nh]*: '*qws* has created'; cf. the Greek form *Kosbanos* from Marisa and from the Idumaean colony at Mitrahineh, Egypt (see Milik, 1958: 240).

3. *pg'qws*: 'entreated of *qws*'; cf. Pagiel (Num. 1.13) and M. Noth, 1928: 90-92, 254.

4. *qwsny*: a hypocoristic form of *qwsntn*, '*qws* has given'; cf. the Greek form *Kosnatanos* from Marisa and Mitrahineh (cf. Milik, *ibid.*).

Of the other names on the list, *r''l* appears in the Old Testament as a Midianite (Exod. 2.18; Num. 10.29) and a son of Esau (Gen. 36.4). *šlm* and *rp'* appear in the O.T. in a variety of forms. For *n'm(n)* (if Glueck's reading is preferred to Naveh's), compare O.T. Naam, Naaman and Naomi.

The purpose of the list remains obscure. Glueck notes that originally it had two further lines at the top, and one at the bottom and that there are traces of the earlier use of the ostracon between lines 1 and 2, 2 and 3, 9 and 10 (Glueck, 1971: 229).

W.F. Albright, 1941, 11-15
N. Glueck, 1941: 3-6; figs 1, 2
N. Glueck, 1971: 228-29; Pl. 3
J. Naveh, 1966: 27-30
J. Naveh, 1982: 102, 104; fig. 93; Pl. 12D
F. Rosenthal, 1942: 8-9

8. Tell el-Kheleifeh (reg. no. 7094)

bršlm

Glueck originally read the final *mem* as a *waw* (*BASOR* 80 [1940], 8), but later interpreted the visible stroke of this letter as the first long stroke of a *mem* comparable with that on ostracon 6043 and the graffito on the juglet (reg. no. 374). The ostracon yields an Aramaic name, and Glueck regards its script as fifth-fourth century BCE cursive Aramaic (following Albright, 1941: 11). Driver (1943: 34) read *bršlp*, comparing Sheleph (Gen. 10.26), Nabataean *slpw*, and Arab. *salaf* ('ancestor').

G.R. Driver, 1943: 34
N. Glueck, 1940c: 9
N. Glueck, 1941: 10-11
N. Glueck, 1971: 233-34; Pl. 12

9. Tell el-Kheleifeh (reg. no. 10,007)

ḥm

Glueck describes the script of this fragment as 'late cursive Edomite', dating it to the fifth-fourth centuries BCE. Only two letters of a larger inscription are visible; Glueck suggests that the following letter may have been a *reš*, giving *ḥmr*, 'wine'.

N. Glueck, 1971: 237; Pl. 12

10. Ḥorvat 'Uza

1. *'mṙ. lmlk. 'mr. lblbl.*
2. *hšlm. 't. whbrktk*
3. *lqws. w't. tn. 't. h'kl*
4. *'šr. 'md. 'ḥ'mh[ ]*
5. [ ]*ḥmr. h'kl*

1. (Thus) said Lumalak (or <E>limelek): Say to *Blbl*!
2. Are you well? I bless you
3. by Qaus. And now give the food (grain)
4. that Aḥi'ma/o . . .
5. And may U[z]iel lift [it] upon (the altar?) . . .
6. [lest] the food become leavened(?)

This transcription and translation are by Itzhaq Beit-Arieh (1985: 96-101). The ostracon was found in a late seventh-century—early sixth-century BCE stratum at Ḥorvat 'Uza in 1983 (Beit-Arieh, Cresson 1983: 271-72) and was adjudged Edomite primarily on grounds of content ('I bless you by Qaus') and of script (similar to the Aramaising script of ostraca from Tell el-Kheleifeh, Umm el-Biyara and Buseira). This ostracon may be added to other evidence indicating an Edomite presence in the Negev of Judah in the seventh-sixth centuries BCE (see above, pp. 142-43). Beit-Arieh and Cresson (1985: 96-101 [99]) interpret the ostracon as 'an instruction issued by a high Edomite official to *Blbl*, apparently a high-ranking officer in an Edomite fort at 'Uza or elsewhere in the Negev, to supply a quantity of food—perhaps dough—to the messenger(s) bearing the inscribed ostracon'. They further note that 'Although the end of the message is not entirely clear, this does not affect the contents as a whole' (Beit-Arieh, Cresson, 1985: 99); but the proposed cultic reference of the last two lines does not relate easily to the suggestion that the previous lines refer to food supplies for the Edomite army. It is worth noting that the opening lines of the text do not necessarily indicate military activity at all. Caution must be exercised in the use of this ostracon as evidence for the reconstruction of border relationships between Edom and Judah in the seventh-sixth centuries BCE.

I. Beit-Arieh and B. Cresson, 1985: 96-101, Pl. 12

Incised Inscriptions

1. Buseira (reg. no. 157)

[... (?)] *lk*

These two letters, possibly the final letters of a name ending in -*mlk*, are incised on a fragment of a stone incense-burner. From palaeographical considerations, Puech suggests a date between the end of the eighth century and the beginning of the sixth century BCE.

E. Puech, 1977: 11-12; fig. 1; Pl. IVA

2. Buseira (reg. no. 487)

'b

Puech interprets these two letters as an abbreviation for *'sryt bt*, 'a tenth of a *bath*', the *bath* being the well known liquid measure of perhaps some 45 litres. The letters are incised on the handle of a jar which might reasonably contain 4-5 litres. The square *'ayin* is reminiscent of Ammonite forms of the eighth—sixth centuries BCE (cf. L.G. Herr, 1980: 22-25) (the form also appears in Moab in the seventh century; Herr, *ibid.*; 27,28). The *bet*, however, with its tail turning sharply to the left in a right-angle, is very similar to that on the *mlklb'bdhmlk* seal (Seal no. 3 above), also from Buseira. These comparisons suggest a seventh century BCE dating.

> C.-M. Bennett, 1975: 12-13; fig. 76
> E. Puech, 1977: 13-14; fig. 3; Pl. IVE

3. Buseira (reg. no. 583)

[b?]rk/qws or *[yb-]rk/qws*

The inscription is incised on a body-fragment of a bichrome bowl, its rim 27 cms diameter and its body painted with concentric bands. The divine name *qws* is preceded by what seems to be a word-divider, and two letters of the preceding word. The whole may be a name, or possibly a phrase indicating that the bowl was used as a votive offering. The lettering suggests a seventh century BCE date. The similar name *qwsbrk*, 'Qws has blessed', appears on a fourth-century BCE Aramaic ostracon from Tel Beersheba (cf. J. Naveh, 1979: 186; Pl. 26 [Ostracon 34]).

> C.-M. Bennett, 1975: 14; fig. 8.1
> E. Puech, 1977: 14-15; fig. 4; Pl. VA

4. Buseira (reg. no. 802)

l'dnš

This graffito is incised on the body of a jug of plain pink ware. The introductory *lamed* suggests that *'dnš* is a personal name. Compare the Phoenician *'dnš'* (*RES* 1239; cf. Benz, 1972: 59, 260f.). The letter forms are angular and lapidary, not cursive, the shank of the *lamed* and the tail of the *nun* being long, the *dalet* triangular. The form of the *šin* suggests Aramaic influence. The graffito probably belongs to the eighth-seventh centuries BCE.

> C.-M. Bennett, 1975: 14; fig. 8.3

5. Tell el-Kheleifeh (reg. no. 374)

l'myrw or *l'myrn*

This graffito is incised on a small, round bottomed jug from Glueck's Period IV of the offsets/insets settlement. The name may be compared with the Punic *'mrn* (*CIS* 5945.1; cf. Benz, 1972: 380) and with the Israelite Omri (1 Kgs 16.16), which Noth suggests is of Arabic origin (1928: 63). The open *'ayin* and *reš* suggest Aramaic influence. The *mem* is most economically incised with two short downward strokes and a longer, curved one. Naveh (1966: 29-30) classifies the script as seventh-sixth century BCE Edomite.

> N. Glueck, 1938b: 17
> N. Glueck, 1938c: 9
> N. Glueck, 1967a: 8-10; fig. 4.13; 5.4
> N. Glueck, 1970: 133; fig. 69
> N. Glueck, 1971: 226 and Pl. 2, 228, 234-5
> J. Naveh, 1966: 29-30

6. Tell el-Kheleifeh (reg. no. 8058)

'rš or *'rš'*

The remains of three lines of script are visible on this small sherd, of which the letters given above form the second. The form *'rš'* may be read if an unaligned *aleph* is added. Another letter, *reš*, appears below the *šin*.

For the name, cf. Benz, 1972: 64-68, 276f. Glueck, following F.L. Cross, notes the script as Phoenician, c. 600-400 BCE (Glueck, 1971: 235f.). The ostracon is perhaps further evidence for Phoenician presence or influence at Tell el-Kheleifeh in the fifth century BCE, to which Glueck dates it from the stratigraphical context.

> N. Glueck, 1971: 235-36; Pl. 9

7. Tell el-Kheleifeh (reg. no. 469)

's

These two letters are inscribed in a South Arabic script which Glueck (1970: 128) identifies as Minean and Albright (1952: 39-45) as Proto-Dedanic on a jar at first dated to the eighth century BCE (Glueck, 1970: 128). Glueck compares the script of these letters with that of inscriptions from the temple of Hureidha in the Hadhramaut in southern Arabia.

W.F. Albright, 1952: 39-45
N. Glueck, 1938b: 16-17
N. Glueck, 1970: 128-30; figs 64, 65
G. Ryckmans, 1939: 247-49

8. Tell el-Kheleifeh (reg. No. 9027)

Two incomplete signs or letters are incised on a sherd found in surface debris. Glueck suggests they are Minaean, and follows Ryckmans in dating them to the sixth century BCE.

P. Boneschi, 1961: 213-23
N. Glueck, 1938b: 19
N. Glueck, 1971b: 236-37; Pl. 10
G. Ryckmans, 1939: 247-47

Cuneiform Tablet

Tawilan

Transliteration

obv. 1 ⌈1⌉X X X X X X NU X⌉ A/šá
      2 ⌈2⌉GUD⌉?⌉[X X]- ⌈ri⌉⌉ MEŠ šá$^{i.d}$UTU-sa-iá-a-bi
      3 3⌉UDU ⌈X X X⌉ šá$^{i.d}$UTU-sa-id-ri
      4 i-bu-ku-u'a-na KÙ⌉.BABBARid-din-nu
      5 $^{i.d}$qu-ú-su- ⌈šá-ma⌉ -a' A⌈šú šá
      6 $^{i.d}$qu-ú-su-ia-da-a'⌈na-ši⌉
      7 ki- ⌈i⌉ laxti⌉X X[   ]
      8 zi-ka-ri A.AN 2[X(X) KÙ.BABBAR]
      9 $^{i.d}$qu-ú-su-šá-ma-[a'   ]
rev. 10 a-na $^{i.d}$UTU-sa-iá-a⌉-bi ⌈i⌉⌉ -[nam⌉-din⌉]
     11 ^{lu}mu-kin-nu ^{1}DÙG.GA-X A-šú ⌈šá⌉
     12 ^{1}ar⌉-ri-iá^{1}ad-du-ra⌉-mu⌉
     13 A-šú šá⌉⌉ar-ri-iá⌉XX
     14 1 ⌈d⌉AG⌉⌉ -KAR⌉-ZI-šú⌉XXX ^{1}NUMUN-iá
     15 KASKAL^{ki}ITI ⌈ŠE⌉ U.24.KAM MU SAG
     16 NAM.LUGAL ^{1}da-ru-ú-me-šú
         LUGAL KUR KUR

Translation
     One (?) . . ., two oxen (?) . . . belonging to Samsa-yabi, three sheep (?) . . . belonging to Samsa-idri, they brought and sold for

silver. Qusu-šama' the son of Qusu-yada' has taken (them). If he does not . . ., Qusu-šama' [shall pay(?)] two [. . . of silver(?)] for each ram to Samsa-yabi.

Witnesses: Ṭab-x son of Arriya; Addu-ramu(?) son of Arriya . . . Nabu(?)-eṭir-napištišu son of(?) Zeriya.

Harran, month of Addar, 24th day, accession year of Darius king of the lands.

The transliteration and translation given above are by Stephanie Dalley (1984: 19-22 [21]). This unbaked clay tablet appears to be a contract of sale drawn up at Harran in the accession year of Darius (possibly but not certainly Darius I, 521-486 BCE). An Edomite, Qusu-šama' son of Qusu-yada', was buying sheep and oxen from men (presumably Aramaeans) with Aramaic names. The reference to some future penalty if certain conditions are not met is unclear (Dalley suggests that 'the sale is made with the condition that the seller takes some offspring after the next breeding season (1984: 10); it seems unlikely, however, that a seller could enforce this, and the condition may perhaps be a device to prevent the buyer welshing on the deal).

There are a number of interesting points raised by this tablet (see Dalley, 1984: 19-22 for discussion), but two stand out for our purposes: (1) that an Edomite (Qusu-šama', presumably from Tawilan) might be found transacting business in Harran, almost 1000 kilometres away; and (2) that he found it important to carry the docket back to Tawilan, where conceivably there were others beside himself who might be able to read this document in Babylonian cuneiform. Dalley points out that a Babylonian personal name appears on the Teima stele from the same period, and concludes from this and her discussion of other contracts (1984: 21) that:

> if Nabonidus kept cuneiform scribes in his royal chancellery at Teima, and if cuneiform contracts were still drawn up in Neirab, Tyre and Qadesh by indigenous scribes with Babylonian names, it is by no means far-fetched to suppose that the occasional cuneiform scribe was to be found in the land of Edom 20 years later, 500 km away along a well-frequented road.

Whether Tawilan boasted a cuneiform scribe or not, it is highly likely (in view of Edom's position as a tributary kingdom of the Assyrian empire and later as subject to Babylonia) that there were cuneiform scribes in Edom, who could both write and decipher contracts when required. Horsfield and Conway (1930: 379, and Pl. X) noted the excavation at Petra of 'five stone pencils, seemingly for writing cuneiform'.

Weights

1. Petra

A small, square bronze weight, inscribed *ḥmšt* and weighing 45.36 gr. The inscription may indicate that the weight is five light shekels (the light shekel was also known, according to R.B.Y. Scott, as the *nṣp*, which was half the heavy Syrian shekel, averaging between 9.5 and 10 gr.).

E.J. Pilcher, 1922: 71-73

2. Umm el-Biyara

A dome shaped stone weight, inscribed with the shekel sign and the sign for 4, and weighing 42.46 gr. As the *nṣp* could weigh as much as 10.63 gr., this weight could be the equivalent of 4 light shekels. If the 'royal shekel' of a little over 11 gr. is meant, then this weight would be somewhat light. Bennett notes that it is the lightest of those weights inscribed '4 shekels'. But the 'royal shekels' belonged to Judah, and there is no need to suppose that this Edomite weight is a 'royal shekel' or that it was brought by some travelling merchant from Judah (Bennett, 1966: 395-96).

C.-M. Bennett, 1966: 395-96; Pl. XXIVB

3. Buseira (reg. no. 621)

A slightly irregular chalk cube, inscribed on one face *n* and on another *nṣ* (crossed through by a horizontal stroke); the inscription probably indicated *nṣp*, the 'half' shekel, or lighter shekel. This weight weighs 9.5 gr., which agrees well with other known *nṣp* weights, which range between 9.28 and 10.63 gr. It seems that on the second side, the engraver tried to write the whole word *nṣp*, but was defeated, perhaps for lack of space, (the *n* and the *ṣ* overlap, but still leave insufficient room for the *p*). Puech dates the weight on palaeographical grounds c. 700 BCE.

D. Diringer, 1958: 227-30; Pl. 13
E. Puech, 1977: 15-17; fig. 5; Pl. VIA
R.B.Y. Scott, 1964: 53-64
R.B.Y. Scott, 1970: 62-66

Edom

Key to sites and natural features on numbered maps

1. es-Ṣāfi
2. Khirbet el-'Akkuza
3. Dhāt Rās
4. el-'Ainā
5. 'Ain 'Arūs
6. Khanazir
7. Feifeh
8. Khirbet et-Tannūr
9. Rujm Jā'īs
10. Rujm Bakhir
11. Qal'at et-Ḥasā
12. Rujm Karaka
13. 'Aima
14. Ṭafīla
15. 'Ain Ḥaṣb
16. Khirbet es-Sil'
17. eth-Thuwāneh
18. Buṣeirā
19. Ruwāth
20. Gharandel
21. Jurf ed-Darāwīsh
22. 'Ain el-Jaladat
23. Khirbet el-Ghuweiba
24. Khirbet el-Jariya
25. Khirbet en-Naḥās
26. Khirbet Hamr Ifdān
27. 'Ain el-Ḥufeira
28. Dānā
29. Khirbet Abū 'Ajāj
30. Shajarat et-Ṭaiyār
31. Feinān
32. Umm el-'Amad
33. Khirbet es-Samrā
34. Shaubak
35. Dūsaq
36. Nijil
37. Khirbet Ishra
38. Shamākh
39. 'Uneiza
40. Bir Khidād
41. Beidā
42. Badibda
43. Umm el-Biyāra
44. Tawilan
45. Udhruh
46. Petra
47. Wadi Mūsā
48. Dḥāha
49. Biṭāḥī
50. Mabrak
51. Basṭa
52. Ma'ān
53. Khirbet el-Megheita
54. Ṣadaqa
55. Ghrareh
56. Dilāgha
57. Bīr Abū el-Lisān
58. Bīr el-Fuweilī
59. Khirbet esh-Shudaiyid
60. Ḥumeima
61. 'Ain Ghadyān
62. el-Quweira
63. Tell el-Kheleifeh
64. 'Aqaba

70. Wadi el-Ḥasā
71. Wadi 'Afra
72. Wadi el-La'bān
73 Wadi Jā'īs
74 Wadi el-'Ali
75. Wadi el-Aḥmar
76. Wadi el-Jeib
77. Wadi el-Fidān
78 Wadi el-Buweirida
79. Wadi Abū Sakākīn
80. Wadi Namala

81. Wadi Abū Khusheiba
82. Naqb er-Rubā'ī
83. Wadi Abū Barqa
84. Wadi Judaiyid
85. Wadi Rummān
86. Wadi Ram
87. Wadi Yutm
88. Jebel Hārūn
89. Jebel Khalāl
90. Jebel el-Jil

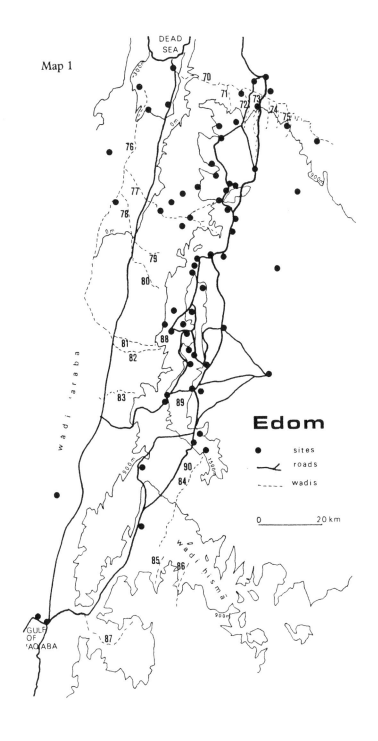

Map 1

DEAD SEA

70
71
72 73
74 75

76

77

78

79

80

81
82

88

83

89

wadi 'araba

90
84

85 86

wadi hisma

GULF
OF
'AQABA

87

Edom

● sites

⌒ roads

--- wadis

0   20 km

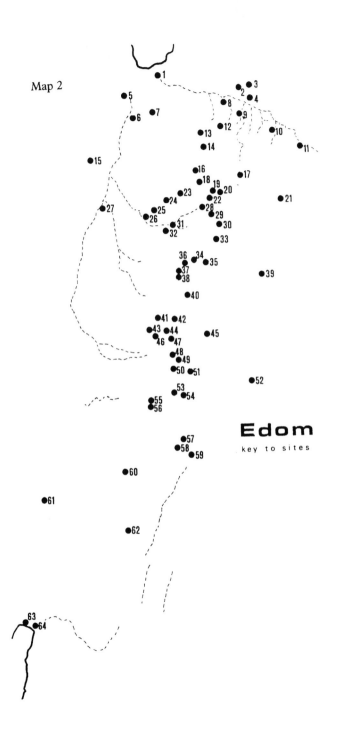

Map 2

Edom
key to sites

BIBLIOGRAPHY

Books

Abel, F.-M.
    1933, 1938   *Géographie de la Palestine*, I, II. Paris: J. Gabalda.
    1973   *Excavations at Tel Beer-sheba*, I. Tel Aviv: Tel Aviv University Institute of Archaeology.
Aharoni, Y.
    1973   *Excavations at Tel Beer-sheba*, I. Tel Aviv: Tel Aviv University Institute of Archaeology.
    1979   *The land of the Bible: a historical geography*. 2nd ed. London: Burns and Oates.
Aharoni, Y., and Naveh, J.
    1981   *Arad inscriptions*. Judaean Desert Studies, Jerusalem: Israel Exploration Society.
Albright, W.F.
    1956   *Archaeology and the religion of Israel*. 4th ed. Baltimore: Johns Hopkins.
Alt, A.
    1953   *Kleine Schriften*, I, II. München: C.H. Beck.
Anati, E.
    1963   *Palestine before the Hebrews*. London: J. Cape.
Avi-Yonah, M., and Stern, E.
    1975-78   *Encyclopedia of archaeological excavations of the Holy Land*, I-IV. London: Oxford University Press.
Axelsson, L.E.
    1987   *The Lord rose up from Seir: studies in the history and traditions of the Negev and Southern Judah*. (CB, Old Testament series 25.) Lund: Almqvist & Wiksell.
Baly, A.D.
    1974   *Geography of the Bible*. 2nd ed. Guildford and London: Lutterworth Press.
Bannister, J.
    1866   *The life of David Roberts, R.A., compiled from his journals and other sources*. Edinburgh: A. & C. Black.
Bartlett, W.J.
    1867   *Forty days in the desert on the track of the Israelites*, or, *A journey from Cairo to Mount Sinai and Petra*. London: Bell and Daldy.
Benz, F.L.
    1972   *Personal names in the Phoenician and Punic inscriptions*. Rome: Pontifical Biblical Institute.
Bernatz, J.M.
    1839   *Bilder aus dem Heiligen Lande: vierzig ausgewählte Original Ansichten biblisch-wichtiger Orte, treu nach der Natur aufgenommen*. Stuttgart: J.F. Steinkopf.
Bernhardt, K.H. (ed.)
    1971   *Schalom: Studien zu Glaube und Geschichte Israels* (Festschrift A. Jepsen). Berlin: Evangelische Verlagsanstalt.

Boling, R.G.
  1975   *Judges* (Anchor Bible). New York: Doubleday.
Breasted, J.H.
  1906-7   *Ancient records of Egypt*, I-V. Chicago: Chicago University Press.
Bright, J.
  1965   *Jeremiah* (Anchor Bible). New York: Doubleday.
  1980   *A history of Israel*. 3rd ed. London: SCM Press.
Brünnow, R.E. and von Domaszewski, A.
  1904, 1905, *Die Provincia Arabia auf grund zweier in den Jahren 1897 und 1898*
  1909   *unternommenen Reisen und der Berichte früheren Reisender*, I, II, III.
            Strasbourg: K.J. Trübner.
Buhl, F.
  1893   *Geschichte der Edomiter*. Leipzig: A. Edelmann.
Burckhardt, J.L.
  1822   *Travels in Syria and the Holy Land*. London: J. Murray.
Burdon, D.J.
  1959   *Handbook of the geology of Jordan*. Amman: Government Publication.
Burney, C.F.
  1903   *Notes on the Hebrew text of the Books of Kings*. Oxford: Clarendon
            Press.
  1918   *The book of Judges*. London: Rivingtons.
Caminos, R.A.
  1954   *Late Egyptian miscellanies* (Bibliotheca Aegyptica 7). London: Oxford
            University Press.
Carmichael, C.M.
  1974   *The laws of Deuteronomy*. Ithaca: Cornell University Press.
Caskel, W.
  1954   *Liḥyan und Liḥyanisch*. Köln: Westdeutscher Verlag.
Cleveland, R.L.
  1960   *The excavation of the Conway High Place (Petra) and soundings at
            Khirbet Ader* (AASOR 34-35), Pt. 2 (1954-56). New Haven: American
            Schools of Oriental Research.
Coogan, M.D.
  1976   *West Semitic personal names in the Murasu documnts* (Harvard
            Semitic Monographs, 7). Missoula, Montana: Scholars Press for
            Harvard Semitic Museum.
Cook, S.A.
  1930   *The religion of Palestine in the light of archaeology*. London: Oxford
            University Press for the British Museum.
Cooke, G.A.
  1936   *A critical and exegetical commentary on the book of Ezekiel* (I C C).
            Edinburgh: T. & T. Clark.
Cowley, A.E.
  1923   *Aramaic papyri of the fifth century B.C.* Oxford: Clarendon Press.
Dahood, M.
  1965, 1968, 1970 *The Psalms*, I-III (Anchor Bible). New York: Doubleday.
Desnoyers, L.
  1922   *L'Histoire du peuple hébreu des Juges à la captivité*. Paris: A.
            Picard.
Dornemann, R.H.
  1983   *The archaeology of the Transjordan in the Bronze and Iron ages*.
            Milwaukee: Milwaukee Public Museum.

Dougherty, R.P.
1929　*Nabonidus and Belshazzar: a study of the closing events of the Neo-Babylonian empire.* New Haven: Yale University Press.
Doughty, C.M.
1888　*Travels in Arabia Deserta.* Cambridge: Cambridge University Press.
1921　*Travels in Arabia Deserta.* New edition, with new preface by the author and an introduction by T.E. Lawrence. London: Medici Society and J. Cape.
Driver, G.R.
1976　*Semitic writing from pictograph to alphabet.* 3rd ed. Oxford: Oxford University Press for the British Academy.
Edgar, C.C.
1925　*Zenon Papyri (Catalogue général des antiquités égyptiennes du Musée de Caire),* I. Cairo: Imprimerie de l'Institut Français.
Efird, J.M. (ed.)
1972　*The use of the Old Testament in the New and other essays* (Festschrift W.F. Stinespring). Durham, N.C.: Duke University Press.
Engnell, I.
1943　*Studies in divine kingship in the ancient Near East.* Uppsala: Almqvist & Wiksell.
Eph'al, I.
1982　*The ancient Arabs: nomads on the borders of the fertile crescent, 9th—5th centuries B.C..* Jerusalem: The Magnes Press; Leiden: E.J. Brill.
Formby, H.
1843　*A visit to the east.* London: J. Burns.
Forrer, E.
1921　*Die Provinzeinteilung des assyrischen Reiches.* Leipzig: J.C. Hinrichs.
Frank, H.T., and Reed, W.L.
1970　*Translating and understanding the Old Testament* (Festschrift H.G. May). Nashville: Abingdon.
Freedman, H., and Simon, M.
1939　*Midrash Rabbah,* I, II. London: Soncino.
Gardiner, A.H.
1961　*Egypt of the Pharaohs.* Oxford: Clarendon Press.
Garstang, J.
1931　*Joshua, Judges.* London: Constable.
Giveon, R.
1971　*Les Bedouins Shosou des documents égyptiens (Documenta et Monumenta Orientis Antiqui* 18). Leiden: E.J. Brill.
Glueck, N.
1966　*Deities and dolphins: the story of the Nabataeans.* London: Cassell.
1970　*The other side of the Jordan.* 2nd ed. Cambridge, Mass.: American Schools of Oriental Research.
Goedicke, H. (ed.)
1971　*Near eastern studies in honor of W.F. Albright.* Baltimore and London: Johns Hopkins University Press.
Görg, M., and Pusch, E.
1979　*Festschrift Elmar Edel, 12 März 1979* (Ägypten und Altes Testament I). Bamberg: M. Görg.
Gottwald, N.
1979　*The tribes of Yahweh: a sociology of the religion of liberated Israel 1250-1950 B.C.* Maryknoll, N.Y.: Orbis.

Grätz, H.
  1866   *Geschichte der Juden von den ältesten Zeiten bis auf die Gegenwart.*
          Leipzig: O. Leiner.
Gray, G.B.
  1903   *A critical and exegetical commentary on the book of Numbers* (ICC).
          Edinburgh: T. & T. Clark.
Gray, J.
  1987   *Joshua, Judges and Ruth* (New Century Bible). 2nd ed. London:
          Marshall, Morgan and Scott.
Gray, J.
  1980   *1 & 2 Kings: a commentary* (OTL). 3rd ed. London: SCM Press.
Gunkel, H.
  1922   *Genesis übersetzt und erklärt* (Göttinger Handkommentar zum Alten
          Testament). 5th ed. Göttingen: Vandenhoeck und Ruprecht.
Hadidi, A. (ed.)
  1982, 1985 *Studies in the history and archaeology of Jordan*, I, II. Amman:
          Department of Antiquities of Jordan.
Harding, G.L., and Littmann, E.
  1952   *Some Thamudic inscriptions from the Hashemite kingdom of Jordan.*
          Leiden: E.J. Brill.
Harper, R.F.
  1902   *Assyrian and Babylonian letters belonging to the Kouyunjik collections
          of the British Museum.* Chicago: Chicago University Press; London:
          Luzac.
Hart, H.C.
  1891   *Some account of the fauna and flora of Sinai, Petra and Wadi 'Arabah.*
          London: Palestine Exploration Fund.
Hayes, J.H., and Miller, J.M.
  1979   *Israelite and Judaean history.* (OTL) London: SCM Press.
Helck, W.
  1971   *Die Beziehungen Ägyptens zu Vorderasien im 3. und 2. Jahrtausend vor
          Chr.* 2nd ed. Wiesbaden: O. Harrassowitz.
Hengel, M.
  1974   *Judaism and Hellenism*, I, II. London: SCM Press.
Hermann, S.
  1975   *A history of Israel in Old Testament times.* London: SCM Press.
Herr, L.G.
  1978   *The scripts of ancient North West Semitic seals* (Harvard Semitic
          Monographs 18). Missoula, Montana: Scholars Press for the Harvard
          Semitic Museum.
Herr, L.G. (ed.)
  1983   *The Amman Airport excavations*, 1976 (AASOR 48).
Hertzberg, H.W.
  1964   *1 & 2 Samuel* (OTL). London: SCM Press.
Hoftijzer, J., and van der Kooij, G.
  1976   *Aramaic texts from Deir 'Alla.* Leiden: E.J. Brill.
Huber, C.
  1891   *Journal d'un voyage en Arabie (1883-1884).* Paris: Imprimerie
          nationale.
Hull, E.
  1889   *Memoir on the geography and geology of Arabia Petraea, Palestine and
          adjoining districts.* London: Palestine Exploration Fund.

Irby, C.L., and Mangles, J.
  1844   *Travels in Egypt and Nubia, Syria, and the Holy Land, including a*
             journey round the Dead Sea, and through the country east of the
             Jordan. London: J. Murray.
Ishida, T.
  1977   *The royal dynasties in ancient Israel* (BZAW 142).
Jamme, A.
  1974   *Miscellanées d'Ancien Arabie.* Washington DC: privately printed.
Jaussen, A., and Savignac, R.
  1909, 1914 *Mission archaeologique en Arabie,* I, II. Paris: Publications de la
             Société Française de Fouilles archéologiques.
Johnson, M.D.
  1969   *The purpose of biblical genealogies—with special reference to the setting*
             of the genealogies of Jesus (SNTS Monograph Series, 8). Cambridge:
             Cambridge University Press.
Jones, A.H.M.
  1971   *Cities of the eastern Roman provinces.* 2nd ed. Oxford: Clarendon
             Press.
Jones, G.H.
  1984   *1 and 2 Kings,* I, II (New Century Bible). London: Marshall, Morgan
             and Scott.
Karmon, Y.
  1971   *Israel: a regional geography.* New York: Wiley Interscience.
Keith, A.
  1823   *Study of the evidence from prophecy: containing an account of those*
             prophecies which were distinctly foretold, and which have been clearly
             or literally fulfilled. Edinburgh: Waugh and Innes.
Kitchen, K.A.
  1973   *The Third Intermediate Period in Egypt 1100-650 B.C.* Warminster:
             Aris and Phillips.
Klostermann, A.
  1896   *Geschichte des Volkes Israel bis zur Restauration unter Ezra und*
             Nehemia. München: G.H. Beck.
Klostermann, E.
  1904   *Eusebius: Das Onomastikon der biblischen Ortsnamen* (Die griechischen
             christlichen Schriftsteller der ersten drei Jahrhunderte: Eusebius
             III.1). Leipzig: J.C. Hinrichs.
Knudzton, J.A.
  1907-15   *Die El-Amarna Tafeln mit Einleitung und Erläuterungen.* Leipzig: J.C.
             Hinrichs.
Laborde, Léon de, et Linant, J.P.
  1830   *Voyage de l'Arabie Pétrée.* Paris: Giard.
Laborde, Léon de
  1836   *Journey through Arabia Petraea to Mount Sinai, and the excavated*
             city of Petra, the Edom of the prophecies. London: J. Murray.
Lartet, L.
  1869   *Essai sur la géologie de la Palestine et des contrées avoisinantes.* Paris:
             V. Masson.
  1876   *Géologie* (= Duc de Luynes, *Voyage d' exploration à la Mer Morte,*
             tome 3). Paris: A. Bertrand.
  1877   *Exploration géologique de la Mer Morte, de la Palestine et de l'Idumée.*
             Paris: A. Bertrand.

Lasko, L.H. (ed.)
> 1986 *Egyptological studies in honor of R.A. Parker*. Hanover and London: University Press of New England for Brown University Press.

Lawrence, A.W.
> 1979 *Greek aims in fortification*. Oxford: Clarendon Press.

Lawrence, T.E.
> 1935 *Seven pillars of wisdom*. London: J. Cape.

Leary, G. (ed.)
> 1935 *From the pyramids to Paul: studies in theology, archaeology and related subjects* (George Livingston Robinson anniversary volume). New York: T. Nelson.

Lemaire, A.
> 1977 *Inscriptions hébraiques. Tome 1: Les ostraca* (Literatures anciennes du Proche-Orient 9). Paris: Les Editions du Cerf.

Libby, W., and Hoskins, F.E.
> 1905 *The Jordan valley and Petra*, I, II. New York: G.W. Putnam's Sons.

Lidzbarski, M.
> 1902-15 *Ephemeris für semitische Epigraphik*, I-III. Giessen: J. Ricker.

Liebermann, S. (ed.)
> 1950 *Alexander Marx Jubilee Volume*. New York: Jewish *Seminary of America*.

Lindner, M. (ed.)
> 1986 *Petra: Neue Angrabungen und Entdeckungen*. München und Bad Windsheim: Delp Verlag.

Lindsay, Lord
> 1847 *Letters on Egypt, Edom and the Holy Land*. 4th ed. London: Henry Colburn.

Luckenbill, D.D.
> 1924 *The annals of Sennacherib* (University of Chicago Oriental Publications, II). Chicago: University of Chicago Press.
> 1926, 1927 *Ancient records of Assyria and Babylonia*, I, II. Chicago: University of Chicago Press.

Lury, J.
> 1896 *Geschichte der Edomiter im biblischen Zeitalter*. Berlin: L. Wechselmann.

de Luynes, Duc (Honore Th. P.J. d'Albert)
> 1874 *Voyage d'exploration àla Mer Morte, à Petra et sur la rive gauche du Jourdain*, I, II, III and *Atlas*. Sous la direction de M. le Comte de Vogüé. Paris: A. Bertrand.

Lynch, W.F.
> 1849 *Narrative of the United States' expedition to the River Jordan*. London: Richard Bentley.

Macintosh, A.A.
> 1980 *Isaiah XXI—a palimpsest*. Cambridge: Cambridge University Press.

Marquart, J.
> 1896 *Fundamente israelitischer und jüdischer Geschichte*. Göttingen: Dieterich.

Matthiae, K., and Thiel, W.
> 1985 *Biblische Zeittafeln*. Neukirchen-Vluyn: Neukirchener Verlag.

Maughan, W.C.
> 1874 *The Alps of Arabia: travels in Egypt, Sinai, Arabia and the Holy Land*. 2nd ed. London: H.S. King.

Maundrell, H.
1703 *A journey from Aleppo to Jerusalem at Easter, A.D. 1697.* Oxford.
McCarter, P.K.
1980 *1 Samuel* (Anchor Bible, 8). New York: Doubleday.
1984 *2 Samuel* (Anchor Bible 9). New York: Doubleday.
Mercer, S.A.B.
1939 *The Tell el-Amarna tablets*, I, II. Toronto: Macmillan.
Meyer, E.
1906 *Die Israeliten und ihre Nachbarstämme.* Halle: M. Niemeyer.
Miller, J.M., and Hayes, J.H.
1986 *A history of ancient Israel and Judah.* London: SCM Press.
Milne, J.G.
1905 *Greek inscriptions* (Catalogue générale des Antiquités égyptiennes du Musée de Caire). Oxford: Oxford University Press.
Montet, P.
1933 *Les nouvelles fouilles de Tanis, 1929-32* (Publications de la Faculté des Lettres de Strasbourg, II. 10). Paris: Les Belles Lettres.
Montgomery, J.A.
1934 *Arabia and the Bible.* Philadelphia: University of Philadelphia Press.
Montgomery, J.A., and Gehman, H.S.
1951 *A critical and exegetical commentary on the Books of Kings* (ICC). Edinburgh: T. & T. Clark.
Moorey, P.R.S., and Parr, P.J.
1978 *Archaeology in the Levant: Essays for Kathleen Kenyon.* Warminster: Aris and Phillips.
Moscati, S.
1961 *L'epigrafia ebraici antica 1935-50.* Rome: Pontificio Istituto Biblico.
Müller, W.M.
1893 *Asien und Europa nach altägyptischen Denkmälern.* Leipzig: J.C. Hinrichs.
Murray, M.A.
1939 *Petra: the rock city of Edom.* London and Glasgow: Blackie.
Musil, A.
1907, 1908 *Arabia Petraea*, II: *Edom. Topographischer Reisebericht*, 1, 2. Wien: Alfred Holder; Kaiserliche Akademie der Wissenschaften.
1910 *Karte von Arabia Petraea.* Wien: Alfred Holder.
1926 *The northern Heğâz.* New York: Czech Academy of Sciences and Arts, and Charles J. Crane
Naveh, J.
1982 *Early history of the alphabet.* Jerusalem: The Magnes Press, Hebrew University, and Leiden: E.J. Brill.
Nöldeke, Th.
1869 *Untersuchungen zur Kritik des Alten Testaments.* Kiel: Schwer'sche Buchhandlung.
North, C.R.
1964 *The Second Isaiah.* Oxford: Clarendon Press.
Noth, M.
1928 *Die israelitische Personennamen im Rahmen der gemeinsemitischen Namengebung.* Stuttgart: W. Kohlhammer.

1957   *Überlieferungsgeschichtliche Studien.* 2nd ed. Tübingen: M. Niemeyer.
1960   *The history of Israel.* 2nd ed. London: A. & C. Black.
1968   *Numbers* (OTL). London: SCM Press.
Olin, S.
1843   *Travels in Egypt, Arabia Petraea and the Holy Land.* 3rd ed. New York: Harper.
Palmer, E.H,
1871   *The desert of the Exodus: journeys on foot in the wilderness of the forty years' wanderings.* Cambridge: Deighton Bell.
Pardee, D.
1982   *Handbook of ancient Hebrew letters* (Society for Biblical Literature Sources for Biblical Study 15). Chico: Scholars Press.
Peters, J.P., and Thiersch, H.
1905   *Painted tombs in the necropolis of Marissa.* London: Palestine Exploration Fund.
Petrie, W.F.M.
1911   *Egypt and Israel.* London: S.P.C.K.
Pritchard, J.B.
1969   *Ancient Near Eastern Texts relating to the Old Testament.* 3rd ed. with Supplement (= *ANET³*). Princeton: Princeton University Press.
Rad, G. von
1972   *Genesis* (OTL). 2nd ed. London: SCM Press.
Rast, W.E.
1986   *Madaba Plains Project: a preliminary report of the 1984 season at Tell el 'Umeiri and its vicinity* (BASOR Supplement 24).
Rawlinson, H.C.
1861-91 *The cuneiform inscriptions of western Asia*, I—V. London: British Museum Department of Egyptian and Asiatic Antiquities.
Reicke, B., and Rost, L.
1979   *Palästina historische-archäologische Karte.* Göttingen: Vandenhoeck und Ruprecht.
Reland, H.
1714   *Palaestina ex monumentis veteribus illustrata.* Trajecti Batavorum ad Rhenum: Giulielmi Broedelet.
Roberts, D.
1842-1849 *The Holy Land, Syria, Idumaea, Arabia, Egypt and Nubia from drawings made on the spot by David Roberts, R.A., with historical description by the Revd. George Croly, LL.D.* London: F.C. Moon.
Robinson, E., and Smith, E.
1841   *Biblical researches in Palestine, Mount Sinai and Arabia Petraea: a journal of travels in the year 1838*, I-III. London: J. Murray.
1856   *Biblical researches in Palestine and the adjacent regions: a journal of travels in the years 1838 and 1852*, I—II. London: J. Murray.
Robinson, G.L.
1930   *The sarcophagus of an ancient civilization: Petra, Edom and the Edomites.* New York: Macmillan.
Rothenberg, B.
1961   *God's wilderness: discoveries in Sinai.* London: Thames and Hudson.
1972   *Timna, valley of the biblical copper mines.* London: Thames and Hudson.

Rüppell, E.
1829   *Reisen in Nubien, Kordofan und dem Peträischen Arabien, vorzüglich in geographischer-statischer Hinsicht.* Frankfurt am Main: Friedrich Wilmans.

Sanders, J.A. (ed.)
1970   *Near Eastern archaeology in the twentieth-century: essays in honor of Nelson Glueck.* New York: Doubleday.

Sawyer, J.F.A., and Clines, D.J.A. (ed.)
1983   *Midian, Moab and Edom: the history and archaeology of Late Bronze and Iron Age Jordan and North-west Arabia* (JSOT Supplement Series 24). Sheffield: JSOT Press.

Schrader, E.
1902-1903   *Die Keilinschriften und das Altes Testament.* 3rd ed. Berlin: Reuther & Reichard.

Schubert, G.H. von
1838, 1839   *Reise in das Morgenland in den Jahren 1836 und 1837.* 3 Bde, Erlangen: J.J. Palm and E. Enke.

Schürer, E.
197 -198   *The history of the Jewish people in the age of Jesus Christ,* I-III, revised ed. by G. Vermes, F. Millar and M. Black. Edinburgh: T. & T. Clark.

Seetzen, U.J.
1810   *A brief account of the countries adjoining the Lake of Tiberias, the Jordan, and the Dead Sea.* Published for the Palestine Association of London. Bath: Mayler.

1854-1859   *Reisen durch Syrien, Palastina, Phonicien, Transjordan-Länder, Arabia Petraea und Unter-Aegypten, herausgegeben und commentiert von Prof. Dr. Fr. Kruse.* Berlin: G. Reimer.

Shenkel, J.D.
1968   *Chronology and recensional development in the Greek text of Kings* (Harvard Semitic Monographs, 1). Cambridge, Mass.: Harvard University Press.

Simons, J.J.
1959   *The geographical and topographical texts of the Old Testament.* Leiden: E.J. Brill.

Skinner, J.
1910   *A critical and exegetical commentary on Genesis* (ICC). Edinburgh: T. & T. Clark.

Smith, G.A.
1931, 1966   *The historical geography of the Holy Land.* 25th ed. London: Hodder and Stoughton. Republished 1966 in the Fontana Library of Theology and Philosophy, London and Glasgow: Collins.

Smith, S.
1944   *Isaiah chapters XL-LV: literary criticism and history* (Schweich Lectures, 1940). London: Oxford University Press for the British Academy.

Smith, W. Robertson
1912   *Lectures and essays,* ed. J.S. Black and G.W. Chrystal. London: A. & C. Black.

Stanley, A.P.
1856   *Sinai and Palestine in connection with their history.* London: J. Murray.

Stephens, J.L. (= Stephens, George)
1838   *Incidents of travel in Egypt, Arabia Petraea, and the Holy Land.* London: Bentley.
Strassmaier, J.N.
1897   *Babylonische Texte: Inschriften von Darius, König von Babylon (521-485 v. Chr.).* Leipzig: Pfeiffer.
Streck, M.
1916   *Assurbanipal und die letzten assyrischen Könige bis zum Untergange Niniveh's,* I-III. Leipzig: J.C. Hinrichs.
Tcherikover, V., and Fuchs, A.
1957   *Corpus Papyrorum Judaicarum.* Cambridge, Mass.: Harvard University Press for Magnes Press, Hebrew University.
Teixidor, J.
1977   *The pagan god: popular religion in the Greco-Roman Near East.* Princeton, N.J.: Princeton University Press.
Thiele, E.
1951   *The mysterious numbers of the Hebrew kings.* 2nd ed. Grand Rapids, Michigan: Eerdmans.
Thomas, D.W. (ed.)
1958   *Documents from Old Testament Times.* London: T. Nelson.
Thomas, D.W.
1967   *Archaeology and Old Testament study.* Oxford: Clarendon Press.
Thompson, H.O. (ed.)
1984   *The answers lie below: essays in honor of Lawrence Edmund Toombs.* Lanham, MD: University Press of America.
Thompson, R.C.
1931   *The prisms of Esarhaddon and Ashurbanipal found at Niniveh 1927-28.* London: British Museum.
Tristram, H.B.
1873   *The land of Moab: travels and discoveries on the east side of the Dead Sea and the Jordan.* London: J. Murray.
Tufnell, O.
1953   *Lachish* III *(Tell ed-Duweir): The Iron Age* (Text). London:
Tushingham, A.D.
1972   *The excavations at Dibon (Dhībân) in Moab: the third campaign, 1952-53* (AASOR 40). Cambridge, Mass.: ASOR.
Vaux, R. de
1961   *Ancient Israel: its life and institutions.* London: Darton, Longman and Todd.
1971, 1973   *Histoire ancienne d'Israel*: I, *Des origines à l'installation en Canaan*; II, *La période des Juges.* Paris: J. Gabalda.
Volney, C.-F.
1793   *Travels through Egypt and Syria in the years 1783, 1784, and 1785,* I, II (translated from the French). Dublin: printed for Messrs White, Byrne, W. Porter, Moore, Dornin, and Wm. Jones.
Vries, S.J. de
1978   *Prophet against prophet: the role of the Micaiah narrative (1 Kings 22) in the development of early prophetic tradition.* Grand Rapids, Michigan: Eerdmans.
Weippert, M.
1971   *Edom: Studien und Materialen zur Geschichte der Edomiter auf*

Grund schriftlicher und archäologischer Quellen. Inaugural dissertation, Tübingen.

Wellesley, G.
1938 *The diary of a desert journey.* London: Putnam.

Wellhausen, J.
1870 *De gentibus et familiis judaeis quae 1 Chr. 2.4. enumerantur.* Dissertation, Göttingen.
1887 *Reste arabischen Heidentum* (= *Skizze und Vorarbeiten* III). Berlin: G. Reimer.

Wellsted, J.R.
1838 *Travels in Arabia,* I, II. London: J. Murray.

Wevers, J.
1969 *Ezekiel* (New Century Bible). London: Marshall, Morgan and Scott.

Wevers, J.W., and Redford, D.B. (ed.)
1972 *Studies on the ancient Palestinian world presented to Professor F.V. Winnett on the occasion of his retirement 1 July 1971* (Toronto Semitic Texts and Studies, 2). Toronto: University of Toronto Press; London: Oxford University Press.

Williamson, H.M.G.
1982 *1 and 2 Chronicles* (New Century Bible). London: Marshall, Morgan and Scott.

Wilson, R.R.
1977 *Genealogy and history in the biblical world.* New Haven: Yale University Press.

Winckler, H.
1895, 1900 *Geschichte Israels in Einzeldarstellungen.* 1-3. Leipzig: E. Pfeiffer.

Winnett, F.V.
1937 *A study of the Lihyanite and Thamudic inscriptions.* Toronto: University of Toronto Press.

Winnett, F.V., and Reed, W.L.
1970 *Ancient records from north Arabia.* Toronto: University of Toronto Press.

Wiseman, D.J.
1956 *Chronicles of Chaldaean kings 626-556 B.C. in the British Museum.* London:

Wiseman, D.J. (ed.)
1973 *Peoples of Old Testament times.* Oxford: Clarendon Press.

Wolff, H.W.
1977 *Joel and Amos* (Hermeneia). Philadelphia: Fortress Press.

Zimmerli, W.
1969 *Ezechiel* (Biblischer Kommentar; Altes Testament Bd. 13). Neukirchen-Vluyn: Neukirchener Verlag.

Articles

Aharoni, Y.
1967 Forerunners of the Limes: Iron Age fortresses in the Negev. *IEJ* 17: 1-17.
1968 Trial excavation in the 'Solar Shrine' at Lachish. Preliminary report. *IEJ* 18: 157-69.

1970   Three Hebrew ostraca from Arad. *BASOR* 197: 16-42.

Ahitub, S.
1973   Review of R. Giveon, *Les Bédouins Shosou des documents égyptiens* (Leiden, 1978). *IEJ* 23: 58-60.

Albright, W.F.
1923   Contributions to the historical geography of Palestine, I: The sites of Ekron, Gath,and Libnah. *AASOR* 2-3: 1-17.
1924   The archaeological results of an expedition to Moab and the Dead Sea. *BASOR* 14: 2-12.
1925   The conquests of Nabonidus in Arabia. *JRAS* 61: 293-95.
1934   Soundings at Ader, a Bronze Age city of Moab. *BASOR* 53: 14.
1935   The Horites in Palestine. Pp. 9-26 in *From the pyramids to Paul: Studies in theology, archaeology and related subjects.* George Livingston Robinson anniversary volume, ed. L.G. Leary. New York: T. Nelson.
1941   Ostracon 6043 from Elath. *BASOR* 82: 11-15.
1944   The oracles of Balaam. *JBL* 63: 207-33.
1953   Dedan, Pp. 1-12 in *Geschichte und Altes Testament.* Beiträge zur historischen Theologie 16. Festschrift A. Alt. Tübingen: J.C.B. Mohr.

Alt, A.
1925   Judas Gaue unter Josia. *PJB* 21: 100-16 (=*KS* II (1953), 276-88).
1931   Judas Nachbarn zur Zeit Nehemias. *PJB* 27: 66-74 (= *KS* II (1953), 338-45).

Astour, M.C.
1979   Yahweh in Egyptian topographic lists. Pp. 17-34 in *Ägypten und Altes Testament* I. Festschrift Elmar Edel, Bamberg: M. Görg.

Avigad, N.
1961   The Jotham seal from Elath. *BASOR* 163: 18-22.

Bachmann, H.-G., and Hauptmann, A.
1984   Zur alten Kupfergewinnung in Fenan und Hirbet en-Nahas im Wadi Arabah in Südjordanien. *ZKKB* 4: 110-123.

Barré, M.L.
1985   Amos 1:11 reconsidered. *CBQ* 47: 420-27.

Bartlett, J.R.
1965   The Edomite king-list of Gen. 36.31-39 and 1 Chron. 1.43-50. *JTS n.s.* 16: 301-14.
1969   The land of Seir and the brotherhood of Edom. *JTS* n.s. 20: 1-20.
1972   The rise and fall of the kingdom of Edom. *PEQ* 104: 26-37.
1973   The Moabites and Edomites. Pp. 229-58 in *Peoples of Old Testament times,* ed. D.J. Wiseman. Oxford: Clarendon Press.
1976   An adversary against Solomon, Hadad the Edomite. *ZAW* 88: 205-26.
1977   The brotherhood of Edom. *JSOT* 4: 2-27.
1978a   Yahweh and Qaus: Reponse to Martin Rose (*JSOT* 4 (1977), 28-34). *JSOT* 5: 29-38.
1978b   The conquest of Sihon's kingdom: a literary re-examination. *JBL* 97: 347-51.
1979   From Edomites to Nabataeans: a study in continuity. *PEQ* 111: 53-66.
1982   Edom and the fall of Jerusalem, 587 B.C. *PEQ* 114: 13-24.

1983   The 'united' campaign against Moab in 2 Kgs 3.4-27. Pp. 135-46 in *Midian, Moab and Edom*, ed. J.F.A. Sawyer and D.J.A. Clines. JSOT Supplement Series 24. Sheffield: JSOT Press.

Baudissin, W.

1898   Edom. *Realencyklopädie für protestantische Theologie und Kirche*[3], 5: 162-70.

1899   Review of J. Lury, *Geschichte der Edomiter im biblischen Zeitalter* (Diss., Bern, 1896). *ThLZ* 24: 132-35.

Beeston, A.F.L.

1974   What did Anah see? *VT* 24: 109-10.

Beit-Arieh, I.

1981   Tell 'Ira, 1980. *IEJ* 31: 243-45.

1982   Tell 'Ira, 1981. *IEJ* 32: 69-70.

1984   Horvat Qiṭmiṭ *ESI* 3: 93.

1985a   H. Qiṭmiṭ. *IEJ* 35: 201-202.

1985b   New data on the relationship between Judah and Edom toward the end of the Iron Age period. Pp. 199, 264, in *Abstracts*: American Academy of Religion/Society of Biblical Literature Annual Meeting 1985. Scholars Press.

Beit-Arieh, I., and Cresson, B.

1983   Horvat 'Uza, 1983. *IEJ* 33: 271-72.

1985   An Edomite ostracon from Horvat 'Uza. *TA* 12: 96-101.

Bekel, H.

1907   Ein vorexilischen Orakel über Edom. *ThStKr* 80: 315-43.

Bennett, C.-M.

1962   The Nabataeans in Petra. *Archaeology* 15: 233-43.

1966   Fouilles d'Umm el-Biyara. Rapport preliminaire. *RB* 73: 372-493.

1967   A cosmetic palette from Umm el-Biyara. *Antiquity* 41: 197-201.

1967/1968   The excavations at Tawilan, Nr Petra. *ADAJ* 12/13: 53-55.

1969   Ṭawilân (Jordanie). *RB* 76: 386-90.

1970   Tawilan (Jordanie). *RB* 77: 371-74.

1971a   A brief note on excavations at Tawilan, Jordan, 1968-1970. *Levant* 3: v-vii.

1971b   An archaeological survey of biblical Edom. *Perspective* 12: 35-44.

1972   Buseira. *RB* 79: 426-30.

1973   Excavations at Buseirah, Southern Jordan, 1971. Preliminary report. *Levant* 5: 1-11.

1974a   Excavations at Buseirah, Southern Jordan, 1972. Preliminary report. *Levant* 6: 1-24.

1974b   Buseira. *RB* 81: 73-76.

1975   Excavations at Buseirah, Southern Jordan, 1973. Third preliminary report. *Levant* 7: 1-15.

1976   Buseirah (Transjordanie). *RB* 83: 63-67.

1977   Excavations at Buseirah, Southern Jordan, 1974. Fourth preliminary report. *Levant* 9: 1-10.

1978   Some reflections on Neo-Assyrian influence in Transjordan. Pp. 165-71 in *Archaeology in the Levant. Essays for Kathleen Kenyon*, ed. P.R.S. Moorey and P.J. Parr. Warminster: Aris and Phillips.

1980a   Tawilan (Jordanie). *RB* 77: 371-74.

1980b   Soundings at Dhra', Jordan. *Levant* 12: 30-39.

1983 Excavations at Buseirah (Biblical Bozrah). Pp. 9-17 in *Midian, Moab and Edom*, ed. J.F.A. Sawyer and D.J.A. Clines. JSOT Supplement Series 24. Sheffield: JSOT Press.

1984 Excavations at Tawilan in Southern Jordan, 1982. *Levant* 16: 1-23.

Bernhardt, K.H.

1971 Der Feldzug der drei Könige. Pp. 11-22 in *Schalom: Studien zu Glaube und Geschichte Israels*. Festschrift A. Jepsen, ed. K.H. Bernhardt. Berlin: Evangelische Verlagsanstalt.

Bertou, Comte de

1839 Notes on a journey from Jerusalem by Hebron, the Dead Sea, El Ghor and Wadi 'Arabah to 'Akabah, and back by Petra; in April, 1838. *JRGS* 9: 277-86.

Bienkowski, P.A.

1984 Tawilan Trench III—preliminary report. Pp. 13-19 in C.-M. Bennett, Excavations at Tawilan in Southern Jordan, 1982. *Levant* 16: 1-23.

Biran, A., and Cohen, R.

1976 Aroer, 1976. *IEJ* 26: 139-40.

1977 Aroër (Negev). *RB* 84: 273-75.

1978 Aroer, 1978. *IEJ* 28: 197-98.

1979 Tel 'Ira. *IEJ* 29: 124-25.

Blank, S.H.

1936 Studies in post-exilic universalism. *HUCA* 11: 159-92.

Boneschi, P.

1968 Encore à propos des monogrammes sud-arabes de la grand jarre de T. el-Ḥeleyfeh. *RSO* 43: 209-14.

Borger, R., and Tadmor, H.

1982 Zwei Beiträge zur alttestamentlichen Wissenschaft aufgrund der Inschriften Tiglatpilesers III. *ZAW* 94: 244-51.

Boschi, G.B.

1967a La Sagezza di Edom: Mito o realta? *RivBib* 15: 357-68.

1967b Tradizioni del Pentateucho su Edom. *RivBib* 15: 369-83.

Broome, E.C.

1973 Nabaiati, Nabaioth and the Nabataeans: the linguistic problem. *JSS* 18: 1-16.

Brünnow, R.

1898 Reisebericht. *MNDPV* 4: 33-39.

du Buit, M.

1977 Qos. *DBS* 9, cols. 674-78.

Byrd, B.F., and Rollefson, G.O.

1984 Natufian occupation in the Wadi el Hasa, Southern Jordan. ADAJ 28: 143-50.

Campbell, E.F., and Wright, G.E.

1969 Tribal league shrines in Amman and Shechem. *BA* 32: 104-16.

Cannon, W.W.

1927 Israel and Edom: the oracle of Obadiah. I, II. *Theology* 15: 129-40, 191-202.

Carmichael, C.M.

1969 A new view of the origin of the Deuteronomic credo. *VT* 19: 273-89.

Cazelles, H.

1959 Tophel (Deut. 1.1). *VT* 9: 412-15.

Clark, V.A.
  1979   Investigations in a prehistoric necropolis near Bab edh-Dhra'. *ADAJ* 23: 57-77.

Clermont-Ganneau, Ch.
  1906   Le marche de Saladin du Caire à Damas avec démonstration sur Kerak. *RB* 15: 464-71.

Cleveland, R.L.
  1960   The excavation of the Conway High Place (Petra) and soundings at Khirbet Ader. *AASOR* 34-35, Pt. 2 (1954-56).

Coote, R.B.
  1971   Amos 1.11: *RḤMYW*. *JBL* 90: 206-08.

Cresson, B.C.
  1972   The condemnation of Edom in post-exilic Judaism. Pp. 125-48 in *The use of the Old Testament in the New and other essays*. Festschrift W.F. Stinespring, ed. J.M. Efrid. Durham, N.C.: Duke University Press.
  1985   Horvat 'Uza excavations, 1982-85. Abstract S87, p. 211 in *Abstracts*: American Academy of Religion/Society of Biblical Literature Annual Meeting 1985. Scholars Press.

Cross, F.M.
  1969   Two notes on Palestinian inscriptions of the Persian age. *BASOR* 193: 19-24.

Cross, F.M., and Freedman, D.N.
  1955   The song of Miriam. *JNES* 14: 237-50.

Crowfoot, J.
  1941   Review of N. Glueck, *Explorations in Eastern Palestine*, III, and *The other side of the Jordan*. *PEQ* 73: 79-83.

Culican, W.
  1970   A palette of Umm el-Biyara type. *PEQ* 102: 65-67.

Dalley, S.
  1984   The cuneiform tablet from Tell Tawilan. *Levant* 16: 19-22.

Davies, G.I.
  1979   The significance of Deuteronomy 1.2 for the location of Mount Horeb. *PEQ* 111: 87-101.

Dayton, J.E.
  1970   The city of Teima and the land of Edom. *BIAUL* 8/9 (1968/69): 253-56.
  1972   Midianite and Edomite pottery. *Proceedings of the Fifth Seminar for Arabian Studies*: 25-33 (published by the Seminar for Arabian Studies, 31-34 Gordon Square, London WC1H OPY).

Dhorme, P.
  1908   Les pays bibliques au temps d'el Amarna. *RB* 5: 500-519.

Diringer, D.
  1958a   Seals. *DOTT*: 218-26.
  1958b   Weights. *DOTT*: 227-30.

Donner, H.
  1957   Neue Quellen zur Geschichte des Staates Moab in der zweiten Hälfte des 8. Jahrh. v. Chr. *MIOF* 5.1: 155-84.

Drioton, E.
  1933   À propos de la stèle du Balou'a. *RB* 42: 353-65.

Driver, G.R.
  1943   Notes on some recently discovered proper names. *BASOR* 90: 34.

1944   Seals from 'Ammān and Petra. *QDAP* 11: 81-82.

1975   Gen. 36: 24. Mules or fishes? *VT* 25: 109-10.

Dumbrell, W.J.

1971   The Tell el Maskhuṭa bowls and the 'kingdom' of Qedar in the Persian period. *BASOR* 203: 33-44.

Edel, E.

1980   Die Ortsnamenlisten in den Tempeln von Aksha, Amara und Soleb im Sudan. *BN*: 63-79.

Eissfeldt, O.

1968   Protektorat der Midianiter über ihre Nachbarn im letzten Viertel des 2. Jahrtausend v. Chr. *JBL* 87: 383-93.

Erman, E.

1892   Der Hiobstein. *ZDPV* 15: 205-11.

Fahd, T.

1978   Ḳaws Ḳuzah. Cols 802-804 of *Encyclopaedia of Islam*. 2nd ed., vol. 4. Ed. H.A.R. Gibb *et al*. Leiden: Brill.

Fairman, H.W.

1939   Preliminary report on the excavations at 'Amarah West, 1938-9. *JEA* 25: 139-44.

Finkelstein, I.

1979   The Holy Lane in the Tabula Peutingeriana: a historical-geographical approach. *PEQ* 111: 27-34.

1984   The Iron Age 'fortresses' of the Negev highlands: sedentarization of the nomads. *TA* 11: 189-209.

Fishbane, M.

1970   The treaty background of Amos 1.11 and related matters. *JBL* 89: 313-18.

1972   Additional remarks on *RḤMYW* (Amos 1.11). *JBL* 91: 391-93.

Flinder, A.

1977   The island of Jezirat Fara'un. *The International Journal of Nautical Archaeology and Underwater Exploration* 6: 127-39.

Frank, F.

1934   Aus der 'Araba, I. *ZDPV* 57: 191-280.

Franken, H.J.

1960   The excavations at Deir 'Alla in Jordan. *VT* 10: 386-93.

1961   The excavations at Deir 'Alla in Jordan: 2nd season. *VT* 11: 361-72.

1962   The excavations at Deir 'Alla in Jordan: 3rd season. *VT* 12: 378-82.

1964a   Excavations at Deir 'Alla, season 1964. *VT* 14: 417-22.

1964b   The stratigraphic context of the clay tablets found at Deir 'Alla. *PEQ* 96: 73-78.

1967   Texts from the Persian period from Tell Deir 'Allā. *VT* 17: 480-88.

Franken, H.J., and Ibrahim, M.M.

1977-78   Two seasons of excavations at Tell Deir 'Alla, 1976-1978. *ADAJ* 22: 57-80.

Franken, H.J., and Power, W.J.A.

1971   Glueck's *Exploration in Eastern Palestine* in the light of recent evidence. *VT* 21: 119-23.

Fritz, V.

1971   Erwägungen zu dem Spätbronzezeitlichen Quadratbau bei Amman. *ZDPV* 87: 140-52.

1975   Ein Ostrakon aus Ḥirbet el-Mšāš. *ZDPV* 91: 131-34.

Fritz, V., and Kempinski, A.
1976   Tel Masos, 1975. *IEJ* 26: 52-54.
Galling, K.
1941   Beschriftete Bildsiegel des ersten Jahrtausends v. Chr. vornehmlich
        aus Syrien und Palästina. *ZDPV* 64: 121-202.
1950   Das Gemeindegesetz in Deuteronomium 23. Pp. 176-91 in *Festschrift
        für A. Bertholet zum 80. Geburtstag*, ed. W. Baumgartner *et al.*
        Tübingen: J.C.B. Mohr.
1967   Das Siegel des Jotham von Tell el Ḥlēfi. *ZDPV* 83: 131-34.
Geraty, L.T.
1975   The Khirbet el-Kôm bilingual ostracon. *BASOR* 220: 57-61.
1986   Madaba Plains Project: a preliminary report of the 1984 season at Tell
        el-'Umeiri and its vicinity. Pp. 117-44 in *Preliminary reports of ASOR-
        sponsored excavations 1980-84*. BASOR Supplement no. 24. Ed. W.E.
        Rast.
Geraty, L.T., and LaBianca. O.
1985   The local environment and human food-procuring strategies in
        Jordan: the case of Tell Hesban and its surrounding region. *SHAJ* II:
        323-30.
de Geus, C.H.J.
1980   Idumaea. *JEOL* 26: 53-74.
Ginsberg, H.L.
1950   Judah and the Transjordan states from 734-582 B.C. Pp. 347-68 in
        Alexander Marx Jubilee Volume, ed. S. Lieberman. New York: Jewish
        Theological Seminary of America.
Ginsberg, H., and Maisler, B. (Mazar, B.)
1934   Semitized Hurrians in Palestine and Syria. *JPOS* 14: 243-67.
Giveon, R.
1979   Remarks on some Egyptian toponym lists concerning Canaan.
        Pp. 135-41 in *Ägypten und Altes Testament* I. Festschrift E. Edel.
        Bamberg: M. Görg.
1983   Schasu. Cols. 533-35 in Lieferung 36, *Lexikon der Ägyptologie*, ed. W.
        Helck and E. Otto. Wiesbaden: O. Harrassowitz.
Glaser, O.
1933   Der wasserspendende Esel (Gen. 36.24). *ZS* 9: 134-36.
Glueck, N.
1934   Explorations in Eastern Palestine I. *AASOR* 14. New Haven:
        University of Pennsylvania Press.
1935   Explorations in Eastern Palestine II. *AASOR* 15. New Haven:
        University of Pennsylvania Press.
1936a   The boundaries of Edom. *HUCA* 11: 141-57.
1936b   The theophany of the God of Sinai. *JAOS* 56: 462-71.
1937a   A newly discovered Nabataean temple of Atargatis and Hadad at
        Khirbet et-Tannur, Transjordania. *AJA* 41: 361-76.
1937b   The Nabataean temple of Khirbet et-Tannur. *BASOR* 67: 6-16.
1938a   The early history of a Nabataean temple (Khirbet et-Tannur). *BASOR*
        69: 7-18.
1938b   The first campaign at Tell el-Kheleifeh (Ezion-Geber). *BASOR* 71: 3-
        18.
1938c   The topography and history of Ezion-Geber and Elath. *BASOR* 72: 2-
        13.

1939a   Explorations in Eastern Palestine III. *AASOR* 18/19 (1937-1939). New Haven: ASOR.

1939b   The second campaign at Tell el-Kheleifeh (Ezion-Geber: Elath). *BASOR* 75: 8-22.

1939c   Surface finds in Edom and Moab. *PEQ* 71: 188-92.

1940a   Kenites and Kenizzites *PEQ* 72: 22-24.

1940b   The third season of excavation at Tell el-Kheleifeh. *BASOR* 79: 2-18.

1940c   Ostraca from Elath. *BASOR* 80: 3-10.

1941   Ostraca from Elath (continued). *BASOR* 82: 3-11.

1942   The excavations of Solomon's seaport: Ezion-Geber. *Annual report of the Board of Regents of the Smithsonian Institution 1941*: 453-78.

1947   The civilization of the Edomites. *BA* 10: 77-84 (= pp. 51-58 in *Biblical Archaeologist Reader 2*. Garden City NY: Doubleday, 1964).

1965   Ezion-geber. *BA* 28: 70-87.

1967a   Some Edomite pottery from Tell el-Kheleifeh. *BASOR* 188: 8-38.

1967b   Some Iron II pottery from Tell el-Kheleifeh. *BIES* 31: 124-27.

1967c   Transjordan. Pp. 429-52 in *Archaeology and Old Testament Study*, ed. D.W. Thomas. Oxford: Clarendon Press.

1969   Some Ezion-geber: Elath Iron II pottery. *EI* 9: 51-59.

1970   Incense altars. Pp. 325-29 in *Translating and understanding the Old Testament*. Festschrift H.G. May, ed. H.T. Frank and W.L. Reed. Nashville: Abingdon.

1971a   Iron II Kenite and Edomite pottery. *Perspective* 12: 45-56.

1971b   Tell el-Kheleifeh inscriptions. Pp. 225-42 in *Near Eastern studies in honor of W.F. Albright*, ed. H. Goedicke. Baltimore and London: Johns Hopkins University.

Görg, M.

1976   Yahwe—ein Toponym? *BN* 1: 7-14.

1979   Tuthmosis III und die *Š3św*-region. *JNES* 38: 199-202.

1980   Namenstudien VIII: *Š3św*-Beduinen und *Sutû*-Nomaden. *BN* 11: 18-20.

1982   Punon: ein weiterer Distrikt der Beduinen? *BN* 19: 15-21.

Graf, D.

1979a   Southern Jordan survey. *BA* 42: 72.

1979b   A preliminary report on a survey of Nabataean-Roman military sites in southern Jordan. *ADAJ* 23: 121-27.

Gray, J.

1953   The god YW in the religion of Canaan. *JNES* 41: 278-83.

1954   The desert sojourn of the Hebrews and the Sinai-Horeb tradition. *VT* 4: 148-54.

Grdseloff, B.

1947   Édom, d'après les sources égyptiennes. *Revue de l'histoire juive en Egypte* 1: 69-99.

Haller, M.

1925   Edom im Urteil den Propheten. *BZAW* 41: 109-17.

Hankey, V.

1967   Mycenaean pottery in the Middle East: notes on finds since 1951. *ABSA* 62: 107-47.

1974   A Late Bronze Age temple at Amman. *Levant* 6: 131-78.

Haran, M.
1968   Observations on the historical background of Amos 1.2–2.6. *IEJ* 18: 201-12.
Harding, G.L.
1937   Some objects from Transjordan. *PEQ* 69: 253-55.
1950   An Iron Age tomb at Meqabelein. *QDAP* 14: 44-48.
Hart, S.
1985   Preliminary report on a survey in Edom 1984. *ADAJ* 29: 255-77.
1986a   Edom survey project (report). *PEQ* 118: 77-78.
1986b   Selaʿ: the rock of Edom? *PEQ* 118: 91-95.
1986c   Some preliminary thoughts on settlement in southern Edom. *Levant* 18: 51-58.
1987   Five soundings in southern Jordan. *Levant* 19: 33-47.
Hartmann, R.
1910   Die Namen von Petra. *ZAW* 30: 143-51.
1913   Materialen für historische Topographie der Palaestina Tertia. *ZDPV* 36: 110-12, 180-98.
Hauptmann, A.
1986   Die Gewinnung von Kupfer: Ein uralter Industriezweig auf der Ostseite des Wadi Arabah. Pp. 31-43 in *Petra: Neue Ausgrabungen und Entdeckungen*, ed. M. Lindner. München und Bad Windsheim: Delp Verlag.
Hauptmann, A.; Weisgerber, G.; and Knauf, E.A.
1985   Archäometallurgische und bergbauarchäologische Untersuchungen im Gebiet von Fenan, Wadi Arabah (Jordanien). *ZKKB* 5/6: 163-95.
1986   Feinan 1984. *RB* 93: 236-38.
Helck, W.
1968   Die Bedrohung Palästinas durch einwandernde Gruppen am Ende der 18. und am Anfang der 19. Dynastie. *VT* 18: 472-80.
Hennessy, J.B.
1966   Excavation of a Late Bronze Age temple at Amman. *PEQ* 98: 155-62.
Henry, D.O.
1979   Palaeolithic sites in the Ras en-Naqb basin, Southern Jordan. *PEQ* 111: 79-85.
1982   The prehistory of southern Jordan and its relationship with the Levant. *JFA* 9: 4-7-44.
Henry, D.O.; Hassan, F.A.; Jones, M.; and Henry, K.C.
1981   An investigation of the prehistory and palaeo-environments of southern Jordan (1979 field season). *ADAJ* 25: 113-46.
1983   An investigation of the prehistory of southern Jordan. *PEQ* 115: 1-24.
Henry, D.O., and Turnbull, P.F.
1985   Archaeological and faunal evidence for Natufian and Timnian sites in southern Jordan with notes on pollen evidence. *BASOR* 257: 45-64.
Herr, L.G.
1980   The formal scripts of Iron Age Transjordan. *BASOR* 238: 21-34.
1983a   The Amman Airport structure and the geopolitics of ancient Transjordan. *BA* 46: 223-29.
1983b   The Amman Airport excavations, 1976. *AASOR* 48.

Hill, G.
    1896   A journey east of the Jordan and the Dead Sea, 1895. *PEFQS* 1896: 24-46.
    1897   A journey to Petra—1896. *PEFQS* 1897: 35-44, 134-44.
Holland, T.A.
    1977   A study of Palestinian Iron Age baked clay figurines, with special reference to Jerusalem: Cave 1. *Levant* 9: 121-55.
Honeyman, A.M.
    1948   The evidence for regnal names among the Hebrews. *JBL* 67: 13-25.
Hornstein, C.A.
    1898   A visit to Kerak and Petra. *PEFQS* 1898: 94-103.
Horsfield, G., and Conway, A.
    1930   Historical and topographical notes on Edom: with an account of the first excavations at Petra. *GJ* 76: 369-90.
Horsfield, G., and Vincent, L.H.
    1932   Une stèle Egypto-Moabite au Balou'a. *RB* 41: 416-44.
Horwitz, W.J.
    1973   Were their twelve Horite tribes? *CBQ* 35: 69-71.
Ibrahim, M.M.
    1972   Archaeological excavations at Sahab, 1972. *ADAJ* 17: 23-36.
    1974   Second season of excavations at Sahab, 1973. *ADAJ* 19: 55-61.
    1975   Third season of excavations at Sahab, 1975. *ADAJ* 20: 69-82.
Ibrahim, M.M.; Sauer, J.A.; and Yassine, Kh.
    1976   The East Jordan Valley survey, 1975. *BASOR* 222: 41-66.
Iktonen, L.
    1925   Edom und Moab in den Psalmen. *StOr* 1: 78-82.
Jacobs, P.F.
    1984   Tell Halif, 1983. *IEJ* 34: 197-200.
Janssen, J.
    1934   Les Monts Se'ir (*śe'îr*) dans les textes égyptiens. *Bib* 15: 537-38.
Jeremias, F.
    1907   Nach Petra! *PJB* 3: 135-76.
Jobling, W.J.
    1981   Preliminary report on the archaeological survey between Ma'an and 'Aqaba, January to February 1980. *ADAJ* 25: 105-12.
    1982   Aqaba-Ma'an survey, Jan-Feb 1981. *ADAJ* 26: 199-209.
    1983a   Recent exploration and survey in southern Jordan: rock art, inscriptions and history. *Berytus* 31: 27-40.
    1983b   The 1982 archaeological and epigraphic survey of the 'Aqaba-Ma'an area of southern Jordan. *ADAJ* 27: 185-96.
    1984   The fifth season of the 'Aqaba-Ma'an survey 1984. *ADAJ* 28: 191-202.
    1985   Preliminary report of the sixth season of the 'Aqaba-Ma'an epigraphic and archaeological survey. *ADAJ* 29: 211-20.
Kafafi, Z.A.
    1985   Egyptian topographical lists of the Late Bronze Age on Jordan (East Bank). *BN* 29: 17-21.
Kalsbeek, J., and London, G.
    1978   A late second millennium B.C. potting puzzle. *BASOR* 232: 47-56.
Kempinski, A.
    1977   Masos, Tel (Khirbet el-Meshash). *EAEHL* 3: 816-19.

Kenna, V.E.G.
1973   A L.B. stamp seal from Jordan. *ADAJ* 18: 79.
Kirk, M.A.
1944   An outline of the ancient cultural history of the Transjordan. *PEQ* 76: 180-98.
1946   Archaeological activities in Transjordan since 1939. *PEQ* 78: 92-102.
Kirkbride, A.S., and Harding, G.L.
1947   Hasma. *PEQ* 79: 7-26.
Kirkbride, D.
1958   A Kebaran rock-shelter near Wadi Madamagh, near Petra (Jordan). *Man* 58: 55-58.
1966   Five seasons at the pre-pottery Neolithic village of Beidha in Jordan. *PEQ* 98: 8-66.
1984   Beidha 1983: an interim report. *ADAJ* 28: 9-12.
1985   The environment of the Petra region during the Pre-Pottery Neolithic. *SHAJ* II: 117-124.
Kitchen, K.A.
1967   Some new light on the Asiatic wars of Ramesses II. *JEA* 50: 47-70.
1976a   A pre-Ramesside cartouche at Timna. *Or* 45: 262-64.
1976b   Two notes on Ramesside history. *OrAnt* 15:311-15.
Knauf, E.A.
1981   Zwei thamudische Inschriften aus der Gegend von Ǧeraš (Der Marwān). *ZDPV* 97: 188-92.
1984a   Qaus. *UF* 16: 93-95.
1984b   Qaus in Ägypten. *GM* 73: 33-36.
1985   Alter und Herkunft der edomitischen Königsliste Gen 36: 31-39. *ZAW* 97: 245-53.
Kochavi, M.
1967   Tel Malḥata. *IEJ* 17: 272-73.
1977   Tel Malḥata. *EAEHL* 3: 771-75.
Köhler, L.
1936   Zum Ortsnamen Ezion-Geber. *ZDPV* 59: 193-95.
Kraeling, E.G.
1928   The real religion of ancient Israel. *JBL* 47: 133-59.
Lapp, P.W.
1966   The cemetery at Bab edh-Dhra', Jordan. *Archaeology* 19: 104-11.
Lear, E.
1897   A leaf from the journals of a landscape painter. *Macmillan's Magazine* 75: 410-30.
Lemaire, A.
1974   Un nouveau roi Arabe de Qedar dans l'inscription de l'autel à l'encens de Lakish. *RB* 81: 63-72.
1975   Note on an Edomite seal-impression from Buseirah. *Levant* 7: 18-19.
Leonard, A., Jr.
1979   Kataret es-Samra: a Late Bronze Age cemetery in Transjordan? *BASOR* 234: 53-65.
Levy, L.
1906   Les Horites, Edom et Jacob dans les monuments égyptiens. *REJ* 51: 32-51.

Lindsay, J.
    1976   The Babylonian kings and Edom, 605-550 B.C. *PEQ* 108: 23-39.
Liver, J.
    1967   The wars of Mesha, king of Moab. *PEQ* 99: 14-31.
Llewellyn, B.
    1980   Petra and the middle east by British artists in the collection of Rodney
                Searight, Esq. *Connoisseur* 204: 123-28.
Lugenbeal, E.N., and Sauer, J.A.
    1972   Seventh-sixth century B.C. pottery from Area B at Heshbon. *AUSS*
                10: 21-69.

Maag, V.
    1957   Jakob-Esau-Edom. *ThZ* 13: 418-29.
MacDonald, B.
    1982a   The Wadi el-Ḥasā archaeological survey, 1982. *LA* 32: 472-79.
    1982b   Edom. Cols. 18-21, *International Standard Bible Encyclopaedia* 2, ed.
                G.W. Bromiley. Grand Rapids, Michigan: Eerdmans.
    1983   The Late Bronze and Iron Age sites of the Wadi el-Ḥasā survey 1979.
                Pp. 18-28 in *Midian, Moab and Edom*, ed. J.F.A. Sawyer and D.J.A.
                Clines. JSOT Supplement Series 24. Sheffield: JSOT Press.
    1984   The Wadi el-Ḥasā archaeological survey. Pp. 113-28 in *The answers lie
                below: essays in honor of Lawrence Edmund Toombs*, ed. H.O.
                Thompson, Lanham, MD: University Press of America.
MacDonald, B.; Banning, E.B.; and Pavlish, L.A.
    1980   The Wadi el-Ḥasā survey, 1979: a preliminary report. *ADAJ* 24: 169-
                83.
MacDonald, B.; Rollefson, G.O.; and Banning, E.B.
    1983   The Wadi el-Ḥasā archaeological survey 1982: a preliminary report.
                ADAJ 27: 311-23.
MacDonald, B.; Rollefson, G.O.; and Roller, W.D.
    1982   The Wadi el-Ḥasā survey 1981: a preliminary report. *ADAJ* 26: 117-
                31.
MacDonald, B.
    1982c   The Wadi el-Ḥasā survey 1979 and previous archaeological work in
                southern Jordan. *BASOR* 245: 35-52.
Macdonald, M.C.A.
    1986   ABC's and letter order in ancient North Arabia. *PSAS* 16:
McCarter, P.K.
    1976   Obadiah 7 and the fall of Edom. *BASOR* 221: 87-91.
McGovern, P.E.
    1980   Explorations in the Umm ad-Danānir region of the Baq'ah valley
                1977-78. *ADAJ* 24: 55-67.
    1981   Baq'ah valley project 1980. *BA* 44: 126-28.
Maisler, B. (Mazar, B.)
    1956   The campaign of Pharaoh Shishak to Palestine. *VTSup* 4: 57-66.
Malamat, A.
    1954   Cushan Rishathaim and the decline of the Near East around 1200
                B.C. *JNES* 13: 231-42.
    1963   Aspects of the foreign policies of David and Solomon. *JNES* 22: 9-
                17.
    1966   Prophetic revelations in new documents from Mari and the Bible.
                VTS 15: 207-27.

Mashal, Z. (Meshel, Z.)
   1961   A casemate wall at Ezion-Geber. *BIES* 25: 157-59 (Hebrew); Eng.
             summary, p. III.
   1975   On the problem of Tell el-Kheleifeh, Elath and Ezion-geber. *EI* 12: 49-
             56 (Hebrew); Eng. summary, p. 120.
Mattingly, G.L.
   1983a   Nelson Glueck and Early Bronze Age Moab. *ADAJ* 27: 481-89.
   1983b   The Exodus-conquest and the archaeology of Transjordan: new light
             on an old problem. *Grace Theological Journal* 4: 245-62.
   198   The role of settlement patterns in Syro-Palestinian archaeology.
Maxwell-Hyslop, R.
   1984   The gold jewellery. *Levant* 16: 22-23.
Mayes, A.D.H.
   1977   The period of the Judges and the rise of the monarchy. Pp. 285-331 in
             Israelite and Judaean history, ed. J.H. Hayes and J.M. Miller. London:
             SCM Press.
Mazar, B.
   1975   Ezion-geber and Ebronah. *EI* 12: 46-48 (Hebrew); 119-20 (English
             summary).
Mazar, E.
   1985   Edomite pottery at the end of the Iron Age. *IEJ* 35: 253-69.
Meisner, O.
   1862   Die Kinder Edom nach der heiligen Schrift. *Zeitschrift für die gesamte
             Lutherische Theologie und Kirche* 23: 201-48.
Mendenhall, G.E.
   1958   The census lists of Numbers 1 and 26. *JBL* 77: 52-66.
Milik, J.T.
   1958   Nouvelles inscriptions nabatéennes. *Syria* 35: 227-51.
   1958/59   Nouvelles inscriptions sémitiques et grecques du pays de Moab.
             SBFLA 9: 331-41.
   1960   Notes d'épigraphie orientale: 2. A propos du dieu édomite Qôs. *Syria*
             37: 95-96.
Miller, E.
   1870   Inscription grecque trouvée à Memphis. *RAr n.s.* 21: 109-25.
Miller, J.M.
   1966   The Elisha cycle and the accounts of the Omride wars. *JBL* 86: 441-
             54.
   1967   Another look at the chronology of the early divided monarchy. *JBL*
             86: 276-88.
   1974   The Moabite Stone as a memorial stela. *PEQ* 106: 9-18.
   1979a   Archaeological survey of central Moab, 1978. *BASOR* 234: 43-52.
   1979b   Archaeological survey south of Wadi Mujib: Glueck's sites revisited.
             ADAJ 23: 79-82.
   1982   Recent archaeological developments relating to ancient Moab. *SHAJ*
             I: 169-73.
Milward, A.
   1975   A fragment of an Egyptian relief chalice from Buseirah, Jordan.
             Levant 7: 16-18.
Mittmann, S.
   1971   Danaba. *ZDPV* 87: 92-94.
   1973a   Das südliche Ostjordanland im Lichte eines neuassyrischer Keilsschrift-
             briefes aus Nimrud. *ZDPV* 89: 15-25.

1973b   Num. 20.14-21—eine redaktionelle Kompilation. Pp. 143-49 in *Wort und Geschichte*. Festschrift K. Elliger. *AOAT* 18.
1982   The ascent of Luhith. *SHAJ* I: 175-80.

Moore, A.M.T.
1982   A four stage sequence for the Levantine Neolithic c. 8500-3750 B.C. *BASOR* 246: 1-34.

Moritz, B.
1926   Edomitische Genealogien I. *ZAW* 44: 81-93.
1937   Die Könige von Edom. Das Verzeichnis der Könige von Edom (Gen 36: 31-39). *Le Muséon* 50: 101-22.
1939   Ergänzungen zu meinem Aufsatz, 'Die Könige von Edom'. *ZAW* 57: 148-50.

Morton, W.H.
1956   Umm el-Biyara. *BA* 19: 26-36.

Muhly, J.D.
1984   Timna and King Solomon. *BiOr* 41: 276-92.

Myers, J.M.
1971   Edom and Judah in the sixth-fifth centuries B.C. Pp. 377-92 in *Near Eastern studies in honor of W.F. Albright*, ed. H. Goedicke. Baltimore and London: Johns Hopkins University.

Naveh, J.
1973   The Aramaic ostraca. Pp. 79-82 in *Beersheba* I. *Excavations at Tel Beersheba, 1969-1971 seasons*, ed. Y. Aharoni. Tel Aviv: Tel Aviv University Institute of Archaeology.
1966   The scripts of two ostraca from Elath. *BASOR* 183: 27-30.
1979   The Aramaic ostraca from Tel Beersheba (Seasons 1971-1976). *TA* 6: 182-98.

Niemann, H.M.
1985   Ein Statuettentorso von der Ḥirbet 'Aṭārūs. *ZDPV* 101: 171-77.

Noth, M.
1938   Die Schoschenkliste. *ZDPV* 61: 277-304.
1944/45   Eine palästinische Lokalüberlieferung in 2 Chr. 20. *ZDPV* 67: 45-71.
1958   Die Einnahme von Jerusalem im Jahre 597 v. Chr. *ZDPV* 74: 133-57 (= *Aufsätze zur biblischen Landes- und Altertumskunde* 1 (1971), II: 111-132).

Oded, B.
1970   Observations on methods of Assyrian rule in Transjordania after the Palestinian campaign of Tiglath-Pileser III. *JNES* 29: 177-86.
1971   Egyptian references to the Edomite deity Qaus. *AUSS* 9: 47-50.
1977   Judah and the exile. Pp. 435-88 in *Israelite and Judaean History*, ed. J.H. Hayes and J.M. Miller. London: SCM Press.
1979   Neighbours on the east. Pp. 247-75 in *The world history of the Jewish people*, IV. *The age of the monarchies*: 1, *Political history*. Ed. A. Malamat and I. Eph'al. Jerusalem: Jewish History Publications and Massada Press.

Ogden, G.S.
1982   Prophetic oracles against foreign nations and Psalms of communal lament: the relationship of Psalm 137 to Jeremiah 49: 7-22 and Obadiah. *JSOT* 24: 89-97.

Olavarri, E.
  1965   Sondages à 'Aro'er sur l'Arnon. *RB* 72: 77-94.
  1969   Fouilles à 'Aro'er sur l'Arnon. *RB* 76: 230-59.
Pardee, D.
  1979   Literary sources for the history of Palestine and Syria, II: Hebrew, Moabite, Ammonite and Edomite inscriptions. *AUSS* 17: 47-69.
Parr, P.J.
  1960   Excavations at Khirbet Iskander. *ADAJ* 4/5: 128-33.
  1962   Petra, the famous desert city. *ILN* (10 Nov. 1962): 747.
Parr, P.J.; Harding, G.L.; and Dayton, J.E.
  1970, 1972 Preliminary survey in north-west Arabia, 1968. *BIAUL* 8/9 (1968/69): 192-242; *BIAUL* 10 (1971): 23-61.
Pfeiffer, R.H.
  1926   Edomitic wisdom. *ZAW* 44: 13-25.
  1928   Judah's tribute to Assyria. *JBL* 47: 185-86.
  1930   A non-Israelite source of the Book of Genesis. *ZAW* 48: 66-73.
Pilcher, E.J.
  1922   Bronze weight from Petra. *PEFQS* 54: 71-73.
Prag, K.
  1974   The Intermediate EB-MB Age: an interpretation of the evidence from Transjordan, Syria, and Lebanon. *Levant* 6: 69-116.
  1985   Ancient and modern pastoral migration in the Levant. *Levant* 17: 81-88.
  1986   The Intermediate Early Bronze—Middle Bronze Age sequences at Jericho and Tell Iktanu reviewed. *BASOR* 264: 61-72.
Pratico, G.
  1982   Tell el-Kheleifeh 1938-40: a forthcoming reappraisal. *BA* 45: 120-21.
  1985   Nelson Glueck's 1938-40 excavations at Tell el-Kheleifeh. A reappraisal. *BASOR* 259: 1-32.
Price, N., and Garrard, A.
  1975   A prehistoric site in the Rum area of the Hisma. *ADAJ* 20: 91-93.
Puech, E.
  1977   Documents épigraphiques de Buseirah. *Levant* 9: 11-20.
Rainey, A.F.
  1975   Toponymic problems: 'Ain-shasu. *TA* 2: 13-16.
Rast, W.E., and Schaub, R.T.
  1974   Survey of the south-eastern plain of the Dead Sea, 1973. *ADAJ* 19: 5-61.
  1976   A preliminary report of excavations at Bab edh-Dhra', 1975. *AASOR* 43: 1-32.
  1980   Preliminary report of the 1979 expedition to the Dead Sea plain, Jordan. *BASOR* 240: 21-61.
Richard, S.
  1980   Towards a consensus of opinion of the end of the EB age in Palestine and Transjordan. *BASOR* 237: 5-34.
  1982   Report on the 1981 season of survey and soundings at Khirbet Iskander. *ADAJ* 26: 289-99.
  1983   Report on the 1982 season of excavations at Khirbet Iskander. *ADAJ* 27: 45-53.
Richard, S., and Boraas, R.
  1984   Preliminary report of the 1981-82 seasons of the expedition to Khirbet Iskander and its vicinity. *BASOR* 254: 63-87.

Robert, L.
  1939   Hellenica. *RPh* 65: 97-217.
Rollefson, G.O.
  1981   A Lower Palaeolithic surface site near Shobak, Wadi el-Bustan,
            Southern Jordan. *ADAJ* 25: 151-68.
  1985   Late Pleistocene environments and seasonal hunting strategies: a case
            study from Fjaje, near Shobak, Southern Jordan. *SHAJ* II: 103-07.
Rollefson, G.O. and Kafafi, Z.
  1985   Khirbet Hammam: a PPNB village in the Wadi el-Hesa, Southern
            Jordan. *BASOR* 258: 63-69.
Rose, M.
  1977   Yahweh in Israel—Qaus in Edom? *JSOT* 4: 28-34.
Rosenthal, F.
  1942   The script of Ostracon no. 6043 from Ezion-geber. *BASOR* 85: 8-9.
Rothenberg, B.
  1962   Ancient copper industries in the western Arabah: an archaeological
            survey of the Arabah. *PEQ* 94: 5-65.
  1965   König Salomon's Hafen im Roten Meer neu entdeckt. *Das Heilige
            Land* 97: 19-28.
Rothenberg, B., and Glass, J.
  1983   The Midianite pottery. Pp. 65-124 in *Midian, Moab and Edom*, ed. by
            J.F.A. Sawyer and D.J.A. Clines. JSOT Supplement Series 24.
            Sheffield: JSOT Press.
Ryckmans, G.
  1939   Un fragment de jarre avec caractères minéens à Tell el-Kheleyfeh. *RB*
            48: 247-49.
Saggs, H.W.F.
  1955   The Nimrud letters, 1952—Part II. *Iraq* 17: 126-54.
Saller, S.
  1966   Iron Age tombs at Nebo, Jordan. *SBF LA* 16: 260-63.
Sauer, J.A.
  1986   Transjordan in the Bronze and Iron Ages: a critique of Glueck's
            synthesis. *BASOR* 263: 1-26.
Savignac, R.
  1937   Le dieu nabatéen de La'aban et son temple. *RB* 46: 401-16.
Schoville, K.N.
  1974   A note on the oracles of Amos against Gaza, Tyre and Edom. *VTS* 26:
            55-63.
Schulman, A.R.
  1979   Diplomatic marriage in the Egyptian New Kingdom. *JNES* 38: 177-
            93.
  1986   The curious case of Hadad the Edomite. Pp 122-35 in *Egyptological
            studies in honor of R.A. Parker*, ed. L.H. Lasko. Hanover and London:
            University Press of New England for Brown University Press.
Schumacher, G.
  1891   Der Hiobstein, Sachrat Eijub, im Hauran. *ZDPV* 14: 142-47.
Scott, R.B.Y.
  1964   Shekel-fraction markings on Hebrew weights. *BASOR* 173: 53-64.
  1970   The n-ṣ-p weights from Judah. *BASOR* 200: 62-66.
Sellin, E.
  1936   Zur Lage von Ezion-geber. *ZDPV* 59: 123-28.

van Seters, J.
1972   The conquest of Sihon's kingdom: a literary examination. *JBL* 91: 182-97.
1980   Once again: the conquest of Sihon's kingdom. *JBL* 99: 117-24.
Shea, W.H.
1979   Nebuchadnezzar's Chronicle and the date of the destruction of Lachish III. *PEQ* 111: 113-16.
Smith, G.A.
1908   The land of Edom. *Expositor* 6: 325-36, 506-17.
Smith, S.
1925   Assyriological notes, Adumu, Adummatu. *JRAS* 61: 508-13.
Speiser, E.A.
1962   Horites. Col. 645a, *IDB* 2.
Spycket, A.
1973   Le culte du dieu-lune à Tell Keisan. *RB* 0: 383-95.
Stade, B.
1885   Miscellen 9: 1 Kön. 22.48f. *ZAW* 5: 178.
1901   König Joram von Juda und der Text von 2 Kön. 8.21-24. *ZAW* 21: 337-40.
Starcky, J.
1965a   Nouvelle épitaph nabatéenne donnant le nom sémitique de Pétra. *RB* 72: 95-97.
1965b   Pétra et la Nabatène. Cols. 886-1017, *DBS* 7.
1975   The Nabataean altar. Appendix I to C.-M. Bennett, Excavations at Buseirah, Southern Jordan, 1973: third preliminary report. *Levant* 7: 1-19 (16).
Stekelis, M.
1960   Villafranchian deposits at Ubaidiya, near Kibbutz Afiqim. *BRCI*, Geological Section 9.
Sumner, W.A.
1968   Israel's encounters with Edom, Moab, Ammon, Sihon and Og, according to the Deuteronomist. *VT* 18: 216-28.
Täubler, E.
1947   Cushan-Rishathaim. *HUCA* 21: 136-42.
Thornton, T.C.G.
1967   Studies in Samuel. *CQR* 168: 413-23.
Tigay, J.H.
1981   Review of T. Ishida, *The royal dynasties in ancient Israel*. *IEJ* 31: 251.
Tomkins, H.G.
1887/88 The name Genubath. *PSBA* 10: 372.
Torrey, C.C.
1898   The Edomites in southern Judah. *JBL* 17: 16-20.
1941a   On the ostraca from Elath (Bulletin No. 90). *BASOR* 82: 15-16.
1941b   A synagogue at Elath? *BASOR* 84: 4-5.
Tushingham, A.D.
1972   The excavations at Dibon (Dhibân) in Moab: the third campaign 1952-53. *AASOR* 40.
Ullendorff, E.
1958   The Moabite Stone. *DOTT*: 195-98.

Vattioni, F.
1969   I sigilli ebraici. *Bib* 50: 357-88.
de Vaux, R.
1967   Les Ḥurrites de l'histoire et les Horites de la Bible. *RB* 74: 481-502.
1969   Téman, ville ou région d'Édom? *RB* 76: 379-85.
Vermes, G.
1975   Ancient Rome in post-biblical Jewish literature. Pp. 215-24 in G. Vermes, *Post-biblical Jewish studies* (Studies in Judaism in late antiquity, 8). Leiden: E.J. Brill.
Vita-Finzi, C.
1982   The prehistory and history of the Jordanian landscape. *SHAJ* I: 23-27.
Vogel, E.K.
1970   Bibliography of Nelson Glueck. Pp. 382-94 in *Near Eastern archaeology in the twentieth century: essays in honor of Nelson Glueck*, ed. J.A. Sanders. New York: Doubleday.
Wallin, G.A.
1854   Narrative of a journey from Cairo to Medina and Mecca by Suez, Araba, Tawila, al-Jauf, Jubba, Hail and Nejd in 1845. *JRGS* 24: 115-207.
Wallis, G.
1969   Die Tradition von den drei Ahnvätern. *ZAW* 81: 18-40.
Ward, W.A.
1972   The Shasu 'Bedouin': notes on a recent publication. *JESHO* 15: 35-60.
1983   A possible new link between Egypt and Jordan during the reign of Amenhotep III. *ADAJ* 18: 45-46.
Ward, W.A., and Martin, M.F.
1964   The Balu'a stele: a new transcription with palaeographical and historical notes. *ADAJ* 8/9: 5-29.
Waterman, L.
1937   The authenticity of conjectural glosses. *JBL* 56: 253-59.
1938   Jacob the forgotten supplanter. *AJSL* 55: 25-43.
Weinberg, S.
1969   Post-exilic Palestine: an archaeological report. The Israel Academy of Sciences and Humanities, *Proceedings* IV.5.
Weippert, H., and Weippert, M.
1982   Die 'Bileam'-Inschrift von Tell Dēr 'Allā. *ZDPV* 98: 77-103.
Weippert, M.
1974   Semitische Nomaden des zweiten Jahrtausends: Über die *Š3św* der ägyptischen Quellen. *Bib* 55: 265-80, 427-33.
1979   The Israelite 'Conquest' and the evidence from Transjordan. Pp. 15-34 in *Symposia celebrating the seventy-fifth anniversary of the founding of the American Schools of Oriental Research (1900-1975)*, ed. F.M. Cross. Cambridge, Mass.: ASOR.
1981   Edom und Israel. Pp. 291-99 in *TRE* 9. 1/2.
1982   Remarks on the history of settlement in southern Jordan during the Early Iron Age. *SHAJ* I: 153-62.
Wellhausen, J.
1870   De gentibus et familiis judaeis quae 1 Chron. 2.4 enumerantur. Göttingen: Dieterich.

Wilson, C.W.
    1899   Address at A.G.M. of P.E.F. *PEFQS* 1899: 304-16.
Wilson, R.R.
    1975   The Old Testament genealogies in recent research. *JBL* 94: 169-89.
Worschech, U.F.Ch.
    1985   Preliminary report on the third survey season in the north-west Ard
                el-Kerak, 1985. *ADAJ* 29: 161-73.
Worschech, U.F.Ch., and Knauf, E.A.
    1985   Alte Strassen in der nordwestlichen Ard el-Kerak. Ein Vorbericht.
                ZDPV 101: 128-33.
Wright, G.R.H.
    1966   The Bronze Age temple at Amman. *ZAW* 78: 350-57.
Yehuda, Eliezer ben
    1920   The Edomite language. *JPOS* 1: 113-15.
Yellin, D.
    1932   Recherches bibliques 1: hayyēmîm, Genèse 36.24. *REJ* 93: 93-94.
Wiener, H.M.
    1928   The historical background of Psalm 83. *JPOS* 9: 180-86.
Woudstra, M.H.
    1968   Edom and Israel in Ezekiel. *CTJ* 111: 21-35.
Zeuner, F.E.; Kirkbride, D.; and Park, B.
    1957   Stone age exploration in Jordan. *PEQ* 89: 17-54.
Zwickel, W.
    1985   Rehobot-Nahar. *BN* 29: 28-34.

Maps

The Hashemite Kingdom of the Jordan. 1: 250,000.
            Sheet 1, Amman; Sheet 2, Karak; Sheet 3, Ma'ān.
            Department of Lands and Surveys of the Jordan. 1949.

The Hashemite Kingdom of Jordan, Archaeological Map. 1: 250,000.
            Sheet 1, Amman; Sheet 2, Karak; Sheet 3, Ma'ān; Sheet 4,
            Maḥaṭṭat el-Jaffūr.
            Jordan National Geographic Centre and Directorate of Military
            Survey with the cooperation of Department of Antiquities.
            1978, 1979, 1982, 1982.

Jordan. 1: 50,000.
            Series K737.
            Defense Mapping Agency, Topographic Centre, Washington D.C.,
            U.S.A. 1972.

INDEX

INDEX OF BIBLICAL REFERENCES

INDEX OF AUTHORS

INDEX OF NAMES

INDEX OF PLACES

JOURNAL FOR THE STUDY OF THE OLD TESTAMENT

Supplement Series

* Out of print